MY BLESSED
BRIDE

A True Story of Love Beyond Death

BY
STEVE FORTNER

First Printing

Author - Steve Fortner

Publisher
Wayne Dementi
Dementi Milestone Publishing, Inc.
Manakin-Sabot, VA 23103
www.dementimilestonepublishing.com

Cataloging-in-publication data for this book is available from
The Library of Congress.

ISBN: 978-1-7350611-4-6

Cover design: Michelle Wilson

Graphic design by Dianne Dementi

Printed in U.S.A.

DEDICATION

This is book is dedicated to my beloved wife, Linda Darlene, who, with much patience and prayer, led me to a personal relationship with Christ Jesus and taught me how to love others, especially our children, unconditionally.

TABLE OF CONTENTS

Proverbs 31:28-29 – Her children arise and call her blessed; her husband also, and he praises her. Many women do noble things, but you surpass them all."

My Blessed

BRIDE

A TRUE STORY OF LOVE BEYOND DEATH

STEVE FORTNER

FOREWORDS

Jonathan and Liz Sawyer

Jonathan Sawyer is a retired Chartered Engineer. In his role as Business Manager – Marine, he worked with Steve and his company QPI supporting the US Navy. He was responsible for the marine business of Aeronautical & General Instruments Limited including commercial sales and product design with the support of his talented and multi-disciplined team.

I have worked with and known the author Steve Fortner for over 20 years and as well as business colleagues, we have become good friends. We built up a successful business together where Steve's company supported and distributed my company's products to the US Navy. I have always admired Steve's direct approach to life, and his faith in God, both of which shine through in his book *My Blessed Bride*.

The book is a captivating story of Steve's life from his first job, his submarine navy career, business career, interwoven throughout his life with his devoted love of wife Darlene and their children during their 49 years together until her death in 2019. He discusses his faith in God, and how he reconciled that with his career and daily life.

The book is easy reading, with some wonderful humour from his navy days. It describes Darlene's long struggle with type 1 diabetes, its complications and how Darlene's faith in God helped her through this challenging life. For Steve too, his faith in God and God's wisdom shines through and there are many examples of this throughout the book, both personal and business related.

He describes how his faith gave him the strength to take on new and varied challenges. Similarly, for Darlene, her life is described in detail, her faith in Jesus Christ, and how she spread the Word of God to those who shared her life.

Steve's life, his devoted love, varied and exciting career is an inspiration to us all. It's a book that will inspire you with hope for the future. Give it a read!

Jonathan Sawyer
CEng MIET BSc

Carol Bretz is the founder and pastor of Jesus is the Light Ministries, aka The Lighthouse Christian Center. Since 1986, she has passionately preached the gospel through street evangelism, kids clubs, multi-cultural parades, crusades, and various events. For over 30 years, she and her Lighthouse Team have hosted its annual Christmas Party for Kids, partnering with local churches to give toys and gifts to over 500 children and their parents. Through the grace of God, her ministry has changed the lives of thousands in the Greater Philadelphia area. Carol has love and compassion for people in need -- who are lonely, depressed, and suffering -- and in all things, gives God the Glory!

Journey with Steve and Darlene Fortner, in his book, "*My Blessed Bride*," that reveals the hand of God is with us, from salvation's call until God calls us home. The hunger for truth in his wife, Darlene's heart was evident the moment I met her. As a passionate Christian, I was immediately aware of her search for God and His love. I told Darlene God loved her, and her family, and wanted them to become a part of His family and she immediately responded. That was the same day Darlene felt the Jehovah's Witnesses may be rejecting her. She felt she was not good enough for God, which left her in tears. When she accepted Christ, the light of God's glory came all over her face. She excitedly shared her faith in Christ with her entire family.

I shared with Steve and Darlene the importance of growing in the knowledge of God's Word and I connected them with a local church family. Darlene loved talking to people about Jesus and participated in the street outreach ministry of Jesus is the Light Ministries in Philadelphia. One weekend Darlene went with me to a Kenneth Copeland meeting in Philadelphia. While we were there, she had a vision and saw a cloud of glory on the stage. Darlene was so excited that God had blessed her in this way. Always encouraging others, she received from the Lord many visions and prophecies that she shared with the people. It was obvious she had a special gift from God.

In "*My Blessed Bride,*" you will observe, that Darlene, as a 'Firebrand' for God was directed, by God, to immediately win souls for Him! She found out He directs our lives from the moment we are born again. The ministry Darlene was called to brought many children and adults to know Christ and be baptized in His name. Darlene and Steve were led by the Holy Spirit through prophecy, visions and dreams from the Lord which opened the door of blessings for them on earth.

Darlene was a lovely person with a passion for Christ. In Steve, I see a man who loves God with all his heart and wants to honor the bride the Lord gave him.

It has been my pleasure to know the Fortner's and call them friends. As the officiating minister at Darlene's Final Service, I was privileged to tell them Darlene's final journey was when Jesus said to her, 'Well Done Thou Good and Faithful Servant.'

This book is so interesting in how God fashions our lives from the beginning to the end. I hope you enjoy it as much as I did!

Carol Bretz

Pastor Carol Bretz
Pastor
'The Lighthouse Christian Center'
Philadelphia, PA

Susan Gayle LaViolette is a widow living in Port Charlotte, Florida. She was married to her husband, Jim, for 42 years. Together they had two sons, Mitchell Shane and Jason Adam. In the mid 1990's Gayle and Jim created a magazine called "*The Gulf Coast Real Estate Guide*," and it flourished until Jim's untimely death in 2018. She drafted her boys to help keep the magazine going but when the Coronavirus attacked the USA in early 2020, she had to shut it down due to no demand. In the early years Gayle held numerous jobs throughout her life, while still managing to be a devoted mother and wife. She even drafted a book, which she called "*God's Word on Sexuality*" to help guide her sons through puberty.

As you read this book, "*My Blessed Bride*," your heart will be touched as Steve shares his deep love and life-long journey with Darlene, a woman after the heart of God. His story will steer your heart to pursue God's heart, too. I am Linda Darlene Fortner's youngest sister, Gayle. I was born 10 months after my sister, so we were very close in age and hopes and in dreams throughout life. Being the youngest of six kids, Darlene felt very protective of me and watched over me like a mother hen all the way through puberty and even after she met and married Steve. Steve was Linda Darlene Fortner's awesome husband for forty-eight years.

Growing up together, we became inseparable, especially at school. Darlene was the best sister anyone could have. She took care of me and protected me from any student who wanted to bully me, and she did it quite well. I remember once when some girl had me on the ground, trying to force me to drink clabbered milk from a baby bottle, Darlene jumped in without hesitation, pulled her off of me and told her if she ever hurt me again, she would beat her up. The bully left the scene without calling Darlene's bluff and never bothered me again.

I looked to Darlene for everything, and I loved her so much. During our times at school, Darlene would save her lunch money and not eat lunch, so she could go by Dairy Queen to get me something to eat and drink on the way home. As we got into Junior High School, she looked after me and kept me from being alone with boys. We always double-dated and Darlene made sure no boys took advantage of me.

As you read this beautiful book about her most wonderful life with her husband Steve, you will see her life explode with God's powerful hand. Her whole life turned from darkness to light, as God touched her and opened her heart to receive His love. God even anointed her to preach and teach others, especially children, about His love. Over the years, she prayed with and led many people to a personal relationship with Jesus, including me and my two sons. "*My Blessed Bride*" will reveal the wonderful spiritual life God did in her, with her and through her.

Susan Gayle LaViolette
Darlene's Sister

Michelle B. Wilson is an award-winning television producer and reporter. She has over 20 years experience in the media industry as a producer of nearly 1,000 stories. She is a media influencer and is best known for producing some of the most prolific transformative stories for CBN in over 139 countries where millions of lives have been encouraged. She is the founder of Millennial Kingdom Publishing and the founder of the world's largest memorial website, My Life Mattered.org. In her spare time, she loves to encourage others through her ministry, Michelle Wilson Ministries, and build businesses to advance God's kingdom.

When I first met Steve Fortner to produce his 700 Club Testimony about his discipline of giving and how God blessed his life as a result, little did I know we would embark on a journey to write and publish his book, *My Blessed Bride.* October 26, 1985, was when God impressed upon Steve through prayer to write about his story and that of his wife. God revealed during their prayer how He would anoint his book to bless every reader. Little did I know as this charge went forth, God had me in mind as his future editor and publisher. The words God gave Steve as he prayed with his wife, Darlene, were prophetic then and a promise to every reader of this book today.

"My words are a sword of fire. As you speak My words, they shall break asunder all evil which bind your finances. For no chains are strong enough to outdo the power of My words. As you write and speak and give my Words in this book, multitudes shall be set free. And as you give out, it shall be met back unto you. And deliverance shall be yours."

As you journey through this incredible true story, you will appreciate how Steve wrote from his heart with full transparency and with one goal in mind, to honor God and his "Blessed Bride"

Darlene. Dar, as he affectionately called her, was the love of his life. She was the inspiration for every dream that ever came true for him as a husband, father, businessman, and in his relationship with God. As you read, *My Blessed Bride*, you will get insight into a love between two Godly people that spanned a lifetime and was strong enough to overcome years of health challenges and even death.

In *My Blessed Bride*, it is evident the heart of God is conveyed in every chapter and will teach you:

How to seek God for your purpose in Life
How to experience God's blessing as a result of giving
How to trust God again when you feel you have failed Him
How to love your spouse with reckless abandonment
How to walk in the prophecies spoken over your life

Steve was blessed to experience life's precious gifts of a loving wife and children, grandchildren, and great-grandchildren, a successful Navy career, and earthly abundance through a successful business he co-founded. Through the inspiration of his Blessed Bride, he learned how to cultivate a personal relationship with God that guides him and gives him comfort today even after her death.

As the editor of *My Blessed Bride*, I can say first-hand that Steve's book about his experiences through life's toughest battles and greatest joys will encourage you on your journey in life that God is with you every step of the way. Buy a copy of *My Blessed Bride* for a friend so the prophetic blessing over this book will be there's as well. God Bless you.

Michelle B. Wilson
Editor

INTRODUCTION

When I met Darlene in the Navy, I knew she was a diamond in the rough. Besides her outward beauty, her greatest attribute was her ardent desire to know and to experience the love of God in a practical way in her daily walk. She said all she ever wanted in life was for someone to just love her as she is and not try to change her into something else. From the very first day I met her, I promised her I would love her forever and a day and that I would never leave her. Sometimes my harsh and cutting words would contradict my earlier vow of unconditional love, yet she continually forgave and prayed for me and our marriage.

Her prayers were unique and spontaneous. In spite of multiple illnesses over the years that weakened her body, when prompted by the spirit of God, she would attend to his calling and pray in the spirit until he released her to rest. Many times, she prayed on her knees and often she wrote down her prayers and God's answers. I still have hundreds of her prayers and answers from God in my home office.

Early on in our marriage, we had a desire to serve God and to know the truth. We just didn't know how to get to the truth. We were both raised in the Christian religion, but we didn't have real peace in our marriage or in our hearts. Eventually, we even tried to find God through the Jehovah witnesses for two years. Over time, they demanded we had to give up certain simple worldly pleasures, like my military patriotism, my Handel's Messiah album, and Darlene's cigarette smoking, to name a few. Fortunately, one day God revealed the demonic activity to Darlene within the two JW visitors in our house. Darlene immediately told them both to leave and never return.

Feeling alone and confused, Darlene wept and prayed for God to help her and God answered her prayer immediately. Carol, our next-door neighbor, came over and talked to her. She told Darlene that God would accept her just as she is and that she didn't have to earn salvation. This message was exactly what Darlene needed to hear. She eagerly prayed with Carol and received Jesus into her heart. When I came home from work, I saw she was different. She was peaceful, no longer anxious or troubled about anything. "Radiant" was the word that popped into my mind. Eight days later, Carol led me and our children to receive Christ into our hearts.

As a believer, Darlene not only had a strong prophetic gift, she was also called as a preacher and teacher of God's word. I do not state this lightly. Even though she was uneducated by the world's standards, small in stature, frail in health, and overlooked by church leaders and other so-called religious people, God used her powerfully to transform the lives of others. Regardless of what other people thought, she was anointed by God to preach and teach. God also endowed her as a prophet in the body of Christ. If you think the aforementioned gifts to Darlene were not real, because she wasn't actually ordained in the church, I must ask you to please consider Saint Paul's own words in scripture:

Romans 1:1 – (kjv) "Paul, a servant of Jesus Christ, called to be an apostle, separated unto the gospel of God..."

Who made Paul an apostle? God called Paul to be an apostle. He wasn't appointed by Peter, James, John or any of the other apostles. Likewise, Darlene was called by God alone to be a Prophet. I witnessed several examples of her prophetic gift throughout our life together. Many are contained within the pages of this book.

Speaking of prophecy, God also had an evangelist speak words over me the day after I accepted Christ in my heart. "God will take you from promotion to promotion to promotion..." he stated. I had no idea what it meant at the time. We were in credit card debt, big time, with no idea how to pay it off. I was also employed as a program manager with a defense contractor, barely making enough money to stay afloat. Darlene continually stressed the need for us to hear and obey God's Word, which included tithing. It was hard, and it didn't make sense; however, I saw the results, and it reminded me of God's faithfulness. Within seven years, I started my own business and 12 years later was competitively awarded a government contract with a potential value of $94,000,000 over the life of the project.

Twenty-seven years after starting the business, I sold the company for millions of dollars. This freedom from work allowed me to be a full-time care giver at home to my beloved bride, Darlene, for the rest of her life on earth. By then, she was confined to a wheelchair unable to care for herself. She had fallen and severely injured her cervical vertebrae and compressed her spinal cord, thereby causing paralysis from the shoulders down. At times, I would lovingly joke with her and tell her I was so thankful God made her small (95 lbs.) so that I could more easily pick her up and carry her when needed without hurting my back. She hated to rely totally on others to meet her basic needs, but I told her she was truly a labor of love.

By the way, she continued to smoke cigarettes all through her life. I asked her continually to quit, and she would say that, unless God asks her himself, she wasn't going to quit. Two weeks before she died, apparently God asked her to quit because she did, cold turkey. It was incredible. She acquired a little chuckle and never really explained to me how she was able to just stop. It was her little secret with Papa God. Someday she may tell me her secret when I see her again in heaven.

On 29 January 2019, at our home on Lake Anna, Virginia, three days after her 67th birthday, heaven met earth when Darlene transitioned into the loving arms of Jesus. We were together as she took her last breath. Darlene's ashes are buried in section 23A at Quantico National Cemetery. Her tombstone has two unusual words (Italy, Holland) engraved on it. These two words, that were our unique love language, were communicated often to each other. They were codes that meant the world to us that no one else understood. She especially used these two words in messages she sent to me when I was on a submarine thousands of miles away underwater on patrol. I would see them and rejoice. Here's what they mean:

Italy – I truly always love you

Holland – hope our love lasts and never dies

I hope you all enjoy the book, *My Blessed Bride*. It is my story about the love of my life.

Front row l to r - Jeff, Theresa, Jimmy
2nd row l to r - Steven, Michael
3rd row l to r - Mom, Mary, Carolyn
Last row l to r - John, Dad, Paul

1
MY YOUTH

"Life is like film. It will develop if you take your best shot!"
Linda Darlene Fortner

1968 was a crazy year when I graduated from Covington Catholic High school (CCH) in Covington, Kentucky. Robert Kennedy and Martin Luther King were both assassinated. The Vietnam War was at its peak with no end in sight. Richard Nixon was leading in the polls and, by November, he would be elected President in one of the closest elections in U.S. history. The Beatles and Rolling Stones were still on top of the music charts. Drug usage, especially LSD, and free sex among baby boomers seemed to be rapidly destroying our culture. Hundreds of cities across the nation were on edge from violent race riots and radical protests over the Vietnam War. Draft dodgers were fleeing to Canada and Mexico to avoid going into the military. The world seemed to be coming apart at the seams.

Despite world chaos that year, I graduated from CCH and was at a crossroads. Should I enter the seminary and pursue the priesthood, like I had promised mom and dad years ago, or should I join the Navy to escape the chaos?

Looking back over my life, I clearly see how God indeed ordered my steps when I was at my crossroads. I had no idea which path to take. The road leading to the priesthood was well organized and highly structured by the Catholic Church. There would be no hidden anomalies in this path. It was well defined and predictable. My older brother, Michael, was already in the seminary and had laid the groundwork for me to follow in his footsteps. It would be a safer journey to take, with less worldly distractions, surrounded by Godly men who dedicated their lives to following Christ in the priesthood.

The other path, which led to the sea, however, was mostly unknown and mysterious. Naval life could be unpredictable and highly dangerous at sea, especially in times of war. I would have to grow up quickly and learn how to survive and work with other sailors in daily routines and emergencies. The fact it was an unknown path, oddly enough, enticed me to consider it. Perhaps I would discover some golden nuggets along the way that would help me grow and learn in order to prosper once I returned to civilian life. Little did I know then, the nautical path I chose was the correct path to take. *My Blessed Bride* was on it, yet to be discovered by me.

Mom and dad were both from Covington, Kentucky. Dad joined the Navy in the fall of 1942 and was trained as an Electrician's Mate. After completing the electrician's training course in April 1943, he received orders to serve on a new aircraft carrier, the *USS Yorktown*, CV-10, which had just been commissioned in Newport News Shipyard. Before he reported aboard, he took a couple of weeks leave and went home to Covington, Kentucky. One night, he decided to go to a dance at Devou Park nearby. It was there that he met his future wife. As the live band played Glenn Miller music, mom and dad fell in love. Mom loved tall men in uniform, especially men who could also dance, and dad met both qualifications. They promised each other they would marry when dad completed his sea duty.

Throughout 1943 and 1944, the *USS Yorktown* was heavily involved in various land assaults and air battles in the South Pacific Theater. In August 1944, the aircraft carrier returned to the U.S. for a two-month overhaul period at Puget Sound Naval Shipyard in San Francisco, California. My dad had been on sea duty for almost 17 straight months. He then received orders for shore duty at San Diego, California. Before traveling there, he corresponded with his future wife and told her to meet him in San Diego, and they would get married right away. Mom, who was only 19 at the time, was under the care of her older sister, Millie. She made a novena and took a train out to San Diego, California to meet her lover and get married in a Catholic chapel on base. They were married on September 17, 1944.

Carolyn, their first child, was born in San Diego on September 3, 1945. Shortly after the war ended, dad was honorably discharged from the Navy, and the family of three returned to Northern Kentucky via a long train ride. Mom was a devout Catholic and dad was a Protestant. She didn't drive, so dad would always take her to church and wait for her. He got to know and like the parish priest and, thanks to mom's prayers and outward witness, a couple of years later, dad converted to Catholicism. Mom wanted to make sure the kids were raised in the Catholic Church.

Like a good Catholic family in the post-WWII days, they had a lot of kids over time; nine, to be exact. As I previously mentioned, Carolyn was born first in September 1945. Michael came next on November 23, 1947. Then I was born on June 6, 1950. The remaining six children to be born included Paul, Mary, John, Jeff, Theresa, and Jimmy, in that order. When I was three, we moved to a new two-story, three-bedroom house with a basement that a contractor friend of my dad had built for us. It was in a growing suburban community called Taylor Mill. We lived around 12 miles south of Covington, off State Route 16. The upstairs and the basement were unfinished when we moved in. Dad continually worked on the interior, especially the second floor, to have rooms for the additional children.

We attended Saint Anthony Catholic Church and never missed Sunday Mass, or so it seemed at the time. It was considered a mortal sin to miss Mass, unless it was due to extenuating circumstances, like illness or pending death. We even prayed the rosary religiously together at times and always took communion each Sunday as a family. Mike, Paul, and I even became altar boys and loved serving Mass, especially during Holy Week.

We believed the Catholic doctrine without question. Each Sunday, during Mass, the congregation would recite the Apostles Creed aloud in church. Near the end of the Creed, it states, "I believe in the Holy Spirit, the holy Catholic Church…" I was taught the word "Catholic" meant "universal." Hence, in my mind, the Catholic Church was the true church Jesus established through Saint Peter.

All other Christian denominations were Protestants, and, therefore, flawed in some way.

From 1962 through 1965, the Second Vatican Council was held in Rome. Significant changes resulted from the council in the Catholic Church. The mass liturgy changed from Latin to English, and the altar was turned around to permit the priest to face the congregation. Another change that greatly affected our family life was the new teaching on tithing. The Pope decreed all parishioners should tithe 10% of their income to the church. My parents were very supportive of this change and decided to begin tithing as they were able. As a young teenager, I immediately noticed the difference in our home life, economically and spiritually. We always seemed to have enough money for our needs even though we were giving more to the church. Plus, our parents seemed more joyful obeying the Word of God.

We all attended Saint Anthony's elementary school for grades 1 – 8. Most of the teachers were Catholic nuns. In the first grade, I remember getting into trouble on the school bus. The next day at school, Mother Benedict made me bend over and touch my knees while hitting my backside with a board three times. All of the students were mustered out of their class to witness this sanctioned display of corporal punishment. I'm not sure if Michael and Carolyn were two of the witnesses that day, as it was so long ago. Nevertheless, I learned from that experience and never had another incident in school that warranted corporal punishment.

My home life was mostly normal, even though there was a lot of chaotic activity with all the kids. Dad worked hard to earn a living and mom was a housewife. In the early years, dad held various jobs as an electrical repair technician of electrical motors in vacuum cleaners and kitchen appliances. When he turned 43, he decided to transition to appliance sales because it offered the potential to earn more commissions. Unfortunately, some weeks he didn't make the minimum amount of commission required, which reduced his pay even more. Despite the lean times, we never went without food, and we usually managed to have just enough of what we needed.

We seemed to do most things together as a family. We always ate together, either around the kitchen table or outside in the backyard, when dad cooked out on the charcoal grill. We never went to restaurants because we couldn't afford it. A lot of the time, mom and dad cooked together, which was great to witness. Mom was also a great baker. Often, she would make home-made bread, dinner rolls, and Danish rolls. She also made snacks for us every day when we came home from school without fail. We generally ate balanced meals with meat, and we never went away hungry. After dinner, we took turns doing the dishes, based on the work schedule mom prepared, which was taped inside one of the kitchen cabinet doors.

On the weekends, we would have additional jobs to do, like cutting the grass. Paul and I would argue over who cuts what section, front or back. The front was easier to cut, but Paul would use reverse psychology to convince me to cut the backyard, and I always fell for it. After we did our chores, we would be free to do whatever we wanted if we were within calling range of our parents. We would often play together and sometimes fight and argue with each other. None of us held grudges against one another for some wrongful act. We loved each other and would defend each other against kids in the neighborhood, who attacked us verbally or physically. When we disobeyed mom or dad, we would get spanked or punished in some way to learn a lesson. There were always consequences for bad behavior.

Sometimes during the summer, we all would sit outside at night on the front porch and listen to mom and dad tell stories or play 20 Questions with us. We especially loved hearing stories about dad's adventures in the Navy during World War II. Sometimes, he would show us photographs of his ship or plane. Our favorite was this one small black-and-white photograph of a Japanese dive bomber that had targeted his aircraft carrier. In the picture, the only thing not encased in smoke and fire was the torpedo itself. The Japanese plane had received a direct hit from dad's ship, causing it to explode in the air and miss the ship. After dad showed us the picture, we looked at him and marveled at his bravery. He never talked much about his Navy experience beyond that. All we mostly knew was he was an Electrician's Mate Petty Officer 1st Class and had worked in an electrical shop that was eight decks below the flight deck. Still, we were all very proud of him.

We had a good life, and there was plenty of love, peace, and security in our house. Mom and dad were always singing and dancing together in the kitchen, as they listened to big band music on the radio. I had never seen my parents argue or fight. I'm sure they did at times, but it must have been away from us kids. The only thing we seemed to lack was money. We had transportation, even though it was always a cheap used car. Dad never kept a car for more than one or two years because usually they would break down and need major repair work. When the vehicles gave out mechanically, he would just trade them in for another "good deal" he found on a used car lot.

As a young kid, I remember we had a 1955 blue-and-white Chevrolet. On the outside, it looked decent. However, the floorboard in the backseat area was so rusty with holes in it that the seat couldn't be mounted anymore. Dad removed the seats and replaced them with small stools. When we went anywhere, we enjoyed watching the ground beneath our feet through the holes in the floorboard. This car also required the engine to be replaced. Dad must have been fond of it because he paid a friend, who was a mechanic, to do the work. It didn't improve the car's performance, however, and it eventually had to be replaced with another used car. Still, we had the necessities of life: food, clothing, shelter, and the love of God and family. I grew up learning from my parents to value relationships with others instead of striving for materialism.

* * *

In 1964, I graduated from the 8th grade at Saint Anthony Elementary School. Although I wanted to attend Covington Catholic High School (CCH), my parents didn't have the money to enroll me in a private school. It was for males only and taught mostly by priests and brothers. CCH was one of the feeder Catholic schools in the diocese for boys who wanted to pursue the priesthood, following graduation, at Saint Pius X Seminary in Erlanger, Kentucky,

15 miles away. My older brother, Michael, who was three years my senior, had already committed to be a priest and was living at Saint Pius X Seminary. Mom and dad were proud of Michael for his decision, and I had always admired my older brother and wanted to follow in his footsteps.

One day, I asked my parents if I could attend CCH. I indicated that I, too, felt that I may have had a calling from God to become a priest. At the time, I wasn't in the dating scene yet and I honestly wanted to serve God in the best way possible. My parents responded by telling me the CCH tuition was more than they could afford. It probably cost less than $1,000 annually, which was a lot of money in those days. Still, my parents had always wanted to push us toward our dreams, so they requested financial assistance from the Catholic diocese. After meeting with the parish priest and discussing their financial limitations, as well as my calling to the priesthood, the diocese agreed to waive the tuition cost for all four years at CCH. Upon graduation, if I decided not to attend the seminary, my parents may be required to reimburse the diocese. I was so relieved and happy I could attend a quality private school and obtain a Catholic education and had looked forward to starting my freshman year at CCH that September.

I had four wonderful years at CCH. Our class size was 194 students and divided into five groups, labeled A through E, with group A containing the "brainiacs." I was in group B for my freshman through junior years. Since I was not an athlete, I had focused more on education and tried my hardest to excel in scholastics and the arts. In my senior year of school (1967-1968), I was promoted to group A, which was both a blessing, and a curse. It was a blessing because I felt I had earned it and a curse because I had to work harder to get passing grades in certain subjects, like physics. Then, during my senior year, I realized I was not called to the priesthood because I had developed an interest in girls and even dated a few. I dreaded the day when I had to tell my parents the bad news, and, while I had no idea what I was going to do after graduation, I was sure that I wasn't going to the seminary.

When I told my parents, I didn't think I was called to be a priest and why and how I was going to meet "Miss Right" and marry her, they were disappointed but not surprised by my decision. Fortunately, they did not have to reimburse the diocese for the cost of my Christian education. Unfortunately, I had no money saved up for college, and I couldn't expect my parents to help pay for it. While most of my high school friends were going on to higher education, I seemed to be lost without direction. Thankfully, God knew the plans He had for me. I just needed to walk it out and allow Him to lead me each step of the way.

2
ANCHORS AWEIGH

Jeremiah 29:11 (NKJV) "For I know the thoughts that I think toward you, says the Lord, thoughts of peace and not of evil, to give you a future and a hope."

Michael, my oldest brother, was in his third year of college at Saint Pius X Seminary when he began to struggle with his calling, as well. One day, the Monsignor, the seminary's head priest, was driving his car around Erlanger, when he stopped next to another vehicle at a traffic light and noticed my brother in the back seat with a girl next to him. Since dating was prohibited for seminarians, Mike was called into the Monsignor's office the next day. He calmly looked at Michael and suggested he reconsider his calling. Within a couple of days, Michael left the seminary and returned home to ponder his future.

Michael and I spent some quality time together in the summer of 1968. We talked about many things, including God, life, military, jobs, and our future hopes and dreams. He decided to join the Marine Corps right away. The recruiter offered him Officer Candidate School (OCS) since he had three years of college, but he turned the recruiter down. He wanted to experience Vietnam as an enlisted man and see for himself if Walter Cronkite, the renowned CBS News reporter, was correct about the Vietnam War being a total mistake. Mike enlisted for three years, but the recruiter told him that he would have to wait a while before he could send him to Camp Pendleton, California, for basic training because of a waiting list due to the high influx of recruits caused by the Vietnam War. I admired my brother's courage and desire to make a difference in the world by serving our country.

Opposite: Steven and Michael Fortner.

That summer, when a neighbor offered Michael and me part-time jobs as laborers with his commercial construction company, we jumped at the offer. It didn't pay much, but we were available. Unfortunately, the job only lasted a month and we were given pink slips and laid off in July. Michael was so upset; he tossed his company-provided hammer down into a wall that was being poured with fresh concrete. Unemployed and still pondering my future that summer, I decided to follow in my brother's footsteps and join the military. The question was which branch of service should I join? I didn't want to go to Vietnam, so I ruled out the Army and the Marine Corps. I was afraid to fly, so I eliminated the Air Force, which left only the Navy. I could swim, so I felt it was the best choice overall for me. A few days later, I drove to the Navy recruiter's office in Newport, across the Licking River from Covington. The Navy recruiter suggested I enlist for six years in order to get certification from the electronic training schools and thus get a better paying job after I left the Navy. Without hesitation, I signed on the dotted line and enlisted for six years.

Little did I know when I enlisted, I would have to volunteer for "submarines" in boot camp to receive the specific electronic training school certification that the Navy recruiter had promised me. He had never mentioned that minor detail. I was claustrophobic as a kid and there was no way I would have volunteered to serve on a submarine willingly. I considered my big brother to be the courageous one in the family, for choosing the USMC, because we both knew he would end up in Vietnam. In contrast, I wanted nothing to do with submarines, which would be my Vietnam, and wasn't so courageous that I wanted to live in a "sewer pipe." I wouldn't have minded riding the ocean waves in a ship, as I never got seasick on the water before. I'm glad I didn't know God's plan for me was to be under the waves in a nuclear-powered submarine with enough nuclear missiles on board to destroy millions of people if we were ever forced to launch them, as I may not have enlisted in the Navy for six years.

When I returned home from the Navy recruiter's office, I told my mom and dad the good news. Mom was somewhat pensive;

however, dad, on the other hand, seemed genuinely happy with my decision. He was proud of my decision to enlist, even if it was for six years of naval service. I wanted to make sure I left for the Navy before my brother left for the Marines. Fortunately, the Navy needed me right away. I was anxious to leave to experience something new and see the world.

On September 12th, the Navy provided me with bus transportation to the military complex in Louisville. There, I was given a physical exam and sworn into the military service. I received basic instructions and, later that day, I caught a flight from Louisville to Chicago aboard a propeller-type commercial airplane. Did I mention I was afraid to fly? I had never flown before and the thought of that airplane leaving the ground with me in it petrified me. Thank God the stewardess allayed my fears through her soothing conversation and snacks during the flight.

Upon arrival at the Chicago O'Hare international airport, I hooked up with several other Navy recruits from around the country. Together, we all boarded a greyhound bus and headed north to Great Lakes, Illinois. When we arrived late that night at the main gate of the Naval Recruit Training Command (RTC), I took notice of how sharp the naval sentries looked. They marched back and forth at the main gate with their rifles on their shoulder. Their steps were crisp, orderly, and synchronized. At the end of the column, they squared the corners each time, by turning 90 degrees and continuing to march. My thought at the time was, "What did I get myself into?"

Eight weeks in Navy boot camp at the RTC in Great Lakes helped me to grow up quite a bit. I had never been away from home for an extended time before. I had to learn to be self-sufficient and, at the same time, work with others to accomplish team goals. I was designated as one of my company's platoon leaders, assigned to manage the clotheslines outdoors. As a platoon leader, I had to ensure all company personnel hung their wet shirts and pants on the correct clotheslines during laundry day. Individual lines were labeled "pants only" and other lines were marked "shirts only." Each recruit was provided small strips of twine to tie their shirts and pants to the lines. Square knots were required. Each article of clothing had to be hung approximately four inches from each other. Our company commander, a Chief Petty Officer (CPO), or one of his seamen, would periodically inspect the clotheslines to make sure all clothes were appropriately hung and on the correct lines. He would then make a fist and place it between articles of clothing to ensure the four-inch width requirement was met. He would also check the knots in the twine to see if any were granny knots.

One day, we failed the clothesline inspection because our company's first recruit hung his wet clothes on the wrong lines. All the other recruits who followed him made the same mistake, and I failed to check the first recruit's work. As a platoon leader, I was called into the company commander's office and chewed out for failing the inspection. I reasoned with the CPO that it was not entirely my fault, but the company's failure, since everyone in the company had messed up. The chief considered my argument and agreed. He then directed me to lead the entire company personnel down to the drill hall with their M1 rifles and have them perform the 96-count manual of arms, which consisted of doing exercises in precision with the M1 rifle, for an hour. Upon arrival at the drill hall, I stood in front of the company and gave orders while they performed the exercises with their rifles. They were not happy campers, but they never did find out I was the reason they all had to muster in the drill hall that day.

During boot camp, I expressed an interest in learning about electronics. I remembered what my recruiter had said about getting a good-paying job when I got out.

USS Simon Bolivar (SSBN-641)

3
RUN SILENT, RUN DEEP

Psalms 139: 9-11 (NKJV) "If I take the wings of the morning, and dwell in the uttermost parts of the sea, even there Your hand shall lead me, and your right hand shall hold me."

Upon graduation from the Navy boot camp, I received orders to Polaris Electronics "A" school in Dam Neck, VA. Dam Neck was a small strip of land owned by the Navy that was on the coast, directly south of Virginia Beach. At the end of 1969, I had completed the 26-week Polaris Electronics "A" School and the 26-week Fire Control Technician Ballistic Missile (FTB) "C" School at the Guided Missile School. Upon graduation from the FTB "C" school, I was promoted to petty officer third class (FTB3).

The next phase of training was supposed to be submarine training in New London, CT, designed to weed out those sailors who are not able, for whatever reason, to serve on submarines. Being claustrophobic, I would surely have failed the submarine training course, especially during the underwater escape portion of the training. The underwater escape training required the trainees to assemble in the escape trunk attached to the water tower 50 feet below the surface. The escape trunk could hold approximately ten sailors at a time. The trunk would then be secured and flooded until the water was above the escape hatch. At that point, each person would be required to exit the escape trunk one sailor at a time into the water tower. As each person ascended to the surface, it was imperative to continually blow out air all the way to the surface, to prevent one's lungs from being injured. God must have had a different plan for my classmates and me, because our "C" school graduating class was waived from having to attend the Naval Submarine Training Center due to an electrical fire at the school. The submarine training school was shut down for repairs and I received orders to report aboard the *USS Lafayette* (SSBN-616), which was homeported in Charleston, South Carolina.

Upon arrival at the Charleston Naval Base, I reported to the yeoman on duty at the Submarine Flotilla (SubFlot). He reviewed my orders and stated that SSBN-616 was fully staffed with six FTB's, and I was not needed on board. He tore up the orders and assigned me to the X Division, which was a temporary duty on base until another submarine needed a trained FTB like me. After a couple of weeks in the X Division, I was bored and biting at the bit to go to sea. Well, little did I know I was going to get my wish soon.

On Saturday, January 7, 1970, I went out to a sports bar with my new yeoman friend from SubFlot. We had dinner and too many beers that night. The next morning, I had a headache and felt terrible. I had duty and was required to stand watch in the barracks until noon. By then, I felt fine, but as I was preparing to leave and go back to my cubicle, I received a call from the yeoman, who I had been out with the night before. He asked me to stop by his office at SubFlot because he wanted to show me something. When I arrived, he pointed out a large wall map of the continents and oceans with stick pin submarines on it.

He asked me if I remembered what I said to him when we were at the sports bar drinking beer.

I said, "No. What did I say?"

He replied, "You said I didn't have the guts to send you to sea."

He then laughed and handed me new orders to the *USS Simon Bolivar* (SSBN-641). He said a sailor had recently gone AWOL. The submarine needed a replacement as soon as possible since they would be going to sea soon.

I said, "How soon?"

He said, "Today. Call your folks and pack your seabag. I'll send a duty driver to pick you up in a few hours."

My mind was spinning. I wasn't given a choice. Didn't he realize I wasn't trained yet for submarine duty? What if I freaked out on board due to claustrophobia? Who would help me? What kind of work would I do? Would I work in Missile Control Center (MCC) on the equipment I had received training in?

"Dear God, I need your help," I prayed silently. I didn't know it at the time, but God had a plan for my life which required me to face my fears of the unknown and trust Him.

With no guidance from anyone, I guessed at what clothes I would need for a two-month patrol at sea. I called my parents long-distance collect to tell them the news. I couldn't disclose how long I would be gone or when I would return because I didn't know. I said goodbye to my parents as a duty driver picked me up in a van and drove me to the Charleston Naval Weapons Station, which was located a few miles north of the Charleston Harbor up the Cooper River, where the *USS Simon Bolivar* was docked pier side. Once we arrived, we had to go through tight security at the gate. After the Marine guards inspected our van and approved our military identification, we entered. From there, it was only a quarter mile to the pier where the submarine was docked.

I was amazed when I saw that vast black submarine sitting quietly in the Cooper River next to the pier. Five lines from the sub kept it secured to the shore. A brow extended from the deck to the shore, allowing people to walk across both ways. As I stared at the submarine in awe, I started to realize it was much larger and longer than I envisioned. Most of the hull itself was still underwater, to give it a low profile on the surface. The most visible part was the sail, which was shaped like a teardrop on its side. The two wings on the sail, one on the port and one on the starboard, were called fairwater planes. The planes helped the sub to stay on depth when submerged. The larger planes, called stern planes, were aft and were presently underwater. The rudder was between the stern planes.

19

When we parked and exited the van near the pier, I continued to gaze at this massive naval war vessel. I looked from one end to the other and thought it had to be a lot longer than a football field. I learned later it was 425 feet long, 33 feet beam, and 32 feet draft on the surface. There were no markings on the hull to indicate it was the SSBN-641, and I wondered how the driver knew this was the right sub. The other unusual thing was no one was topside on the boat to greet us and all the hatches were secured. I asked the driver about this, and he said the submarine was simulating an at-sea experience for two days. This scenario was called "fast cruise" and, once completed, the sub would get underway.

Once we arrived, the driver walked over to a pier-side phone booth and called the submarine. A moment later, the main hatch opened in the sail, and a sailor stepped out on the deck. He yelled for me to come aboard with my seabag. Once I crossed the brow, he took my bag and told me to proceed in and go down the ladder into the control room, and I followed his command. He was right behind me on the ladder with my seabag draped over his shoulder. As soon as I dropped down to the deck and got out of the way, the sailor who greeted me topside came down the ladder and stood right next to me and handed me my seabag. Then he left without saying anything else, and I was on my own.

I stood in the Control Room and looked around, trying to understand where I was and where to go. No one gave me any guidance and everyone seemed busy doing various tasks. Finally, I asked another sailor nearby where MCC was located. He told me it was two levels down in the lower-level operations. I found a stairway outside of the control room and proceeded down to the middle-level operations. Once there, I looked straight ahead and saw what looked like the torpedo room, and I turned and went aft. As I passed the galley, which was on my right, I saw a ladder that went down to a lower deck and decided to take it. Once I was standing in the lower level operations, I looked right, and there was a closed-door with the words "Missile Control Center" engraved on a plaque. I knocked on the door, and someone opened it and told me to enter. I sauntered in and immediately felt more comfortable with the surroundings. I recognized the Fire Control System (FCS) electronic equipment on which I was trained. As I looked around, several sailors in the small compartment seemed very busy with their duties. I tried to stay out of everyone's way, so I sat on my seabag in one corner and made small talk with the other FTB's in MCC. Within a few minutes, a sailor wearing blue dungarees, a white tee-shirt, and a white puffy cook's hat entered the room.

He looked directly at me and asked loudly, "Are you the new guy?"

"Yes, sir," I replied confidently.

"Get changed out of those dress blues and put on dungarees and a white tee-shirt," he said. "You're going mess cooking."

I felt like I had been punched in the gut, and surely, he had made a mistake. I thought, why can't I work in MCC with the other FTB's? Surely, seniority in rank meant something, didn't it? Then I remembered when the yeoman at SubFlot had said: I was to replace the sailor that went AWOL. His rank must have been a seaman or seaman apprentice (E-3 or E-2). He was assigned to the Deck Division and I was now his replacement as a mess cook. Seniority in rank didn't matter when the Navy had a need. I was the warm body that met the need and mess cooking was my first duty. Thankfully, my new FTB friends allowed me to change in MCC from dress blues into dungarees. They also allowed me to temporarily store my seabag until I got assigned a bed with a locker. After I changed, I hurried to the Galley in the middle-level operations to begin my new job as the mess cook. There were several seamen in the Deck Division. Some mess cooks and others were assigned to other jobs, like planesmen, who operated the fairwater and stern planes to control the sub's course and depth.

The submarine completed fast cruise in a couple of days, and then we got underway on patrol. For the next six weeks, I mess cooked, sometimes working 12 hours a day. A mess cook was like a waiter who got no tips and little respect from the crew. It was a high-pressure job with no time to rest during mealtimes. Tasks included scrubbing the deck, cleaning tables, washing the dishes, and wait-ing on all tables to ensure everyone was happy with the service and food, both in quality and quantity. It was the kind of job that either built character or destroyed a person. The good news was I was so busy mess cooking, I had no time to worry about claustrophobia or any other fears for that matter.

During my first patrol, I thought my mess cooking days were over. I remember, one day, when I was retrieving a heavy carton of canned food from the bilge in the lower-level operations birthing compartment, the submarine inadvertently took a roll and a deck plate I had propped open slammed down onto my right ankle. The pain was unbelievable and my scream woke up several men that were sleeping. I hobbled back to the sickbay in the middle-level missile compartment to see the medical doctor. Dr. Smith asked me to roll up my pants leg above my knee and he started to examine my knee. I told him there was nothing wrong with my knee and I had injured my ankle, but he ignored me. He hardly looked at my ankle and then told me to tell my supervisor I was to go to bed until the swelling came down. A couple of days went by, and the swelling remained and the pain got worse. I went back to the sickbay and showed the doctor my ankle, and he told me to put ice on it. I won-dered why he didn't tell me that in the first place. I also wondered why Dr. Smith, a Navy Lieutenant, was trained as an OB-GYN spe-cialty on a submarine with all males aboard. I guess to meet the needs of the Navy. Wasn't I doing the same thing?

Another incident that occurred with this same doctor on this patrol was even more bizarre. Apparently, a couple of enlisted men had tampered with Dr. Smith's stateroom bunk, loosening the bolts holding up the bed. When Dr. Smith had gotten into bed later that day to sleep, the entire frame had collapsed and he had rolled out onto the deck. He was quite upset about the incident and suspected the culprit worked in the missile compartment. He got a screwdriver and went into the upper-level missile compartment, where he tam-pered with one of the valves and caused it to misalign, alerting the Missile Technician (MT) at the Launch Control Panel in the middle-level missile compartment of a valve-misalignment red indicator.

Immediately, the MT set off the missile emergency alarm, which caused the doctor to panic and lock himself in the Head (i.e., bathroom) in the upper-level missile compartment.

The missile emergency alarm should only be used when there is fire or flooding in the missile tubes, so the MT on watch at the Launcher Control Panel had made a mistake, but the alarm still had the effect he'd sought. It caused immediate action by the officers and crew on board. All-access doors to every compartment were closed and locked, including the missile compartment. In the missile compartment, the roving patrol technician discovered the head door locked and notified the MT on watch, who then informed the Officer of the Deck (OOD). Within minutes, a security detail was dispatched to the upper-level missile compartment. The hinges on the head were removed because Dr. Smith would not unlock the door. There, sitting on the stainless-steel sink with his legs crossed and screwdriver in hand as a makeshift weapon, was Dr. Smith. That was his last and only patrol he ever made. I never knew whatever happened to him. Incidents like these were rare, but when they did happen, it provided a combination of excitement, fear, and entertainment for the crew.

∼

4
LOVE AT FIRST SIGHT

Psalms 37: 23 (NKJV) "The steps of a good man are ordered by the Lord, and He delights in his way..."

Near the end of the patrol, I learned one of the FTB's was being transferred off the boat, which opened an FTB slot for me. That meant on the next patrol, I would no longer mess cook but work in the MCC in my field of training. After two months underway, we returned to the Charleston Naval Weapons Station. It was mid-April 1970. I had no car, so I hitched a ride to the Charleston Naval Base barracks with a seaman whom I had worked with onboard. As we approached the naval base, my friend told me he wanted to stop at his trailer to greet his wife and change clothes before taking me the rest of the way to the barracks at the naval base. I told him that was fine and I was in no hurry. After all, I had nowhere to go and nothing to do.

As he entered his trailer, he affectionately embraced his wife and went back to the bedroom to change clothes and converse with her. After entering, I noticed an angelic-like figure sitting in a recliner to my right. She was so beautiful and radiant I could hardly keep my eyes off her. I sat down in a small nondescript chair in the small living room area and stared at the gorgeous woman sitting less than 10 feet away. She was dressed in light green pants with white polka dots and a white turtleneck shirt with a long-sleeve pull-over top that accented her figure. I could tell she was petite in stature because the recliner seemed too large for her small size. She was like Goldilocks sitting in Papa Bear's chair.

As I continued to stare, I noticed her facial features were flawless, and her dark brown eyes were the main attraction. They were large and captivating. One could not turn away once her eyes captured your soul. The eyeliner she wore enhanced them and her light beige makeup complimented her skin tone and was blended to perfection so that even her freckles peeked through the tapestry. Her lips appeared soft and tender, covered with a light shade of lipstick, as to not draw much attention. Her dark brown hair was neatly parted down the middle and pulled away from her face to allow the full beauty of her facial features to be exposed. The hair on top of her head was puffed up somewhat and resembled a natural crown, reserved only for a princess of royalty. Her hair gently flowed down her neck just above her shoulders.

She had a pensive look on her face as she glanced over at me. It was almost like something was on her mind, but she wasn't about to let her guard down. She was holding a lit cigarette so naturally that it was like an extension of her hand. Her right elbow rested comfortably on the recliner arm, and her right hand, with the cigarette in her first two fingers, was tilted back with the palm facing the ceiling. The smoke seemed to form angelic rings above her head and curl away from her body, so as not to cloud nor deface her beauty. I noticed she wore colorful yellow sandals with an artificial daisy on top that matched her lovely outfit. The open-toed sandals exposed her beautiful feet and bright red-colored toenails. Likewise, her fingernails were sculpted and the same color as her toenails.

I noticed a couple of rings on her fingers, but wasn't sure if she wore a wedding band. Before I uttered a word, hundreds of thoughts raced through my mind. Who is she? Where does she live? How old is she? Is she married? Does she have kids? I started to answer my questions in my mind. I imagined she was around 24-years old. I was 19 at that point and, surely, a woman five years my senior would have had nothing to do with me, would she?

After a few seconds, which seemed like minutes, I initiated small talk with her. I learned her name was Darlene and she lived in the trailer next door. She said she often came over to have coffee with her girlfriend. I didn't learn it then, but I later found out she was only 18-years-old. I also don't think I learned at that time if she was married or had children. My mind was racing, and I was in a fog of wonder. I was captivated by her angelic presence and the fact we were talking together in that small living room. She carried herself like a princess and was very pleasant but brief and measured in her responses, as if she wasn't sure she could trust me with information about her.

About that time, my buddy and his wife appeared from the back bedroom. He was ready to go. As I got up to leave, Darlene got up from the recliner and followed us out the door. Before getting into my friend's car, I turned to face her and mentioned I would like to see her again to talk with her. She asked me what I wanted to talk about, and I said, "life." Although she didn't respond verbally to my request, I knew from our initial small talk in the trailer and the fact she came outside to see us off, I would soon meet her again. I said good-bye and got into the car. On the way to the naval base, which was only a few miles away, my friend discouraged me from seeing her again. He told me she was married to a sailor, who was attached to a minesweeper operating out of the naval base. He also indicated they had no children, but he thought she was pregnant. I asked him if she was happy in the marriage and he said even though they were not happy and divorce was possible, he wanted me to stay away from her. He said she would be trouble for me. I didn't know what he meant by that, and, frankly, I didn't care.

I could not stop thinking about my brief encounter with Darlene. I was smitten by this mysterious and beautiful woman. The more I thought about her, the more I wanted to get to know her. It was irrational and I understood that. Yet, when I told her I wanted to see her again and talk to her about life, she had not shut me down. I saw a spark of life in her beautiful brown eyes and face. I cannot explain the determination I had within me to see her again, but I was driven by an inner force I did not understand.

I took two weeks leave and caught a flight home to Kentucky. While there, I told my folks and siblings I had met the girl I was going to marry. Of course, my parents thought I wasn't serious and tried to overlook my exuberance. Perhaps they thought the Navy's worldly experience was corrupting me, and who could blame them? I was young and barely out of high school and I had never acted this way about any of the girls I had dated growing up. The only real girlfriend I had had was named Maureen and we had dated when we were attending Catholic grade school. We also dated a little during our high school years. The more I had hung out with Maureen, the more we had become like brother and sister, but Darlene was different. I was just trying to communicate how I felt about her with my parents, that she was the girl I was destined to marry.

Being in the Navy assured me I was on a new journey in life. Hopefully, this journey would include the most beautiful and mystifying woman I had ever met. I could hardly wait to return to Charleston to locate her.

In early May, I took a return flight to Charleston. The first order of business was to visit my dream girl again. To see Darlene, I needed to acquire a mode of transportation. I only had around $1,200 saved up from six Navy paychecks earned during my two months at sea. I decided the only vehicle I could afford to buy was a motorcycle. I went to the local motorcycle shop, and, with $750 cash, I bought a yellow 250cc Suzuki and two helmets. I told the salesman I had never ridden a motorcycle before and he gave me verbal instructions on how to shift gears, accelerate, and brake. Then he suggested I practice in his parking lot. After a few minutes of learning to ride and not injuring myself or wrecking the motorcycle, I left and headed out to find Darlene. Oddly, I had no problems operating the motorcycle and felt very comfortable and in control.

Later that day, when I met up with my friend who lived in the trailer next to Darlene, he refused to give me his home address or tell me the exact location of where Darlene lived. He reminded me that she was married to a sailor and pregnant with their first child. He did, however, admit her husband was abusive to her and occasionally took pills to get high, and I couldn't understand how he could be in the Navy with such a terrible character and profile. He also mentioned her husband was currently out to sea and wouldn't be back until the following week. That was great news, and it lit a fire for me to begin the search, with or without his help.

It was a beautiful Saturday morning in early May when I began my search for Darlene. The sun was shining brightly and there were only a few white clouds in the sky. The temperature was mild that morning and I wore a light windbreaker jacket on the cycle. I brought an extra helmet in case she wanted to ride. I knew she lived in a trailer park a few miles from the base, next door to my friend in a smaller trailer. I remembered that the trailer park was located off a street named Spruill Avenue. Using a map, I found Spruill Avenue and decided to drive it, starting from the downtown area going north.

It was a long highway that ran for several miles, and it took me over an hour of searching before I finally located the small trailer park in question. I was able to identify my friend's trailer and noticed a smaller trailer in the adjacent lot. It was faded yellow and silver and looked rather old and run down. A metal awning extended from the front door about four feet and was held up by two rusty poles on each side. The trailer itself was small and only around 50 feet long. At one end, there was a propane canister propped next to the structure. The yard was worn and rather small, with no driveway. No vehicle was present that day. I surmised this run-down trailer had to be Darlene's residence.

Without any fear or hesitation, I parked my motorcycle and knocked on the door of the small trailer. I was hoping her husband was still out to sea. I hadn't thought about what I was going to say to her if she answered the door. I hadn't even practiced or rehearsed any lines. I was acting on impulse and an inner desire to get to know her. After a moment, which seemed like an eternity, the door opened a few inches, and there, peeking out behind the cracked door, was my dream girl. It seemed heaven invaded earth and time stood still. She was as beautiful as I had remembered. All I saw at that moment was her face because her body was hidden behind the door. It was uncanny that she didn't seem to recognize me at all, even though it had only been two weeks since I had first met her.

"Hi. Do you remember me?" I asked.

"No, I don't think so. What do you want?" she asked.

Her lack of recall didn't deter me. It only made me more determined to jog her memory of our first encounter.

"I met you a couple of weeks ago when I stopped by my friend's trailer next door. You were in their living room."

"Oh, okay. What do you want?" she asked.

"I just wanted to stop by and talk to you," I said.

"Talk to me about what?"

At this point, I felt like a door-to-door salesman. It was like I was trying to convince her to buy a product that she didn't need. I didn't want to be overly pushy about wanting to talk to her, yet, I wanted the opportunity to sit down with her and discuss life in general. The key was to jog her memory of our initial contact and small talk so that she could feel safe and secure about my presence. I thought if I showed too much enthusiasm, she might slam the door in my face. So, I tried hard to control my emotions and display even temperament.

"I would like to talk to you about life," I said.

She thought for a moment and then opened the door wide and invited me in.

I almost couldn't believe my eyes. The door was wide opened, and I could enter her world. I came in quickly for fear she would change her mind if I hesitated. Once inside, I knew I had crossed the Rubicon and there was no going back. I had committed within myself to invest in her life, regardless of the consequences. I somehow knew this moment was right and it was meant to be. I needed to listen and learn about her life and share my life experiences with her. I know it may be hard to believe, but I had no other motive but to get to know her a little at a time. She told me the door had to be wide open and I didn't care since I was now in her presence. I assumed she wanted to make a quick escape if she feared for her safety, but she had nothing to fear from me.

Once inside, I took a moment to survey the interior. I didn't want to move far from the entrance for fear it would frighten her. I noticed that even though the trailer was old, the interior looked clean and tidy. In the main area, where I was standing, there was an eat-in kitchenette and a small living area off to the right with a sofa against the trailer wall. A small kitchen table separated the two areas. Being petite and around 5' 1" tall, I could see Darlene would have no trouble navigating through the trailer.

She offered me coffee, which I gladly accepted. She made herself a cup as well. We sat at the kitchen table that was a few feet from the main door. I started our conversation with general small talk. I learned that her name, Darlene, was her middle name. Her first name was Linda, which she said people rarely used. I loved the name Darlene. I never knew any girl by that name, except for one on the Mickey Mouse Club Show. I used to love to watch that TV series and that beautiful name made her even more special and unique to me.

She let me know she was unhappily married and a couple of months pregnant. Her husband was abusive, both physically and mentally. She said he would take prescription medication to get a cheap high. He was a Navy corpsman who served on a minesweeper and was presently out to sea. Thank God, for my sake!

We talked all afternoon until early evening about our lives. The hours passed effortlessly as I discovered many personal things about her and challenges she had endured. She poured out her heart to me, and I listened and showed compassion and a desire to understand her. She told me her marriage to Tom was over even before she met me, and I knew then that meeting Darlene was no accident.

⸺◦◦⸺

5
DARLENE'S YOUTH

Psalm 147: 3 (NASB) "He heals the brokenhearted
and binds up their wounds."

Darlene, who was born on January 26, 1952, was the second youngest of four children born to Wilbur Frederick "WF" Parks
and Bertha "Geraldine" (Brown) Parks. Darlene's siblings included
Gayle, ten months her junior, and David and Shirley, who were six
and nine years older than her, respectively. WF, as he was commonly
known by his friends, grew up with his grandparents in southeastern
Ohio. As a teenager, he met a traveling evangelist affiliated with the
Church of Christ denomination, who witnessed to him about Jesus
Christ.

After graduating from high school, WF left home and attended Harding College, a Christian school in Searcy, Arkansas. He
attended from 1938 through 1940 and majored in Liberal Arts curriculum with an emphasis on the Bible. He left college before attain-
ing a degree and ended up moving to central Florida. There, he met
Geraldine, and they married in the Church of Christ on June 8, 1942.
He held various secular jobs, like a vegetable salesman and general
maintenance and repairman in a warehouse. It wasn't long before
he was hired as a pastor of a local "Church of Christ" assembly. He
was a good preacher of the Gospel who helped others have a passion
for God's word. The family always attended church together every
Sunday and Wednesday night.

Unfortunately, several years later, WF became unfaithful
to Geraldine and committed adultery with another woman, who he
would later marry. In 1957, when Darlene was around five years

Opposite: Darlene at 16.

old, Geraldine was awarded a legal separation from WF. She retained sole custody of the children and WF was required to pay child support. WF was fired as the pastor of the church and had to seek employment elsewhere. He moved in with his lover in Lakeland, Florida, and got a job working in the orchards as a fruit picker. It was a seasonal job and dependent on the weather, which meant he barely made enough money to survive, much less pay monthly court-ordered child support. Five years after filing for legal separation, the divorce decree was granted.

Geraldine was forced to get a job to support the four kids. She was a dispatcher for a trucking company, and didn't make much money, either. Thankfully, the Florida Department of Public Welfare did approve a grant of $78 a month. It was all she could do to pay the monthly bills and feed the kids. Geraldine's mother bought her a very small, two-bedroom house for $3,000 in Winter Haven, which Darlene would tell me, years later, was the 2nd house built in Winter Haven after WWII.

Geraldine's mother was a landlady of many residential properties. She expected her daughter to make mortgage payments to her, which she did. Eventually, Geraldine paid the entire mortgage and owned it outright. The small non-discrete house was constructed of concrete block and had less than 1,000 square feet of living space. Fortunately, the backyard was fenced in and large enough for the kids to play outside. There was also a large oak tree in the back that Darlene loved to climb, sometimes out of necessity to escape her mother's wrath when she was angry at her. Her mother's stressors came from several things, including her diabetes, a broken marriage, and raising kids on her own, as well as her son David having diabetes.

Geraldine thought it was important to raise her children in the Church of Christ religion. She faithfully took the kids to church every Sunday and Wednesday night. Over time, each of the children would go up front to the altar and say the sinner's prayer with the pastor, asking Jesus to come into their heart. Following that action, the church would baptize each of them in water. The Church of

Christ, however, did not believe in the baptism of the Holy Spirit, so the children may have been saved by grace if they genuinely believed, but they did not have the Comforter within to lead and guide them daily.

In 1961, Shirley, the oldest child, married and moved away to Orlando, leaving David, Darlene, and Gayle at home. David was now the oldest child at home. Even though he was six years older than Darlene, he would always protect her and play with her. He taught her many things, including how to fish using a cane pole with a string tied to a bent nail. Together, they would go to Lake Silver nearby and dig up earthworms for bait. He even taught her how to box during playtime. David, like his father, was very open and vocal about his love for God.

He would tell Darlene about God and his love for Jesus. He would also encourage Darlene to call out to God when she needed help. He even suggested she climb the tree in the backyard to get closer to God. On one occasion, Darlene told me she climbed the tree to the uppermost branches and talked to Father God. It was on one of these climbs that Darlene asked Jesus into her heart. David and Darlene grew very close and became inseparable. On the other hand, Gayle was sick a lot with asthma and had to stay inside most of the time.

David's health took a toll, as well, when he developed type I diabetes at around 12 years old. He had to take insulin injections several times a day. His mother had a difficult time teaching him how to manage diabetes and the importance of monitoring his blood sugar. Fortunately, she connected with an organization in Mobile, Alabama that ran a summer camp program for kids with diabetes. She received financial assistance and sent him to the diabetic summer camp for the next two years. The camp experience was a blessing to David because he was around other kids with the same medical challenges. The camp also helped David to better understand how to live with this disease.

Upon returning home after camp, however, David still struggled with managing his blood sugar. As a diabetic teenager on insulin, coupled with hormonal changes through puberty, his life was challenging. His mother thought he was getting too rebellious and disrespectful because he often argued with her over his grades at school. She also scolded him for misbehaving and missing a lot of classes due to poor health. Others accused him of stealing their property like a pocket-knife, a comb, a wristwatch, and other personal items from time to time. The victims would confront his mother and complain about his behavior. It got to the point where she didn't think that she could handle David anymore.

At 16-years-old, Geraldine asked her oldest brother if David could live with him and his wife in their home in Winter Garden, and they agreed to take him in. She loved this new arrangement because her brother also had diabetes and could help him learn how to live with this disease. Darlene was very distraught when David left because he was her best friend, mentor, and father figure. Soon, she would have to face one of the most challenging times in her life. After Thanksgiving dinner in 1963, while still living with his aunt and uncle, David got very ill and was rushed to the hospital. Early the next morning, he slipped into a coma and died. The cause of death was determined to be heart failure due to diabetic ketoacidosis.

David was only 17 years old and Darlene was emotionally devastated. Her best friend and protector was dead. During the funeral service, she attempted to kiss David good-bye as he lay in the coffin. Her mother got very anxious when she saw her and yelled for someone to get her away from the coffin. Geraldine simply didn't understand the deep love Darlene had had for her brother.

At 11 years of age, Darlene was now the oldest child at home and her mother held her responsible for Gayle's welfare. Darlene accepted this role with vigor. She took care of Gayle and protected her from any harm, especially when they had to walk 2.5 miles each way to school. Since Gayle was only ten months younger than Darlene, they were in the same class at school. Darlene would make sure no kid picked on her and, if someone did, she would jump in straight away and try to break it up. She also wouldn't use the money their mother gave her for lunch at school. Instead, she would fast for lunch and then on the way home, stop at a Dairy Queen and buy Gayle a cold drink and a snack. Afterward, they would walk close to Lake Silver, remove their shoes and socks and wade through the shallow water, laughing.

As they got older, Darlene switched to trying to keep boys away from Gayle so that they wouldn't take advantage of her. Their mother mandated they were only allowed to double-date when they went out with boys and, before any date, Darlene would read the riot act to Gayle's boyfriend to make sure he was proper and on his best behavior.

Just as David before her, Darlene continued to have a rocky relationship with her mother. No matter how hard Darlene tried to please her, she failed. Her mother could not accept her as herself and only saw Darlene's actions as reminders of her ex-husband, WF, a fact of which she would cruelly remind her daughter. Darlene could do nothing right in her mother's eyes.

One day Darlene's mother was so angry with her over some issue concerning Gayle. She took Darlene in the bathroom, locked the door so Gayle couldn't interfere, and switched her 38 times on her bottom and lower backside. Gayle counted all the strikes. Only by God's grace was Darlene able to take this abuse without uttering a word.

Gayle, however, was outside the door crying and begging her mother to stop beating her sister. She even admitted it was her and not Darlene who did the wrong, but their mother would not relent. The next day at school, the teachers saw Darlene was bleeding through her dress and suspected abuse from her mother. It was a small town and word got around about others suspecting her mom of abuse. Darlene had also mentioned some of the previous abuse to her teachers. The authorities only gave Geraldine a warning and, afterward, when Darlene ran away from home, she was returned by the police.

Despite the authorities getting involved, the abuse continued. In 1969, when Darlene and Gayle were in the 11th grade, Darlene had enough of the abuse and decided to quit school and go live with her father. She thought she would have a better life with him. Her mother often said terrible things about her father, but she never believed them.

Darlene had always wanted her father's love, and she didn't want to put off the wait any longer. She contacted him and he agreed for her to come and live with him. He had remarried and was living in Lakeland, which was around 30 miles away. The first order of business was for her father to get custody of Darlene. Her mother and father went to court, and the court agreed to give WF legal custody.

Darlene moved in with her father and his wife, but little did she know the type of man her father truly was. It wasn't long before Darlene's father violated her sexually and her dreams of unconditional love from her parents were shattered beyond repair. The only father who could protect her and who she could count on now was God.

After her father violated her, she had a nervous breakdown from the assault. At this point, she was feeling depressed, hopeless, and anxious. She needed to get out of her father's house immediately because she could no longer trust him. In survival mode, she called a young man named Tom, whom she had known and dated in high school. He was one of the few men Darlene knew who hadn't hurt her at that time. Without hesitation, Tom agreed to come and get her only if she would marry him. In her traumatized condition, Darlene saw no other option for survival and agreed to his proposal.

As a young woman of 17-years-old, she thought by marrying Tom, she would finally be loved unconditionally and no longer abused. Tom and Darlene went to the local courthouse with her mother, who signed for her. They got married by the Justice of the Peace. Shortly after that, Tom joined the Navy and got orders to a minesweeper homeported in Charleston, South Carolina. Darlene went with her new husband, even though she was still experiencing an emotional breakdown caused by her father's actions.

The last thing she remembered was waking up one morning with a wedding band on her finger and living in a small trailer in Charleston. Eventually, by the grace of God, she recovered her senses. She didn't take any medication during this time, nor did she go to the hospital for treatment. Despite Tom rescuing her from her abusive situation with her father, he turned out to be a monster, as well. Tom took pills to get high and he was a womanizer. Often, he would get drunk before coming home from work on the ship. Upon arrival, he would swear and strike out at Darlene if he didn't get his way on something.

When he wasn't drinking, he would take pills. He was especially keen on Darvon medication. He would take the capsule apart and empty the powder and take the small b-b size pill only, thereby getting a quicker high. Some nights he would go to a local strip club and carry on with the prostitutes.

Sometime in early 1970, Darlene became pregnant with Tom's baby. Tom wasn't happy about the pregnancy because he didn't want a child. One day, during a ride in the family car, Tom, unexpectedly and purposely slammed on the brakes, causing Darlene to crash into the dashboard, hurting her stomach and chest. Seat belts were rarely used in those days and she wasn't wearing hers. She was around two or three months pregnant. Perhaps, Tom wanted to terminate the pregnancy in this manner. That incident occurred just around the time I first met Darlene in the early spring of 1970.

That day in the trailer, as I listened to her share her pain and sorrow, she told me she did not remember marrying Tom or moving to Charleston. In her small trailer on that beautiful Saturday afternoon in early May, with the sun's rays shining brightly into that little room through the open trailer door, we talked into the evening hours. She told me about her love for God and how He had saved her from dying at the hands of her mother, father, and her husband.

6
THE PROPOSAL

Psalm 37:4 (NKJV) "Delight yourself also in the Lord, and He shall give you the desires of your heart."

I cherished every moment as Darlene shared all her hopes and dreams and fears with me in that small 50-foot trailer, sitting at that tiny fold down kitchen area table, with the door wide open. She said all she ever wanted in life was for a man to love her and accept her for who she was. She was so tired of trying to please others only to have her dreams shattered when they would hurt or desert her. Despite all the disappointments in life, though, she retained hope for a better future, hope for a good marriage, and hope that her mother would finally love her unconditionally. It was a very emotionally-filled day. We cried together, and she allowed me to hug and embrace her. She emptied herself of her cares and I poured into her person new hopes and dreams. We even spoke of our future, together, forever, and it seemed natural to talk about it. Everything we shared made it easy to transition into the next step of what we were to do.

We lost track of time. I fell in love with her. I'm not sure if she fell in love with me then, but she certainly felt safer having me there to protect her. That evening, I got the courage to ask her out on a date on my new motorcycle. As we got ready to go out and ride, I reached into the closet to get her jacket.

With my back to her and facing the closet, I asked her, "Will you marry me?"

There seemed like an eternity between the time I posed the question and her reply. Meanwhile, my whole life passed in front of

Opposite: The Proposal ~ spring 1970.

me before she responded. It was like I was in a foxhole and the mortar round explosions were getting closer and closer to my position. I went through all of my life experiences like one panoramic display in a split second. I knew I loved her, even though I hardly knew her. It's hard to explain and it didn't make any sense, but I wasn't dealing with reason. It was a deep yearning within my heart to live the rest of my life with this precious and beautiful young woman. All these feelings were bubbling up within me. It was as if I was being propelled by an inner force too difficult to keep within. Within a moment, I was back to reality.

She then replied, "What did you say?"

I turned around with her jacket in my hands and, looking into her beautiful brown eyes, I repeated, "Will you marry me?"

After another pause, which seemed to last forever, she said, "Yes."

Later in our life together, I would find out that when she had said "yes" to marrying me, she was testing me. She wanted to see if her response would scare me away. She wanted to know if I was serious. Was I going to hang in there and wait for Tom's divorce to be final, which could take a year? Was I going to get her a ring? Would I be a faithful, kind, loving, and protective husband, or would I be like all the others who abused her? I was ready for the challenge and was happy. I was the one God chose to help bring stability, love, and protection into her life as well as into my life.

After I helped her put on her jacket, we went outside and I showed her my new yellow motorcycle, which she loved. I didn't tell her I was a beginner. I felt that in this fairy tale, in which we were both living in real-time, there would be no mishaps. We rode together to a local nightclub and bar and danced the night away. Time seemed to stand still that night. We laughed and we cried. We danced and we dreamed of our future together. We loved our time together, wishing it would never end.

I stayed with Darlene that Saturday night in her little mobile home. We slept in the same bed, but we were not intimate. I respected her when she asked me not to move close. It was almost an impossible challenge, but I endured the test.

The next morning was Sunday, and she woke up before me. She got dressed, fixed her hair, and put on makeup, lipstick, and perfume. Only then did she prepare us coffee and breakfast. I noticed during breakfast that she looked so fresh and radiant and she appeared very happy with a bright smile. It was like weights had come off her shoulders. She told me Tom was out to sea and was supposed to return later that week. She wasn't sure exactly what day, but she permitted me to stay with her until he returned. Hearing her say I could stay with her was a joy to my ears.

I got some clean clothes from the Navy barracks and temporarily moved in with my future wife. That Sunday night, we lay together in bed and were intimate for the first time. The next morning, she rose early again, dressed, applied makeup and perfume, and fixed her hair. Then she made us coffee and breakfast and lovingly woke me up. Cooking me breakfast became her standard modus operandi during our first week together. She had a servant's heart and she wanted to bless me. As the days went by, the more beautiful she looked to me.

On Tuesday night, while we were lying in bed together, Darlene had a strong feeling Tom would come home early the next day. She told me to get dressed and take my clothes and go back to the Navy barracks immediately, which I did. The next day, just as she predicted, Tom arrived home. Despite his arrival, nothing could keep us apart. On Thursday, we talked on the phone when Tom was at work. The next day, she asked me to come over to take her motorcycle riding. She also mentioned she told Tom about us, and she wanted a divorce as soon as possible. She asked me to talk to Tom and tell him myself, and I said I would.

I was hoping when I visited Darlene on Friday, Tom would be gone, perhaps back out to sea again, but that wasn't the case.

When I knocked on the door, Tom opened it and introduced himself. I almost died. All courage drained from my soul as I nervously introduced myself. He appeared angry, and I wasn't sure what he was going to say or do.

Darlene pushed past him through the open door and told him we were going riding and we would be back later. Her bold behavior dumbfounded me, and I didn't know what was going to happen next. She was transformed into a lioness by my presence and I was transformed into a kitten. Now that I was in her life, she found new hope and courage. I quickly followed her lead, got on the bike with her, and sped off to the club. She mentioned again I needed to tell Tom that I loved her and we were going to get married. I said I would tell him when we returned home and she was pleased.

She also told me that as a matter of safety, she kept a knife under her pillow to help stave off physical beatings from her abusive husband. I was hoping the abuse would stop and he would just leave her life forever as soon as possible. When we returned to her trailer later that night, I waited until she got safely into her residence before I left. I did not have a conversation with Tom about his wife and me. I put it off because of fear, but I would soon get the chance to have this dreaded conversation.

A few days later, Darlene invited me back over to have dinner with her and Tom, and I accepted the invitation. I was quite nervous to sit in that small trailer at the same fold-down table where Darlene had poured her heart out to me a week or so prior. I don't remember what we had for dinner that night, but I do remember Darlene playing footsie with me under the table. Again, fear began to rise within me, and I was hoping Tom would not see our contact with each other. Darlene was bold and I was shaking like a leaf. Nevertheless, Darlene gave me courage because she saw me as her champion. I was starting to realize soon I was going to have to tell Tom I was going to marry his wife. Thankfully that was not the night I needed to do it. I left and returned to the barracks without telling him.

A couple of nights later, I stopped by, and Darlene suggested we go riding. We just rode around downtown Charleston near the Battery. Upon returning to the trailer, when we opened the door, we saw Tom, unconscious on the floor just inside the trailer on his stomach. Darlene entered first and, with disgust, kicked him in the side and told him sternly to get up. I started to panic because I thought he was dead. I knew I would be blamed and would go to prison for causing the death of this man.

I rolled him over and noticed a steak knife under his gut and a small puncture wound in his stomach. I immediately checked to make sure he was breathing. After reviving him, I drove him to the naval hospital emergency room in his car, while Darlene stayed behind. She seemed apathetic to his condition and I didn't blame her because of everything he had put her through. Still, I wanted to make sure he got medical attention right away. I also wanted witnesses to see he was alive and I was trying to help him.

The naval hospital corpsmen in the ER treated Tom's superficial stomach wound. They wanted him to answer a series of questions about the cause and take a drug test. He refused both requests and specified he wanted to leave right away after the wound was treated. He checked himself out and told me we were leaving, and I just listened. He decided to drive, and I rode with him. We didn't talk about anything on the way home, nor did he thank me for taking him to the hospital.

When we returned him to his trailer, Darlene asked me if I had told him we wanted to marry. I indicated that I did talk to him about it. That was my first lie to my beloved. I lied because I was afraid, and I didn't know how to face my fear. I just wanted Tom to go away and I was hoping he would just leave her life for good. Believing my lie, Darlene confronted Tom in the back bedroom while I was there. I was sitting on the couch near the front of the trailer, and I could hear their conversation.

She brought the subject up and said she knew I told him we were getting married. He denied I said to him that fact, which left

Darlene confused and angry. She believed me and she wanted him to hear it from me again. Darlene and Tom exited the bedroom and came directly towards me sitting on the couch.

Darlene asked, "Steve, did you tell Tom we were getting married?"

"I was going to tell him," I replied. "I haven't done it yet."

I could tell by her demeanor she was very disappointed in me. She then turned and looked directly at Tom and said, "Steve and I are getting married, and you'll have to leave right away and give me a divorce."

Tom looked at me, and I nodded in agreement. That's when he got the message loud and clear. Later, I apologized to her for my lie. I left that evening and went back to the barracks, asking God to forgive me for the lie I had told and to protect Darlene from Tom. I didn't call Darlene for several days to allow her time to heal from the hurt.

Unfortunately, Tom did take his anger out on her that night. He physically and sexually abused her. She finally had had enough, and when he turned his back to her, she smacked him in the head with an 8" cast iron skillet, knocking him out cold. When he came to, he knew to never hurt her again and finally left for good. On the way out the door, he threatened Darlene, saying he was going to have his way with her younger sister, Gayle, the next time he went home to Winter Haven.

Darlene called me and gave me the good news. The nightmare was finally over, and the next day I moved in permanently with my beloved. I bought an engagement ring for $25 from a buddy named John, who I served with on the last patrol. As luck would have it, he had just broken up with his girl and the ring was returned to him. I was thankful the ring fit perfectly on Darlene's finger, and she wore it with pride. The ring made it official. We belonged to each other, and we planned to marry as soon as she was legally divorced. We moved into each other's hearts for good.

In June, Darlene started having menstrual cramps and bleeding. We were worried she might miscarry her first child. She hadn't gotten any bigger over the past month and didn't look very pregnant. When the bleeding started, I took her to the naval clinic to be checked. They hooked her up to the fetal doppler and couldn't detect the baby's heartbeat.

A couple of days later, Darlene miscarried at home. She went into a funk for a while and was very sad about losing her first baby. She believed Tom had killed the fetus when he slammed on the brakes that one day in the car and hurt her lower stomach. To help alleviate her painful loss, Darlene gradually removed all baby items from the spare room and donated them to the local charity. She did not want to be reminded of this precious baby's lost life.

7
BONDING

Proverbs 31:10 (NASB) "An excellent wife, who can find? For her worth is far above jewels."

Living together with Darlene was a dream come true, and we already considered ourselves a married couple. We shared everything, and we were committed to each other on every matter. We promised to love, honor, and cherish each other until death do us part.

We contacted a local attorney in Charleston, who practiced family law. I gave him a check for $250 for Darlene to file for divorce. He said it might take a year to finalize since she filed it on the grounds of desertion. I also changed my pay status to include Darlene as my dependent. This action would ensure my bi-monthly paychecks would be sent to her when I was at sea. She was also added to my bank checking account, which would allow her to cash the paychecks, pay the bills, buy food, and engage in other matters involving finance. We trusted each other completely.

My submarine buddies thought I was crazy to trust her with my paychecks while I was out to sea. I didn't care what they thought and ignored their advice and went with my gut instinct. I believed it was God leading me to take care of Darlene. After all, we were in love, forever and a day.

During June and July of 1970, the Gold Crew was out to sea on the *USS Simon Bolivar*, while the Blue Crew, of which I was a member, was ashore. During the week, I had to physically report every day to the SSBN-641 submarine office on base. Some days, I

Opposite: Darlene and Steve 1970.

had some type of training to attend. Other days, I had work projects to accomplish. Still other times, we had nothing much to do but to hang out at the office. Every day I was away from Darlene was a challenge for me. I thought about her all the time and usually had a hard time concentrating on my job.

During our first year together, it was as if time stood still, as we always seemed to stay in the moment. I loved that we only had eyes and hearts for each other. Whenever I had the opportunity to go off base for a lunch break, I would often get on my motorcycle and race over to our trailer to see her. We loved to surprise each other. On the way home, I would sometimes stop by someone's yard and pick their flowers, stuffing them in my shirt, to protect the petals from falling off as I drove the cycle. Upon arrival, I would present them to her, never revealing how I had acquired them. Her face would light up with joy as she gently arranged the flowers in a vase and placed them on our fold down kitchen table.

I would often write love notes to her, hiding them in her coffee cup, shoes, and other discreet places, hoping she would find them early and read them before the day began. The little gifts would surprise her and brighten her days. She also left me love notes in the morning, hidden in my shoes or under my coffee cup or in other out-of-the-way places. We acted like newlyweds all the time, and I cherished those moments.

We created a special language to express our love to each other with minimum words. We used two unique acronyms the most: ITALY and HOLLAND. ITALY meant "I Truly Always Love You," and HOLLAND was "Hope Our Love Lasts and Never Dies." These two acronyms were written on all presents and cards and notes we gave each other. Darlene also used these two acronyms in family grams she sent me when I was on submarine patrol. Each family gram was limited to 25 words or less, which included both of our names, so the two coded words allowed us more use of our love language beyond the 25-word limitation.

Most of our time during that first year together in 1970, we went everywhere on my motorcycle. We even visited grocery stores and carried our groceries back on the bike. Dar would hold the bag in front of me, and we always made it home with our food intact. We also enjoyed riding our motorcycle and going to the Charleston beaches. Darlene loved the ocean and said that, when she was near the ocean, she could hear God's voice more easily, and I believed my beloved. Our favorite beach was on Mount Pleasant, located directly east of the Charleston Battery area. To get there, we would have to cross the Cooper River Bridge, which only had a two lane span at the time. The bridge was designed to allow tall military ships to pass under it. Hence, it was very high and the lanes were narrow. God truly protected us as we drove everywhere on our motorcycle. We traveled back-and-forth over that bridge many times on the motorcycle without fear.

On one particular day, we had had a great time in the sun on Mount Pleasant Beach, and Darlene was unusually tired and wanted to go home. She took her normal position on the back of our cycle and wrapped her arms around my waist, locking her fingers together. As usual, she rested her head sideways on my upper back. When we got home, which took around 20 minutes, I turned off the motorcycle and started to assist Darlene, but she wouldn't release her grip around my waist. After a moment, I turned around and saw her eyes were closed. In shock, I woke her up and helped her dismount from the bike. Once inside, she mentioned she must have fallen asleep as soon as she climbed on the cycle behind me. I could hardly believe it. The bike had no sissy bar to support the passenger, and if her hands had let go, she might have fallen off the bike. Being asleep on the back of a small motorcycle and riding across the Cooper River Bridge, makes this event worthy of the Guinness Book of Records. I thanked God for His protection.

When we weren't riding our "motor," as she called it, and having picnics in the country or frolicking on the beach, we took long walks around the neighborhood or into town. During our walks, she would bring healthy snacks to eat along the way, like boiled peanuts, cherry tomatoes, celery sticks, or other fresh vegetables. I tried boiled peanuts when she offered me some, but I hated them. I thought they were too squishy and tasteless. Also, I was never interested in eating tomatoes by themselves or raw vegetables. Still, I learned to like them over time. My favorite snacks on our walks were ice cream cones. We would stop at a custard vendor with a pushcart on wheels along the way and buy flavored ice in a cup or soft ice custard in cones or cups. Darlene loved crushed ice without any additives. It didn't have to have flavor additives for her to enjoy it. She just loved crunching the cold chips in her mouth. When she did desire a flavor on those rare occasions, she always chose grape.

In our small trailer, we would play many games to entertain ourselves. I hated playing gin rummy with her because she always seemed to get the best cards. In fact, this was also true with Poker, Pinochle, Rook, and many other card games. When I learned how to play Bridge, I taught her hoping her luck with cards would continue, and it did. Through the years, when we played Bridge with our neighbors and friends, she invariably continued to get the best hands. We also played various board games, like Sorry, Scrabble, Aggravation, and Life. Other times we would just make up games, like ice fighting, where we would get ice chips from the freezer and chase each other around the trailer inside and out, throwing ice at each other, while laughing hysterically   .

Darlene and I were so in love, we rarely argued about anything. Still, oddly enough, our first verbal fight was over a silly card game. I called her a name and quickly apologized, but never forgot her look of disappointment at my unthoughtful barb. I made sure that that would never happen again.

One of her absolute favorite hobbies was reading. We made sure to visit consignment shops and used bookstores regularly. She especially loved romance novels and mystery thrillers, and would curl up with a good book and read for hours. Often, she would read through the night while I slept, and she never forgot the details in the books she read. Years would go by, and she could still see a book and recount to me some details within it. I was amazed by her memory.

She also had a fantastic memory when it came to movies. Once she saw a movie, she committed it to memory, even the most trivial details. In those early days, we didn't see many movies because we didn't have much money to spend and we didn't own a TV. We did have a little portable record player with a built-in speaker that played 45 and 33 records, though. She loved all kinds of music, including romantic love songs as well as rock music and gospel. She never really liked Opera and tolerated Classical music until the violins would play. The sound would pierce her ears with the high notes.

And, like my father and mother, we loved to dance. On most weekends, we would ride to the Navy enlisted club or the Air Force officer club and dance the night away. She was small, and I was tall and lanky. We looked like the odd couple on the dance floor, but we didn't care what people thought, because we had each other and that's all that mattered. During our first year together, Darlene was very healthy and active. It was as if her body was renewed and refreshed by hope and our love

* * *

Darlene was a southern girl from Florida and held fast to some traditions. She loved to get together with other neighborhood ladies for coffee and fellowship in the morning. She was a great listener of their problems, usually having to do with their kids or husbands. Even though it was natural for them to gossip about others, Darlene would try to steer the conversation to more wholesome topics or, if that was not possible, she would ask them if she could pray for any of their needs. Darlene believed that God answered prayers, regardless of the severity. She would also never pass along the gossip to me when we were together. She kept the issues in her prayer book and shared them with God alone.

I didn't want Darlene to have to work outside the home because I wanted to provide for her, and she appreciated being a stay-at-home "wife." Each morning, she would get up early and fix her hair, put on makeup, and cook me breakfast. She never wanted me to see her in curlers or without makeup on, and I loved the fact she made me breakfast while looking good. It made me feel good before I went to work on my motorcycle.

One morning, I woke up very late for work at the naval base. We were scheduled to have a personnel inspection after quarters around 8:00 am and I had to rush to get dressed in my dress whites, hurrying off to work on my motorcycle. It had rained the night before and the moisture from the roadways splashed up onto my shoes and pants. When I was almost to the base, I ran out of gas and switched to the reserve tank. Upon arrival at the base, I had to park the motorcycle at the front gate because they weren't permitted. I hitched a ride to the office and arrived around an hour late. As I entered the office, I noticed the personnel inspection had just finished. The duty officer wrote me up for being late and missing inspection. He also made a note that my uniform was dirty and I was told I would have an XO's mast later that day to explain why I was late.

Around 1:00 pm, I was ordered to stand at parade rest outside the XO's office. A couple of minutes later, the XO ordered me to report. As I stood at attention in front of him, he asked me to explain my tardiness. I apologized for being late and told him it would never happen again. I proceeded to tell him I had acquired two extra alarm clocks as back up. He ordered me to do two hours of community service on base, and then dismissed the charges, and I was free to go. A couple of hours later, I completed the community service. On the way home, I bought a couple of alarm clocks, one electric and one battery, to help me never to be late for duty again.

* * *

It had been a year since Darlene had seen her sister, Gayle, and she was always worried about her safety due to Tom's threat to hurt her when he returned to Winter Haven that summer. Gayle had just graduated from high school and wasn't getting along with their mom. When Darlene called her and warned her about Tom, she ended up giving Gayle permission to stay with us until the dust settled back home. By late June, Gayle had saved enough money working at her uncle's jewelry store to buy a one-way train ticket to Charleston. Once she arrived at our trailer by cab, our honeymoon came to an end.

Darlene felt responsible for Gayle's welfare, which I understood. She became a pseudo-mom to Gayle and looked after her welfare since David's death. Darlene thought if Gayle was close by, she could continue to counsel her and help her get started on a new life. We gave her the small bedroom next to our room in the trailer. It wasn't long before a couple of sailor friends of mine discovered the new girl in town. Gayle had hardly dated in high school and was very naïve when it came to men. When she was around men, she was too outgoing and flirtatious, despite our warnings to be careful. She felt free, now that she was away from her mom.

One sailor named Bob caught her eye. He also had a motorcycle, like me, and would take her riding, which she loved. Gayle wanted to be like her older sister, Darlene, in every way. She had a good man now that Tom was gone, and Gayle wanted one, too. Darlene, however, was getting frustrated that Gayle wouldn't listen to her warnings about guys and hanging out with strangers. In addition to this, Gayle also wasn't motivated to get a job and start being productive. During the week, I spent every day at the submarine office on base, and I didn't witness all of the drama Gayle was creating. I did, however, sense Darlene's frustration and was hoping Gayle would be responsible and get a job and save up some money. None of that happened that summer of 1970.

8
BATTLE STATIONS

Isaiah 43:2 (NKJV) "When you pass through the waters, I will be with you; and through the rivers, they shall not overflow you."

I wasn't due to make another submarine patrol until August. I knew I would be gone for two months, so I made sure Darlene and Gayle would be taken care of financially by having my paychecks sent to them. Getting letters from your loved ones helped to pass the time at sea, and I made sure to let Darlene know I wanted her to communicate with me when I was out on my next patrol. I reminded her she could send me messages of 25 words or less. These messages were known as "family grams."

She would have to provide the family gram to the radioman on base at the SSBN-641 office and was allowed five family grams per patrol period. The radioman on base would review each family gram to make sure it contained no bad news. Any information that would adversely affect the sailor's attitude or behavior aboard was prohibited. Once approved, the radioman would transmit the family gram messages to the submarine, and the sub's radioman on watch would then print the family grams and hand them out to the recipients.

Many times, messages received were sketchy due to words that were removed by the shore-based radioman. Darlene made sure the two acronyms we created, ITALY and HOLLAND, were always inserted into each family gram while I was on patrol. The shore-based radioman never caught on to our scheme. Some sentences were incoherent, but ITALY and HOLLAND remained, which meant a lot to me, thousands of miles away, underwater somewhere.

In early August, we prepared to get underway for patrol. It was my 2nd submarine patrol on the *USS Simon Bolivar*, and this time I was going to work in the field in which I had trained as an FTB in MCC. Underway, the submarine operated on 18-hour days. Each FTB was paired up with another FTB and stood watch in the MCC for six hours. All assigned preventive and corrective maintenance of the Mk-84 Fire Control System (FCS) equipment would be completed by the two FTB's on watch. At the end of the sixth-hour watch, the two FTB's would be relieved by another pair of FTB's, and they would assume watch. The pair that was relieved of duty had 12 hours off to do what they wanted, including eating, sleeping, and recreation, like playing cards. Of course, when there were planned and unplanned drills and emergencies, all hands had to be awake and in their battle stations.

On this patrol, I was honored to stand watch in MCC with Walt Norris. He was an FTB1, the leading petty officer (LPO) of our FTB gang. I was only an FTB3. Walt had a reputation of being a good listener and providing guidance to sailors to help solve their problems. This unique gift was especially needed on long underwater submarine patrol periods. Sailors had a lot of downtime on their hands after their watch, and plenty of stuff to think about when they were underway. As previously mentioned, we couldn't transmit any messages or make phone calls to our loved ones when we were out to sea, so having Walt available to share our problems with was a real blessing. Many shipmates visited him in MCC, while I stood watch with him, and took advantage of his good nature and wisdom.

Walt had been in the Navy for 16 years and only needed four more years before he could retire and draw a pension. Years before, when he was an LPO on another submarine, he had had a nervous breakdown. The Navy had grounded him and considered giving him a medical discharge. After recovering, he had asked the Navy to give him another chance to serve at sea on subs and they had consented. All was well when Walt wasn't the LPO. On this patrol, however, he became the LPO again, due to his seniority in rate. Life was about to radically change for him once again.

While underway on patrol in some remote part of the world, deep within the ocean, I was standing watch with Walt in MCC. Earlier in the watch period, a couple of guys had visited with Walt in MCC. They had talked to him about issues in their life, and Walt had listened and given them advice. I was focused on running tests, so I didn't pay much attention to the discussion or Walt's demeanor.

After they left, he asked me to get him a cup of coffee. He had never requested that I get him coffee before, but I didn't think it was unusual because he was my boss and LPO. I immediately left MCC, shut the door and went to the crew's mess, one deck up, and made two cups of coffee. I was only gone for a couple of minutes. Upon my return, I tried the combination on the door keypad three times, but it wouldn't open. I started to get concerned. I then knocked on the door and yelled his name, but there was no answer. About that time, a few guys who were playing cards nearby sauntered over and asked what was going on. I told them that Walt wouldn't unlock the door and let me back in. I then tried to call him on the phone outside the MCC door. Walt answered the phone, and I told him I had his coffee and he needed to unlock the door and let me in.

He said to me, "Why should I? When you're in here, you don't do any work anyway."

I said, "C'mon, Walt. Stop kiddin' around. Open the door." He abruptly hung up.

By this time, more guys had assembled around the door, including the Engineering Officer. Bill Hankison (aka Hank), one of the FTB's, who also worked in MCC, decided to take matters into his own hands. I heard him say he could gain access into MCC via the MCC fan room access door. He hurried around the corner and located a small access door near the deck in the laundry room. He removed the access cover and slid himself inside the MCC fan room. He climbed around, over, and under various ductworks until he reached another small access door that opened into MCC. Fortunately, the door was unlocked, and he entered. When Walt heard the door close, he turned towards Hank.

Hank calmly talked to Walt as he slowly moved towards the main door. He reminded Walt he shouldn't be in MCC alone with the door locked. As Hank rounded a corner and started towards the door, Walt leaped up and grabbed Hank's right arm, trying to pull him back. Hank continued to pull and, with his left arm fully extended, managed to unlock and open the door. Being the most senior person present, the Engineer took charge of the scene and stepped inside MCC. He was not as tall or as big as Walt and was no match for him. The Engineer looked up into Walt's face and yelled, "What the hell is going on, Petty Officer Norris?"

With his right-hand, Walt reached out and roughly grabbed the Engineer's shirt near the collar and pushed him away. At that moment, the XO and the Weapons Officer entered MCC. Both were armed with .45 caliber semiautomatic pistols. They confronted Walt and escorted him out of MCC and led him to the XO's stateroom, which was in the upper-level operations. The XO talked calmly to Walt and asked him what had happened. Walt said he felt someone was messing around with the switchboard in the middle-level missile compartment. The XO verified with the roving patrol that such an incident had never occurred.

The XO listened more and, after a while, Walt seemed to calm down and become more lucid. He then told Walt to go to bed and get some sleep. As Walt was leaving the XO's stateroom, he said offhandedly he had to go back on watch in MCC. At that point, the XO jumped up and darted out to the passageway, grabbing Walt and trying to prevent him from leaving. It was a battle between two big men. The XO yelled loudly for help. Upon hearing the XO's cry, three or four men rushed out from the Control Room and leaped on Walt, trying to restrain him. The Corpsman arrived in the nick of time and injected a syringe filled with a sedative into his leg. Within a minute, Walt went limp and lay motionless on the deck.

Per the XO's direction, the sailors picked him up and carried him to the Torpedo Room. Once there, they put him on a stretcher and laid him on his back on a small bench just inside the room. Using rope and high-pressure tape, they secured him to the bench, and he remained in that configuration for three days. We surfaced near the coast of Cape Race, Newfoundland, and attempted a helicopter transfer of Walt in a stretcher. However, the waves were too high to try a helicopter transfer, so the Captain decided to submerge and head south to Bermuda for calmer seas.

During that transit, I got permission to visit Walt in the Torpedo Room. When I saw how he was restrained securely to the bench, I couldn't believe it. I didn't say anything about it because I didn't want to upset him any further. Instead, I told him I appreciated everything he had taught me in MCC and I hoped he would get well soon. He spoke softly and asked me to get closer to his face.

I leaned down, and he whispered, "They think I'm crazy."

I laughed a little and said, "Walt, you're not crazy. You're going to be okay."

He said, "I know I'm not crazy. I'm getting off this boat. You're staying."

I wondered at that time if he had faked the incident so he could get off the boat.

A couple of days later, we surfaced off the coast of Bermuda. A Navy tugboat came alongside our missile deck and Walt was carefully transferred to it on a stretcher. Years later, I heard through the rumor mill that Walt had received a medical discharge from the Navy. He was a good man who had tried to help everyone who had asked for his advice, but, sadly, the only one he couldn't help at that time was himself. He only had four more years to retire, but the strain of being the leading petty officer in charge of the FTB's was too much for him.

On that same patrol, we had a new medical doctor on board. He was a Navy lieutenant and had replaced the MD we had had on the previous patrol. During this patrol, the doctor handed out a survey form to all crew members, asking questions about the use of illicit drugs, like marijuana. For some reason, he wanted to find out if drug usage was a problem in the Navy on submarines. Once the Captain found out about the drug survey, he ordered the doctor to collect all the surveys and dispose of them at sea. Later, I found out from some friends that the doctor took a personal interest in marijuana and some even believed he smoked it underway in the sickbay where he worked most days, though I had never witnessed it.

When our patrol was complete, we surfaced and docked in Rota, Spain. We had to take a crew flight back to Charleston, SC, but the doctor decided to stay and take leave in Europe. When we left, he visited the island of Gibraltar and bought several kilos of marijuana and packaged it in his luggage. When he returned to Charleston on a separate flight, the drug-sniffing dogs at the Charleston airport discovered the drugs and he was promptly arrested. From then on, the Navy stopped assigning medical doctors for submarine duty. The Navy corpsman could handle the assignment better, anyway.

* * *

Near the end of my second patrol, I officially "qualified in Submarines" and received my silver dolphins pin, which was presented to me by Captain Browder, the Commanding Officer, at an official ceremony in the Control Room. He pinned the dolphins on my chest and congratulated me. After the ceremony, I went to the crew's mess and bought a lot of cokes and handed them out to qualified sailors. Then, I walked a gauntlet between two rows of sailors who had the honor of tacking the dolphins on my chest with their fists as a congratulatory gesture. Most punches were gentle, but a couple seemed determined to literally pin the dolphins onto my chest. Fortunately, they didn't draw blood.

* * *

We returned from patrol in early October, and when we came into port, we tied up alongside a submarine tender. Wives and families of the Blue Crew were waiting on the ship for their spouses to depart the sub. Darlene was there waiting for me as well, and I was so thrilled to see her. I rushed into her loving arms and we held each other close as we kissed deeply.

Upon arrival back at our trailer, Gayle was there. She commented that she was glad I was back as well, as she was tired of eating macaroni and cheese for breakfast, lunch, and dinner. I didn't understand why they only had mac and cheese to eat the whole time I was away until Darlene produced all the paychecks she had received while I was out. None of them had been cashed or deposited. She said she had wanted to prove to me she could be trusted with my money, but I couldn't understand how they survived. She said her girlfriend in the trailer next door gave them food to eat many times, and they had also picked and ate field corn from the local farms. I convinced my beloved never to do that again because I trusted her emphatically. She didn't need to prove her loyalty to me.

* * *

In October, we decided to move from our little silver trailer and start a new life and leave the past behind. Riding around on our motorcycle, we saw a small concrete block type single-story house with a small "For Rent" sign out front. On the outside, the place looked tiny and run down, but we decided to check it out anyway. We met with the landlord and he showed us the interior, which was a square-shaped room about 24 x 24 feet in diameter. It was a multi-purpose room containing a kitchen area, dining area, and living room. On the far side was a door that opened into a bedroom. We also had a small bathroom that was attached to the bedroom. The house, or "shack," as we humorously named it later-on, was somewhat furnished with the essentials, including a refrigerator and bed. Overall, it looked clean and tidy and livable on the inside.

The exterior, however, looked like a building that had barely survived the Depression years. The siding was moldy and chipped or missing in many places. Weeds and other vegetation had married itself to the structure and appeared to be assisting in holding it up. The house was also located on a main street with hardly any frontage. What yard there was was completely bare of grass. Red clay and weeds were nature's covering out front. The great thing was that we didn't care about how it looked on the outside. We were in love and all we wanted was a place of refuge, a place of peace, and a place to start our life together. After agreeing to pay $70 a month, we signed a month-to-month lease, and the three of us moved in.

Unfortunately, we couldn't stay in the shack for more than a couple of months, as it was too small and run down, and also had mice. We wanted to move to a better location and still stay within my tight Navy budget. Fortunately, we were able to find a lovely mobile home in a quiet area of town. The monthly rent was a little more, around $125 a month, but we could still afford it and moved in right away.

* * *

One night, we had a strange encounter with an evil presence in our mobile home. Darlene and I were resting in bed, holding hands and talking quietly to each other. Gayle was asleep in her bedroom. Besides our voices, the only other sound we heard was the turning of the wheel by Gayle's pet hamster running in his cage. Suddenly, I audibly heard laughter and the clinking of cocktail glasses together. It was the sound of people partying and laughing with each other. I sensed Darlene heard this noise at the same time because her body jumped slightly and her hand squeezed mine. I released my hands from hers and placed them over my ears, and the sound level didn't change. It was as if it originated from within our beings.

I then heard a voice within me clearly say the following: "I think we got them now."

At that moment, Darlene and I hugged one another tightly. All I wanted to do was escape the pending terror by leaving the trailer immediately that night and never returning. I even yelled out to Gayle to wake up and come into our room. When she entered, I asked her if she heard anything unusual. She said she hadn't because she was asleep.

I told her and Darlene we needed to leave immediately for our safety. Then, Darlene and I heard another loud noise outside the trailer. It sounded like someone had hit the trailer one time with a baseball bat or some other large object, but Gayle didn't hear a thing. Then the noise stopped completely. We waited and whispered to each other, not knowing what was going to happen next. If we left and the enemy was outside, we could get hurt.

I remember Darlene and I prayed together that day for God's protection and peace. We were both raised in the Christian faith, so we believed both good and evil existed. For some reason, evil had manifested itself to us in the natural realm and Gayle was spared the experience. This evil encounter left a significant and lasting impression on Darlene and me, as we recognized that this evil had wanted to terrorize and possibly kill us. Why had we been singled out? Why did it manifest itself? Was it our fault?

We didn't have the answers. We only knew we wanted God's protection, and we didn't know how to have a personal relationship with God to be fully saved and protected from the evil one. We had been churchgoers when we were young but had drifted away as we had gotten older. I had been raised Catholic, and she had been raised in the Church of Christ. Wasn't that good enough? Apparently not. We didn't know the way or the truth. (John14:6 NKJV - Jesus said to him, "I am the way, the truth, and the life. No one comes to the Father except through Me.")

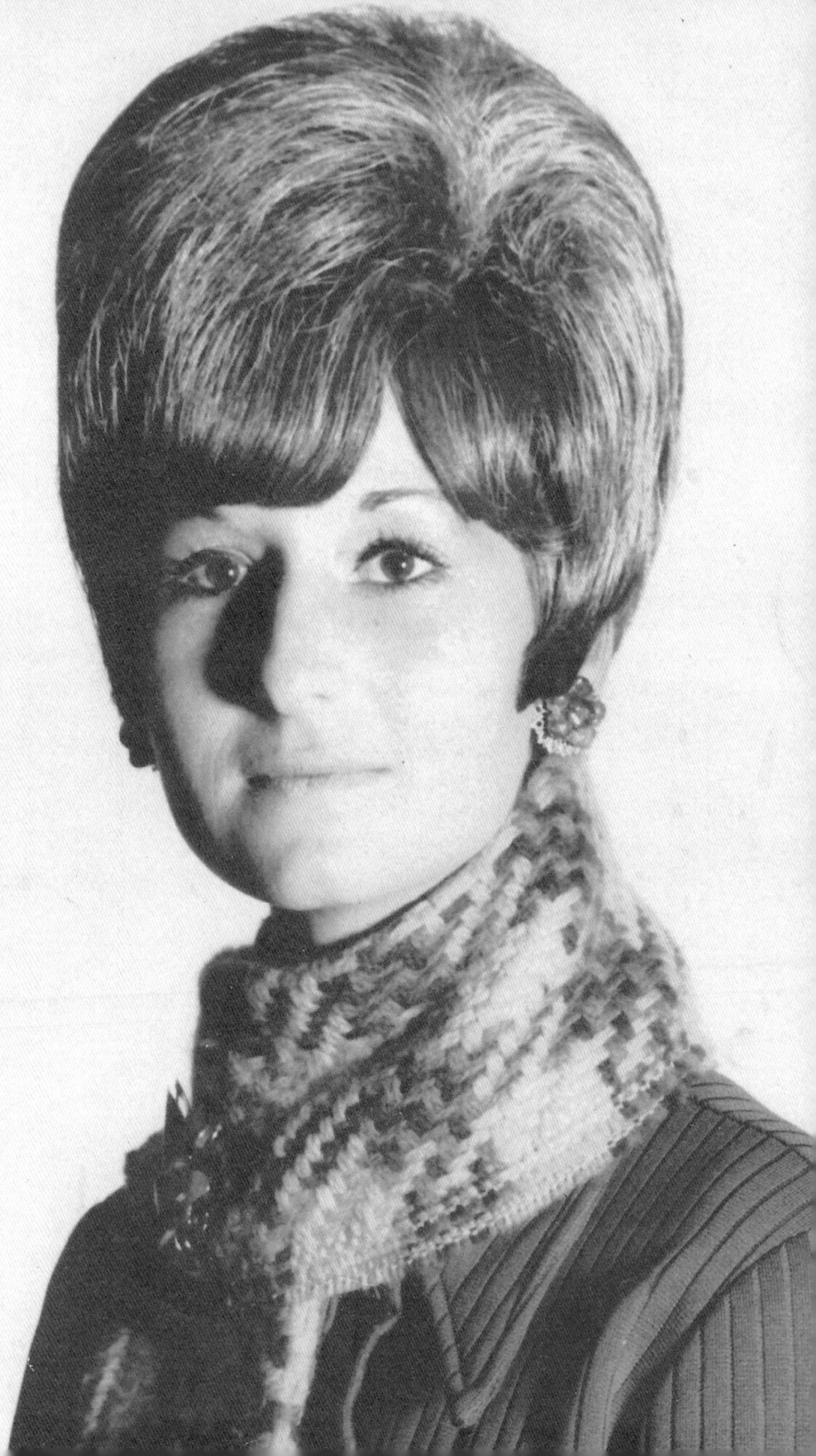

9
MY BLESSED BRIDE

Genesis 2:24 – (NKJV) "Therefore a man shall leave
his father and mother and be joined to his wife, and
they shall become one flesh."

In January 1971, the *USS Simon Bolivar* (SSBN-641) came out of operation and went into the Newport News Shipyard for a year of overhaul and modernization. Even though I was still assigned to the submarine while it was in the shipyard, we needed to relocate to the Newport News area and find a place to live during this overhaul period. Every day, I would still have to go to work on the boat or the Navy barge nearby. The barge had a make-shift office set up inside for the officers and crew. Most of the time in the shipyard, we had very little to do but to sit around, tell sea stories, and shuffle administrative paperwork. The shipyard itself was responsible for overhauling and modernizing our submarine. Besides replacing the existing nuclear reactor with a new one, they had to convert all of the missile tubes from a Polaris Missile A-3 configuration to the new Poseidon C-4 Missile, which had a longer range and greater destructive power.

Once our submarine initially went into the Newport News Shipyard and was dry docked by the Gold crew, I was then able to carpool with a couple of other shipmates back to Charleston to get Darlene. We left on Sunday and drove south on US-17. When we got to Smithfield, Virginia, our car broke down, and we pulled off on the side of the road with no idea what to do about the situation. I suggested we should pray and ask God to bring us a mechanic to help. I remember one of the guys laughing about what I said, and he started openly mocking God in a blasphemous way. I felt very uncomfortable with his behavior and wanted to get away from him for fear God would bring a greater disaster on us.

I stepped out of the car and said a prayer silently to God, and it wasn't long before a vehicle stopped and asked us if we needed help. He said he owned a car repair shop in town and would be more than happy to diagnose the problem and repair our vehicle so we could continue on our way. After towing our vehicle to his shop, he determined the problem to be a clogged fuel pump, for which he just happened to have a replacement part in stock. Within the hour we were back on the road and I was amazed by God's answer to my prayer. I later reminded the mocker of God's goodness, and he shrugged it off as a coincidence.

* * *

I was so glad to see Darlene when I arrived back in Charleston. I decided to sell my motorcycle and buy us a car. A shipmate wanted to buy my motorcycle, and he wanted to take it out for a ride first. After he admitted, he had very little experience with a motorcycle, I refused to let him ride it. I told him to give me the cash first, and then I'd sign over the title and give him the keys.

He finally agreed and gave me the money. After handing him the title and keys, I explained how to operate the motorcycle and cautioned him to be careful, especially in first gear. Then, I stepped back, and he got on the cycle. He started the engine, revved it up, and popped the clutch. Without warning, the motorcycle leaped forward with the front wheel coming off the ground dragging my friend across the street. He barely missed a vehicle that was driving by, and the motorcycle slammed into the building on the opposite side of the road. After he flipped over the handlebars and landed on his back, I ran over to make sure he was okay. He was fine but very embarrassed about the accident. He turned off the cycle and noticed the front wheel was bent. He then asked for his money back, and I refused and reminded him he owned it.

We used the money to buy a used 1966 Chevrolet Caprice from another friend in town. It was dark blue with a white vinyl top and tan leather seats. It was a very nice car that rode well, and Darlene enjoyed driving it, too.

It wasn't long before we left Charleston and headed north to Newport News. Gayle wasn't going with us because, in early December, she had married Bob and they stayed in Charleston. Also, since we didn't have any furniture to transport, we were able to bring everything we owned in the car. Upon arrival in Newport News, we looked around for an apartment to rent. We found a lovely one-bedroom that was quite small but fully furnished and suited our needs. We signed a one-year lease and looked forward to living in our new home.

We could hardly wait to make our marriage official. Darlene's lawyer in Charleston was trying to expedite the divorce, but Tom continually refused to sign the divorce paperwork that the court had served him. At another hearing in Charleston, Darlene's lawyer finally convinced the judge to honor her divorce request on the terms of desertion, as Tom had not responded to any of the court's requests. The judge set a date for the divorce hearing for late March 1971, and we were elated. I immediately started making plans and wanted us to marry in the Catholic Church, to which Darlene agreed. It was the only faith I knew, and I wanted to make sure we started with a sure foundation. Also, I knew my parents would attend the wedding because I needed my dad to sign for me since I was only 20 years old; I also wanted their blessing. I wasn't concerned about Darlene's parents attending the ceremony because we weren't going to invite them anyway.

We immediately contacted Saint Vincent DePaul, a local Catholic Church in downtown Newport News and made plans to marry with the parish priest. The date we chose for our wedding was Saturday, April 3, 1971. The pastor required us to meet with him a few times in March for marriage counseling, which we agreed to do. We verified with the local county marriage license office that to get a marriage license, I would need my father to sign for me. Even though Darlene was 19, she didn't need her parent's permission because she had been previously married.

One interesting fact about our wedding date that came to light many years later during my private Bible study was that according to the Roman calendar, Jesus Christ was crucified on April 3, 33 A.D. This is noted on page 200 in Josh McDowell's book, "The New Evidence That Demands A Verdict". Was our wedding date a coincidence or did Father God guide us? I may ask Him when we meet in heaven.

After I told my parents the good news, they agreed to come to the wedding. They would need to arrive no later than Friday, April 2, during the business day to allow dad and me to go to the county marriage license office for a license. The challenge was my parents lived in northern Kentucky, about 600 miles away from Newport News, Virginia, and my father was unable to get off work until that very day. It would take around 12 hours for them to drive to our apartment, assuming they had no incidents or accidents along the way. The family car was a brown and white 1958 Oldsmobile with large tail fins and was not in good running condition but it was all they had to make the trip. Fortunately, it was large enough to transport five kids and two adults. John, Jeff, Theresa and Jimmy sat in the back seat and Mary, who drove most of the way, was next to mom and dad in the front. My other brothers, Paul and Mike, decided to bring their girlfriends and carpool together. My sister, Carolyn, couldn't come, however, because she was married and had to take care of her husband and children.

Before we could marry, the other challenge was for Darlene to obtain the official divorce decree from the court. The hearing was set for Friday, March 26, and I was hoping there would be no delay. I bought her a round trip airplane ticket from Norfolk to Charleston. She flew to Charleston on Thursday and stayed at a motel near the courthouse. The next day, she met her lawyer and, together, they went to the divorce hearing. Tom never showed up and the hearing only lasted around a half hour. The judge ruled in Darlene's favor, and she was granted the divorce from Tom. On Saturday, Darlene flew back to Norfolk, and I picked her up. She could hardly wait to show me the divorce papers and we celebrated her freedom in our apartment.

Friday, April 2 finally arrived. We awoke early that day and were both quite anxious, as my parents were on their way to our place. I was very concerned they may be late, but Darlene seemed more worried about the cleanliness of our apartment and, all morning, she cleaned everything in sight. She even waxed and polished all the wood furniture to make it look shiny and bright. When I tried to rest my elbows on the wooden dinner table, she yelled at me to not touch it for fear it would smudge her work. I jokingly replied we should set up stanchions and rope off the furniture and treat our apartment like a museum, a comment that was not well received by my beloved.

Finally, at 4:30 pm, my parents' 1958 Oldsmobile pulled into our parking lot. It was a minor miracle they made it at all. On the way to our place, the car had broken down on a mountain in West Virginia. Dad had added STP gas additive to the fuel tank and that had seemingly given the old car new life. My younger sister, Mary, took over driving duties at that stage of the trip. She was only 18 with no experience driving across the country, but, by God's grace, they made it safely to our place in the nick of time. When they arrived, I ran out and kissed mom, then grabbed dad and stuffed him into my car. Darlene came along, as well. We only had 30 minutes until the county marriage license office closed for the weekend and thankfully, we made it with five minutes to spare. With the marriage license in hand, we went back to our apartment to rest.

The next morning, Saturday, April 3, was a glorious day to be alive. Finally, my beloved was going to be my bride, not just for that day, but forever and a day. It was the best day of our lives, bright and sunny out with hardly a cloud in the sky. Darlene and I had made our wedding vows a few nights before, with permission from the priest. We took the standard vows and changed them to be more personal to our deep love and devotion to each other. We had practiced saying our vows at home and made a couple of revisions before we were satisfied with them.

It had only been a year when I first met my blessed bride in that small trailer in Charleston. Over time, she had blossomed into a vibrant and outgoing young woman with hopes and dreams for the future. We had even talked about how many kids we would like to have. I suggested five kids—enough to form a basketball team. I teased her and said, we may go all the way and have nine children, like my mom and dad. From her reply, however, I could tell she didn't like that idea. Five was okay, but nine? I wanted her to know she would never have to work outside the home. I was going to be her sole provider and I would take care of her and the children, so she could focus on being at home with them as she desired. I told her I would always be her helpmate, and we would make all major decisions together. On our wedding day, we started a new journey, to be knitted together, under the blessing of Father God in holy matrimony.

Since Darlene had been previously married, she didn't think she should wear a white wedding gown. Instead, she chose a beautiful sky-blue colored dress, which was a few inches above the knee, and a purple plaid wool scarf, which she draped around her shoulders and she held together with one hand, giving her the appearance of royalty and beauty. I didn't own a suit at that time, so I wore a dark blue pin striped suit jacket, a long sleeve buttoned down light blue shirt, and a dark blue and white tie with gray dress pants. Our colors and our hearts matched the radiance of that special wedding day.

* * *

Gayle, sadly, wasn't able to attend our wedding. Right after we had left Charleston, she had run away from her husband, Bob, who had abused her. Sometime after she left, he filed for divorce. Gayle hitched a ride with a stranger to Rhode Island in the hope of starting a new life by herself. Upon arrival, she got a job right away and rented a small apartment close by. A year later, her mom convinced her to return to Florida and live with her at home. Darlene and Gayle kept in touch regularly over the years, mostly via phone calls.

* * *

Early Saturday morning, everyone left our apartment and drove their cars to the church. The priest, who was going to do the wedding, led us over to the chapel to show us where the actual ceremony would take place. We hadn't practiced the ceremony and he wanted to make sure we knew what to expect. It was going to be a simple wedding without a Catholic Mass. The entire wedding would be in the chapel, a small room just off the main sanctuary. Darlene and I would stand together up front, facing the priest for the entire ceremony. There would be no processional, no organist, no flowers or other decorations, no photographer, or any of the other niceties that were traditional in most weddings. It was going to be a simple yet serious affair because it was for life. We planned to exchange our vows and place a wedding ring on each other's fingers. Michael and Mary were to be our two witnesses, and besides my immediate family and my brothers' girlfriends, the only other attendees were my two best friends and shipmates: Ken Rice and Bill "Hank" Hankison.

After the priest explained the ceremony to us, he called me aside to partake in the sacrament of confession, a Catholic tradition. He didn't ask Darlene to join in because she was non-Catholic. He asked me quietly if I had any sins to confess before the ceremony, and I told him I couldn't think of any. I hadn't thought to confess to living with Darlene out of wedlock for the year leading up to that day. In truth, it had just never crossed my mind as a sin, because I was too excited about our marriage to take place. After confession, I walked over to see Darlene, and she asked me what he said. In jest, I said he offered me the keys to his car in case I wanted to make a quick getaway. She thought I was serious.

The priest did a great job of orchestrating the wedding. When it came time for me to read my wedding vows to Darlene and place the ring on her finger, it went flawlessly. I slipped the paper out of my inside jacket pocket at the right time and read the words with sincerity and purpose. When Darlene's turn came, there was a little problem. When she started to read her vows aloud, I looked over at the paper she was holding and noticed she was reading from an earlier draft we had changed the night before.

I interrupted her, and I quietly said to her, "Honey, you're reading the wrong version."

She turned and looked at me and said, "What?"

I repeated, "You're reading the wrong version. We updated it."

She paused and then said emphatically, loud enough for all to hear, "I'm going to kill you."

Everyone broke out laughing, including the priest. I felt like an idiot because I should have just let her read the draft, as no one would have known the difference, and, besides, God knew what was in our hearts. Nevertheless, my beloved finished reading her vows from the draft, and it came out perfectly anyway. Even though it wasn't OUR final product, it was God's, and that was all that mattered. When the priest gave me permission to kiss my bride, we warmly embraced, closed our eyes, and kissed each other for a moment that seemed eternal. After the ceremony, my brother, Mike, asked me if I had some money as an offering to give the priest, which I hadn't even considered. I gave Mike all I had, which was around $20. He contributed another $6 and handed the small amount of cash to the priest and thanked him. The priest seemed genuinely thankful for our offering.

We all stood in the churchyard for a while, laughing and talking about the ceremony. Mike, a natural-born entertainer, decided to do a cartwheel, and he managed not to hurt himself or ruin his clothes. When we left the church, we all went to a local Howard Johnson's Restaurant for lunch and fellowship. There were many great memories that day, including our time at lunch. Kathy, Mike's girlfriend and future wife, played with an olive from her martini during lunch. She inadvertently flipped it out, and it landed in my mom's tea glass, a perfect ending to a perfect day.

The next day, Sunday, my family said their good-byes and departed for their long road trip back to Kentucky. Darlene and I were finally alone together again to share the moment of being husband and wife.

~

10
OUR JOURNEY TOGETHER

1 Corinthians 13:4-8 (NASB) "Love is patient,
love is kind and is not jealous; love does not brag and is
not arrogant, does not act unbecomingly; it does not
seek its own, is not provoked, does not take into account
a wrong suffered, does not rejoice in unrighteousness,
but rejoices with the truth; bears all things, believes
all things, hopes all things, endures all things.
Love never fails; but if there are gifts of prophecy,
they will be done away; if there are tongues, they will
cease; if there is knowledge, it will be done away."

Darlene and I discussed traveling to Florida in the week that followed to meet her mom for the first time. We didn't have money to go on a real honeymoon, and I thought the trip to Florida would be a good substitute, especially since I had never been there before.

We decided to take a day trip to Washington, DC, which neither of us had ever visited, before we left for Florida. It was only a couple hours north of Newport News, but I had had no idea how congested the traffic would be both while getting there and while negotiating our way around town to see the various memorials. It took us around four hours just to drive to DC through the terrible traffic. Upon our arrival, we attempted to visit the Arlington National Cemetery, but we could not figure out how to enter it. We finally gave up, pulled over to the side of the highway, and parked. I asked Darlene to get out and pose with the Washington Monument in the background over her right shoulder. I snapped a couple of pictures and handed her the camera so she could do the same for me. We then got back in the car, drove around, and looked at the various monuments as we drove by. After an hour or so, we decided that was enough sightseeing for one day, and we headed back to our apartment in Newport News.

The next day, we packed and headed off to Florida. Rather than take I-95 to Winter Haven, Florida, I decided we should take a more scenic route via US-17. This was the route I had partially traveled with my buddies on our way to Charleston, and it hadn't been so bad, save for the breakdown in Smithfield. Overall, it was a more scenic route than I-95, because of all the small towns we had to travel through. And, while it was going to be a much longer road trip we didn't mind since we would be together. We talked the whole way about many things, including "flying roaches," which Darlene warned me were in her mother's house. They were aggressive, she said, and would fly at you. I was familiar with cockroaches because we had had them in our house growing up, but those had never flown and certainly hadn't been aggressive. In fact, they had always scattered as soon as the lights had been turned on. I didn't know if Darlene was kidding, but I was going to be careful anyway.

Upon arrival, her mom came outside to greet us. She hugged and kissed Darlene and me. We had a pleasant day with her, talking about our love and marriage, and she invited us to spend the night, to which we agreed. She even offered us to sleep in her bedroom since it had a queen-sized bed and the most privacy, and we accepted. Of course, after the long trip, I had to use the bathroom. I looked around thoroughly and didn't spot any roaches. However, as soon as I started to pee, a giant cockroach came out of hiding and launched itself towards me with vigor. It was all I could do to finish quickly and not urinate all over the floor. When I exited the bathroom and shared that scary experience with Darlene privately, we laughed about that incident, both then and several more times before we went to bed. Then as we lay down together in bed and was drifting off to sleep, she mentioned that I needed to make sure my mouth remained closed while sleeping, because a roach may fly in. At that instant my eyes failed open, my mouth closed tightly and I don't remember sleeping a wink that night for fear of the aggressive creatures from hell. Darlene slept like a baby and I stood guard.

Years later, after doing some research, I discovered the so-called "flying roach" was really a Florida palmetto bug. It was still in the cockroach family, but native to Florida and other southern states. I made sure Darlene knew I was right. Cockroaches don't fly, palmetto bugs do. I won't tell you all that she said about Florida, "Love Bugs", however. I'll save that for another book .

* * *

The phrase "time flies" is often used by people to express their disappointment in events or happenings that end, in their minds, all too soon. They wish these memorable and joyful events would continue forever. Time, in contrast, doesn't seem to pass quickly when you are bored or suffering.   Even though time seemed to fly by on our honeymoon, we had each other, and that's all that mattered. The first couple of years together were filled with love and joy and motorcycle rides and very little spending money, though that hadn't seemed to matter because love was all we had and needed in those early days. We enjoyed just being with each other, blocking out the rest of the world and its distractions. Time stood still, but that would change, and it had to. We weren't in heaven. We were in heaven on earth. God had a plan for our lives, and we had to discover what it was. (Jeremiah 29:11 For I know the plans and thoughts that I have for you, says the Lord, plans for peace and well-being and not for disaster, to give you a future and a hope.)

11
THE BIRTHING YEARS

Ephesians 6:1-4 (NASB) "Children, obey your
parents in the Lord, for this is right. Honor
Your Father And Mother (which is
the first commandment with a promise), O That
It May Be Well With You, And
That You May Live Long On
The Earth. Fathers, do not provoke your
children to anger, but bring them up in the discipline
and instruction of the Lord. "

Darlene and I had always talked about the number of children we would have and looked forward to becoming parents. I initially told her I wanted nine, enough to field a baseball team. She didn't like that idea and overruled me. Basketball was my favorite sport anyway, and we only needed five. I kept those thoughts to myself. I didn't want to be ejected from the game of life. One day, Darlene told me she didn't get her period and thought she was pregnant. The rabbit test showed a little life was growing within my beloved and would enter our world and change our lives forever. Darlene became pregnant with our first child during the summer of 1971. We were still living in our one-bedroom apartment in Newport News, and my submarine was halfway finished with the overhaul period at the Newport News Shipyard. The closest military hospital was at Fort Eustis, which was around 13 miles away.

Darlene's pregnancy was uneventful with no morning sickness or swollen legs. She looked beautiful and I made sure she had every food craving she desired. I really got off easy, however, when it came to late night cravings. It seemed the only craving she had was for crushed ice. In those days we didn't have a blender. So, I

Opposite: 1979 Clearwater, Florida. Darlene with Alita (4), Shane (2) and Joe (7).

decided to improvise. I would take three or four ice cubes and roll them in a clean dish towel. Then placing the towel on the kitchen counter with both ends folded, I would strike the towel sharply with a ball peen hammer until only ice chips remained within. I would then unfold the towel and carefully scrape the ice chips into a cup with a spoon making sure to not lose any of the frozen slivers. To see my wife's face light up as I presented her with her heart's desire, was worth the effort of my task.

In late March 1972, we felt the baby was long overdue. In March, we had made several trips to Fort Eustis Army hospital, only to be told after the pelvic examination that she hadn't dilated enough, and we could go back home. One day, in late March, after timing her contractions to consistent two-minute intervals, we were convinced this was the real thing. She was going to give birth with no more false alarms.

We rushed to the hospital and waited in the car until a contraction ended and I guessed that we would have around two minutes or less to get her into the hospital before another contraction would start. I hurried her into the lobby, and a nurse wheeled her back to an ER examination room, where she examined her and stated Darlene had only dilated a couple of centimeters and, therefore, I should take her home again, but I refused. I explained how this time was different because the contractions were increasing in frequency, and they were constant and measurable. The nurse could tell that Darlene was feeling very bad with abdominal pain, which prevented her from walking very easily. Even though she hadn't dilated, the nurse reluctantly relented, and Darlene was admitted into the military hospital.

I stayed with Darlene and waited for her to give birth, but nothing happened for several hours and I finally went out to the waiting room, laid back in a recliner, and fell asleep. Finally, as morning approached, Darlene was examined, and it was found that she had dilated a little more, prompting the medical team to move her to the delivery room. All the while, Darlene was screaming in pain. She told me later there were a few candy stripers nearby, who were observing the ordeal, and she also mentioned that the delivery room smelled of fresh paint, which made her sick to her stomach. The Army doctor finally gave her an epidural injection in her lower spine to numb her lower body and, approximately 24 hours after we visited the hospital, Joseph David Fortner was born. He weighed 8 lbs. 15 ounces and was 22 inches long.

The doctor came out to the waiting room, woke me up in the recliner, and gave me the great news. I was relieved that finally our baby was born. I made sure to ask him if momma and baby were healthy. When I arrived in my wife's recovery room to see her and our baby, however, I was surprised to find that our son wasn't there. Darlene told me they had taken him to the nursery. But, when I wanted both of us to go to the nursery together to welcome our son to his new life, Darlene could hardly get out of bed and into a wheelchair, even with my help. I pushed her slowly down the hall-way. At the nursery, I positioned her wheelchair in front to clearly see the infants on display. At the same time, another couple joined us at the window.

I read the name tags and noticed our son was in the center of the front row. As I pointed him out to Darlene, she commented aloud that our baby did not look good, because he was wrinkled and pale. I didn't understand her comment since he looked beautiful to me, but then I realized that she was looking off to her left at another infant. When I pointed out her mistake, the other couple next to us spoke up and said the infant she was talking about was their baby. I chuckled to myself quietly and moved us to another window to avoid further embarrassment. Even though I was a little chagrined by Darlene's mistaken identity, she wasn't because it was an honest mistake.

At this point, I observed that Joseph was in an incubator. He was so large that he almost filled the entire container. His face was turned towards us and I observed two small white nubs in his mouth that appeared to be baby teeth. I asked the nurse to check him and she inserted her hand into the glove attached to the incubator. With her index finger, she extended it gently into his mouth along the lower gum. She immediately pulled her hand out and turned to face us. With wonder and surprise, she stated emphatically that there were two teeth in his lower gum. However, they were pre-natal and would probably fall out when his actual baby teeth emerge. It turned out that she was wrong, as they were his real baby teeth. It was truly amazing! I was not surprised when Darlene chose not to breastfeed.

Joe was a very healthy baby boy and ate like a horse. When Darlene would bottle feed him, he seemed to always want more, and he was eating strained baby food in almost no time. Darlene started with the small Gerber infant jars, but had to quickly graduate to the larger baby jars, and, even then, he would eat more than one serving, washed down by a full bottle of milk. Once satisfied, Joe would immediately want to be put down. Even after he was a few months old, he never liked to be held and cuddled. When he was full, he would arch his back to try to get free and down from his mom, and it was all she could do to hold and feed him at the rate he wanted to be fed.

One of our greatest joys, when Joe was around seven months old, was winning first place in a baby beauty contest. His beautiful smile displaying two bottom teeth, wavy light brown hair, naturally rosy cheeks, and bright blue eyes must have won over the judges. Joe grew quickly and learned how to walk by nine months, and he loved to be free. Over time, this independent trait became more of a challenge to us.

Even as a toddler, Joe loved the outdoors. I remember once when he was around two years old, he was in our fenced-in back-yard. We had felt he was safe, but, when I checked on him, he was suddenly nowhere in sight. I ran around the backyard and discovered a very small section of the fence he must have squeezed through. I then ran around to the front yard and saw him walking casually and confidently up the road. After retrieving our son, I made sure to secure the weak area of our fencing. That was a scary day I never wanted to repeat. It was such a helpless feeling not being in control and not knowing where our little boy was and if he was safe.

* * *

On May 12, 1972, the *USS Simon Bolivar* completed the overhaul. We departed Newport News for post-overhaul shakedown operations, including various sea trials and sound trials. The sound trials were conducted off the Florida coast. During the submarine's post-overhaul shakedown operations at sea, our wives needed to relocate to Charleston. With our then-two-month-old son, Darlene had to drive our Chevrolet Caprice from Newport News to Charleston. Two other Navy wives, Kathy and Jeannie, whose husbands served with me on the submarine, wanted to accompany Darlene in this journey. Kathy rode with Darlene to help with our baby and Jeannie drove her own car. Darlene was in the trailing vehicle and was a nervous wreck for the entire trip. Jeannie, the lead driver, was determined to get there as quickly as possible.

Before they had left, Darlene had pleaded with Jeannie to drive the speed limit, and, while she had agreed, she seemed to forget her promise as soon as the journey began. Darlene, however, refused to drive more than five miles over the speed limit and found herself alone on most of the long trip. When Jeannie finally slowed down to allow Darlene to catch up, they stopped for gas. Darlene was so stressed, she wanted to kill Jeannie, so she got out of her car and pinned Jeannie up against her own with her hands around her throat. Kathy saw what was going on and freaked out. Luckily, Darlene scared Jeannie and Kathy so much that Jeannie finally got the message and slowed down to a reasonable speed the rest of the way.

Once the post-overhaul sound trials were completed, the boat returned to Charleston's home port, where we reunited with our spouses. In early June, I was promoted to 2nd class petty officer. Refresher training for both crews continued until the middle of September. By the end of 1972, the *Simon Bolivar* was back on the regular patrol cycles with the Blue and Gold crews alternating patrols, and I remained in the Blue crew. The submarines had two identical crews of about 125 crew members each, consisting of officers and enlisted men. Two different crews were assigned to the same submarine. Three months would be the Blue crew, and the next three would be the Gold crew. There was a one-month overlap period in which they loaded stores like food and material goods, missiles, and torpedoes. The schedule was two months at sea and one month in port. In 1973 and 1974, I made four more deterrent submarine patrols, for a total of six altogether.

Preparing for the sixth patrol in late 1974 was very stressful for Darlene and me. My wife was 36 weeks pregnant with our second child when we left on patrol on Sunday, December 8, 1974. Only three days later, our beautiful baby girl was born. My wife barely made it to the hospital in time for delivery. The woman next-door, who was married to a Marine, understood the call of duty and dropped everything to rush her safely and quickly to the Charleston Naval Hospital. It only took three pushes for Alita Maria Fortner to enter this world. She had dark brown hair and weighed around 8 lbs. 7 ounces, measuring at 21 inches long. I didn't see her until she was two months old, because I was out to sea. I didn't receive any family gram message from her to indicate that she had given birth. She swears that she did message me the good news, but the radioman who reviewed and transmitted the message must have eliminated that bit of news fearing that it might cause me stress and concern. Regardless, my wife assured me that I hadn't missed much because she hardly moved and ate very little, in contrast with her older brother.

When Alita was born, Joe was 2 ½ years old. He was a handful and seemed to be getting into everything at that age, throwing temper tantrums if he didn't get his way on everything. Often, he would hold his breath or bite his arm until it bruised or bled, to show his frustration. Sometimes, he would walk off the carpet and bang his head against the floor, or hit his head against the wall. We were worried about him, but the Navy pediatrician assured us that he would grow out of it. It was a stage that lasted a long time.

One morning, when I got up to go to work, I noticed Joe was already up and playing in the kitchen. I went in to see what he was doing and found that he was playing with his trucks and cars on the floor and had gotten into the flour, coffee grounds, and sugar. He had mountains of foodstuff all over himself and everything else. He had also gotten Alita out of her crib somehow, and she was lying in all this mess. When Darlene came into the kitchen, she just about died over the scene, but, fortunately, Alita was not injured.

* * *

I made another submarine patrol in early 1975. By the end of April, I had served five consecutive years on the *USS Simon Bolivar* (SSBN-641) Blue crew. That consisted of seven deterrent submarine patrols and one shipyard overhaul-modernization period. I had also been promoted to 1st class petty officer and was ready for a change. On May 1, 1975, I left the *USS Simon Bolivar* for good. I transferred to the Fleet Ballistic Missile Training Center at Dam Neck, Virginia. This base was located on the ocean, directly south of Virginia Beach. It was a three-year tour as a Navy instructor at the FTB "C" School, where I would teach FTB students how to operate and maintain the Mk-88 FCS, which was installed on nuclear-powered FBM submarines containing Poseidon Missiles.

When we moved to Virginia Beach in May 1975, we bought our first house. It was a three-bedroom, two-story Cape Cod home located off Witchduck Road. It had hedges that bordered our property on three sides. I hated trimming those hedges and trying to keep them evenly cut and low enough to see over was a hopeless task. On one occasion, I almost electrocuted myself using the electric hedge cutter by accidentally cutting the cord. Fortunately, I cut it completely in half, thereby shutting off the power entirely. We lived in that house for the last three years of my Navy career. It was a nice neighborhood with neighbors who looked out for each other.

As a three-year-old, Joe kept us on our toes. He hated going to bed, so I would have to take him on a walk around the neighborhood to try to tire him out enough to go to sleep. Many times, when that wouldn't work, I would lean over his crib and rub his head gently and sing lullabies to try to coax him to sleep. Eventually, he would give up and doze off. One day, a neighbor across the street called us on the phone and said she feared our son was trying to jump out of the window upstairs. I asked her what gave her that idea and she said he had already pushed out the glass pane and shoved a bed sheet out the window. I rushed upstairs to catch him in the act. His crib was not supposed to be near the window. He must have rocked the bed from one side to the other until it was positioned near the window in order to escape. I'm thankful I got the call from a caring neighbor   .

In late 1975, Darlene became pregnant with our third child, and we couldn't have been more excited. When her water broke in late July 1976, I took her to the Portsmouth Naval Hospital, where I stayed with her in the labor room until around midnight, when they took her on back to delivery. Early the next morning, on July 22, my beloved wife gave birth to our third child, a boy, who we named Shane Louis Fortner. He weighed 8 lbs. 5 ounces and measured 21 inches long.

A nurse wheeled him out for me to see him. When I first laid eyes on him, my first thought was that he was beautiful. They had placed him on his back in a small carrier, and he had his eyes open and seemed to be very content. His hair was brown, and his skin was pink and healthy-looking. I quickly counted all of his fingers and toes and found that everything looked normal. The only concern I had was, where was his mother? Where could she be? Was she still in the recovery room or had they already moved her to an in-patient room? The nurse attending my son did not know the answers but indicated she would ask another nurse to help. I was worried and quite anxious because no one told me anything about her condition. After a couple of hours, another nurse finally met with me in the waiting room and told me I could see my wife now in the recovery room.

Darlene told me she had a tough time giving birth because Shane had been breach within her. The doctor had had to manipulate his body within the womb and the birth had been touch-and-go for my wife. At one point, her vital signs had dropped to code blue status. Also, during the birthing process, the Navy Obstetrician had dropped an instrument, which ended up under the operating table Darlene was laying on. She told me that she had an out-of-body experience and was floating above her physical body. She could see the instrument on the floor and had wondered why the doctor wouldn't retrieve it.

After the delivery, they had covered my wife's body from head to toe with a sheet and placed her in another room with the lights out. When my wife had re-entered her body, sometime later, she had screamed loudly for help and the medical staff on duty had been shocked to see she was alive. They put her hospital gown back on and took her to the recovery room. While no one at the naval hospital ever confirmed or denied this near-death experience to us, we saw it as a miracle, as God had saved her life.

Shane was a healthy and good-natured child. As he grew and learned to move around, though, he had a very unusual way of crawling. He would crawl on his hands and feet with his butt sticking up in the air, and could move around quickly like a spider. He figured out that this method of spider crawl was the fastest way to get from point A to point B. Before turning one year old, by observing his two siblings, he realized that he could even move quicker by standing and taking steps toward his target.

* * *

I enjoyed my final three-year tour of shore duty at Dam Neck as a Navy instructor. I especially liked teaching the FTB technicians about missile targeting, as the targeting classes were a highly classified subject, and I would require the students' full attention on the material. One day, as I was preparing to teach, I noticed a student in the hallway who had a book in his hand, which appeared to be a Bible. I confronted him before going into the classroom and asked him what he was carrying. He proudly announced for all within earshot to hear that he was a Christian and would read scripture during breaks in class. I couldn't believe what I was hearing. I told him a Bible was not allowed in the room and only the student activity books he was provided on the subject matter of targeting would be allowed. Prohibiting his Bible reading didn't seem to discourage him, however. He answered he would obey me and keep the Bible closed during the lesson. He also commented that he was a "born-again Christian," and he knew Jesus as his Savior and Lord. I had no further problem with this young man in the course   He was very respectful, did what was expected of him and graduated from the course with satisfactory grades. Even though I never saw him again, his words about being a "born-again Christian" always remained with me. At the time, as a lifelong Catholic, I had no idea what this young sailor meant by that phrase. I had never heard a Catholic priest, nun, or any other Catholic laity use the phrase, "born-again Christian."

* * *

After Darlene and I were married in 1971 in the Catholic Church, we never really connected to Catholicism or any other Christian denomination, for that matter. We were not anti-religion, we just did not take the time for church. To compound on that, I made seven submarine patrols in the early '70s, so I was home only half the time. In addition, I attended George Washington University (off-campus) and earned an Associate's Degree in General Studies. Our family life changed in 1975, when I got orders to the Guided Missile School in Dam Neck. As a Navy instructor, I worked from 8:00 am to 4:00 pm Monday through Friday. I was free on the weekend to take our family to church, but I didn't.

It wasn't long before a couple of Jehovah's Witnesses (JW) knocked on our door, and we made the mistake of inviting them in. We had never met or talked to any JWs before that time. They seemed friendly and genuinely interested in our welfare, and spoke to us about their religion and understanding of God and other JW doctrine. They kept the discussion focused only on their religious beliefs and even gave us a couple of their JW booklets and a Bible to read. At that time, we did not own any personal Bibles, so we gladly accepted the books. And, while we did have a large family Bible in our house, we hardly opened it because it was meant to be displayed on the coffee table.

I later found out that the JW Bible was a New World Version (NWV), which varied significantly from the authorized King James Version (KJV).

For example, John 1:1 reads as follows in both versions:

NWV – In the beginning was the Word and the Word was with God, and the Word was a god. The same was in the beginning.

KJV – In the beginning was the Word, and the Word was with God, and the Word was God. The same was in the beginning.

Take notice of the difference between both scripture versions. The NWV states the Word (i.e., Jesus) was a god. In other words, He was a mighty one, like an archangel. We discovered that, in the JW religious doctrine, Jesus is not God. The KJV, in contrast, clearly states the Word (Jesus) is God. Although I did not agree with the JW interpretation, I did grow to like other things about the religion. We also found out they don't believe in hell and they don't mind if you partake in alcohol responsibly. They also like sports, including the Olympics.

We ended up forming a relationship with them and attended their Kingdom Hall for around two years. During our time together, whether it be in their Kingdom Hall, door-to-door witnessing, or fellowshipping, I tended to focus only on the things I liked about them and stayed away from the verses we disagreed upon, like John 1:1.

The main reason they were in our life to begin with, was because my wife was searching for spiritual truth, and I followed her lead in these matters. Since she was happy with them, I didn't complain. Each Sunday, we attended the services at the local Kingdom Hall. When I was at work during the week, my wife would go door-to-door with a female JW elder to spread their doctrine. She got used to the doors slamming in her face. We became brainwashed and started to believe in their propaganda.

Over time I became passionate about their doctrine and tried to convince my mother, father, and siblings to read and study it. That effort was fruitless, and I only managed to alienate my family from us. Gradually, the JW leaders applied more pressure on us to comply with their doctrine, but my wife and I had certain things we believed in and were unwilling to give up. My primary red line was everything pertaining to the military, and my wife's red line was everything relating to her cigarettes and coffee. It finally got to the point, after a couple of years, that rather than hide our "prohibited stuff" and pretend to comply, we decided to walk away from them, which we happily did.

I couldn't understand why cigarette smoking bothered the JW's so much when drinking beer was considered an acceptable beverage. I didn't mind if Darlene smoked because it was her choice and her life. She enjoyed smoking and would go through at least a pack a day. She had been a cigarette smoker from the time she was a preteen and especially enjoyed smoking when she drank coffee, which she did all day. When I brought Darlene home with me to meet my parents before we married, my dad bet me $10 that I couldn't quit smoking. At that time, I was also a cigarette smoker. He bragged about how he was able to quit cold turkey when he was 40 years old. He went on to challenge my manhood and said that I wasn't half the man that he was. I knew that my father was only half-joking with me. However, he said these fighting words in front of my fiancee and I couldn't let him get away with it. So, to prove to my dad that I could do anything that he could do, I decided to quit smoking cold turkey and told him to pay me the $10 a year from that date if I kept my word. He agreed and Darlene promised him that she would help to keep me honest. On the flight back to Charleston, I did try to light up, but Darlene took the cigarette out of mouth and told me that I was going to keep my word. A year later, my father paid me that $10.

12
A NEW PATH

Deuteronomy 2:3 (NASB) "You have circled this mountain long enough. Now turn north."

In my last year of service, I took the test for Chief Petty Officer and passed it. The Navy Board approved me for the promotion to E-7, but I would have to extend my enlistment by at least six months. Even though I had invested many years into the Navy, I decided not to accept the promotion. I was ready for a change to civilian life and that was forefront on my mind. On August 11, 1978, I was honorably discharged from the U.S. Navy, having served nine years and eleven months. Before I left the service, I applied for a job at Data-Design Laboratories (DDL) in Virginia Beach. When I interviewed for the job, I also had to complete an employment application. On the form, there was a line item that stated, "Minimum Salary Required." I asked an employee nearby what it meant, and he told me to either put a dollar figure or write the word "negotiable." Not leaving anything to chance, I did both. I wrote "$16-$18k (NEG)."

During the interview, looking over the application, the interviewer offered me a $16,000 annual salary. When I tried to negotiate for a higher amount, he said he would only give me what I needed and what I wrote on the application. I felt foolish knowing I had been hoodwinked by this ambiguous statement on the application. However, I accepted the job because I had no other options at that time. Ironically, when I filed our federal income taxes for 1978 (my final year in the Navy), we had only earned around $12,000. We did not pay any additional federal income taxes that year. Still, we received an additional amount of money from the IRS, under a new program called "earned income tax credit." It was a refundable tax credit for

Opposite: Darlene and Steve at Disney World - 1979.

low income working individuals and couples with children. To summarize, the $16,000 salary I accepted at DDL was almost equal to what I had earned in my last year in the military if you include the Government tax credit. Since we were no longer allowed to use the Navy medical system nor shop at the commissary for groceries, we started to struggle financially to make ends meet. The only credit card we could get at that time was a Sears credit card and we used it and accumulated debt. We paid the minimum amount required each month and Sears would automatically raise our credit limit.

After I left the Navy, we decided to sell our Cape Cod house and bought a nicer home a few miles closer to the job. It was a four-bedroom, single-story, L-shaped ranch with an attached single-car garage. This house was larger than our previous one and the neighborhood was newer. The one problem it had was it was closer to the Naval Air Station in Oceana, a suburb of Virginia Beach. Late at night, the Navy would test the fighter jets' engines, like the F-4 Phantom and the engine noise was so loud it would wake us up. During the daylight hours, the F-4 Phantoms would fly very low over our neighborhood with their afterburners screaming through the sky. The sound was so loud and powerful it was deafening, and it would shake the house windows. It was always an impressive display of power and might.

DDL provided me with an office to share with another employee. My task was to develop technical training material for the Navy FTB's under a government contract. I had no difficulty doing the work and exceeded company goals. Every day, for the entire day, I would do the same task. The only variable was the technical equipment the training material addressed. It wasn't long before I became bored with my work's repetitive nature and wanted a new challenge. I learned DDL was developing some robotic devices for military application. I asked my supervisor if there was any way I could transfer to that department, as I thought I could learn to market and sell this new technology to the Navy. My supervisor turned down my request and suggested I focus on my present job. I was deflated and saw no future for me at DDL. Another area that frustrated me was that the bi-monthly paychecks would occasionally be late, sometimes one or two days, because of weather related problems in mailing them across the country from DDL headquarters in California. This was unacceptable to me. In the Navy my paychecks were always on time. I knew that I would be paid on the 1st and 16th of each month. As a government contractor, I realized that this company didn't consider that issue as an important factor. They were dead wrong.

In January 1979, six months after joining the company, my officemate told me about a great job opportunity with SEACOR (Systems Engineering Associates Corporation), a small business defense contractor in Cherry Hill, New Jersey. The job entailed writing technical training curricula materials on various naval weapons systems and equipment that would be installed on small high-speed vessels built by a U.S. Shipyard for the Saudi Arabian Navy. The prime contractor was Sperry Microwave in Clearwater, Florida. SEACOR was one of its subcontractors, who provided personnel to develop the technical training material. The prime contract was called the Saudi Naval Expansion Program (SNEP). SEACOR functioned as a "headhunter" for Sperry in support of the SNEP. Sperry had filled most of the positions already and this final push was to hire and organize a new five-person team to develop a training course for the ship's 3" 50-caliber gun system. A new SEACOR curriculum development team would be formed in the Cherry Hill office with its own project manager.

On that Friday, with the urging of my DDL office mate, I immediately called SEACOR direct and confirmed the employment opportunity. After faxing my resume to him, within a half-an-hour, I received a phone call from SEACOR. The SEACOR representative offered me a starting salary of $19,200. He indicated I would have to work at SEACOR in Cherry Hill for six weeks initially. There, I would be joined by four other new employees to form a gun system training development team for the SNEP. We would organize and begin the process of course development at SEACOR.

After six weeks, we would transfer to Sperry's Clearwater, Florida facility and continue course development work for 39 more weeks and receive an additional $7,200 per diem, which was tax free. Upon completion of the task, we had two choices: 1) teach the course to the Saudi officers and crew in Saudi Arabia or 2) resign. I wasn't excited about either option. I believed a lot could change once we were working in Florida. Darlene's family was living in central Florida, and we thought it would be good to reconnect with them. This job sounded like a golden opportunity. When I spoke to Darlene about the opportunity, she was as anxious as me for a new beginning, especially since we would be making a lot more money. On the following Monday morning in early January 1979, I submitted my two-week resignation notice to DDL.

My family and I were excited for this new adventure. We had never been to New Jersey and had no idea where we would live or where Joe and Alita would go to school during the six weeks we were there, but the excitement remained. We sold our house by ourselves within a couple of weeks and, even though we had only lived there for a year, we made a few thousand dollars on the sale. We then rented a U-Haul truck, stored our household furniture in a local storage facility, and packed only enough clothes and essentials to live in New Jersey for six weeks.

It was a new beginning, and Darlene and I were not afraid of the challenge facing us. New Jersey was known as the Garden State, which sounded lovely, and we had never been north of the Mason-Dixon line before. Upon arrival, we surveyed the area and settled on an efficiency motel on SR-70 in Camden, a few miles from the SEACOR office. It was a furnished two-bedroom place, sufficient for our short stay, and we arranged for Joe and Alita to attend a nearby elementary public school.

* * *

My first day at work was exciting. I arrived early and was given a desk among many others in a large room. There were very few people in this bull pin area at that time of day. I noticed a coffee pot nearby and went over and got a cup. While I was standing there adding cream, a man with a full head of grey hair came over for a refill and we exchanged greetings. I could tell he was one of the executives—he had on a white shirt and tie with his sleeves rolled up his arms, and there was a pencil behind one of his ears, which gave the impression he had been at work for a while. I also noticed his coffee cup was the size of a cereal bowl. After pouring his coffee, he made another pot without hesitation, then walked away, whistling a familiar tune aloud. He could tell that he enjoyed his job and made me feel very welcomed to join the company. Later, I found out this man was Bob Carr, the founder and president of SEACOR.

The other four men I would be working with arrived on time. After meeting each other and sharing some of our backgrounds, we decided to begin work right away. We met daily and worked feverishly on the project, gathering and studying technical material on the 3" gun mount planned for the Saudi fast patrol boat. SEACOR was a rather small company and the work environment was quite relaxed, and, as I had already observed, even the president would make coffee when it was needed. Near the end of the six weeks, the president briefed us on our mission as valued SEACOR employees. He told us they would provide subcontract services to Sperry Microwave in Clearwater and designated me as the project manager of our team, requesting that I keep him posted on our progress.

* * *

Two weeks before my assignment was up at SEACOR, my wife and I made plans to move our family back to Florida. My brother, Michael, and his family were living in Bradenton, Florida at that time, which was about 45 miles south of Clearwater. My brother insisted Darlene and the kids stay with them until I arrived. About a week before I left Cherry Hill, my wife and three children took a one-way flight from Philadelphia to Tampa, and, there, Michael picked them up and drove them to his house. He and his wife had a couple of children, and my kids enjoyed playing with them, especially on the beach.

Back in New Jersey, we completed our work that week. The four team members and I organized a convoy and started our road trip south. The road trip to Florida was going to be long and arduous. Just as we began, a team member whose car was in front of me hit a piece of metal on the road, which sliced a hole in his gas tank, emptying all of his fuel immediately. His car shut off and coasted off the road to the shoulder. I pulled off behind him and stopped and got out and told him what had happened. He suggested the rest of us continue our way. He had AAA support, so he would be able to replace the gas tank, but it would take a couple of days to complete. When I arrived in Virginia Beach later that day, I rented a 24-foot Ryder truck with a car trailer hitch. I attached my car to the truck and went to the storage unit to load our furniture and one of the other guys from our SNEP team Calvin, helped me load up the truck. When we finished, the two of us were so tired we decided to spend the night in a motel and get a fresh start in the morning, so our remaining two team members continued the journey without us.

The next morning, Calvin and I left Virginia Beach early. I drove the 24' truck with my car in tow and Calvin followed in his own car. It was about 860 miles to Bradenton, and we stopped again for the night somewhere in South Carolina. We only had about 400 miles left. During the entire trip, we did not have any problems on the road, thank God. When my friend and I arrived in Bradenton, it had been nine days since I had last seen my wife and children. To my surprise, my youngest son, Shane, who was only three years old, didn't want anything to do with me. He cried when I picked him up and kissed him and seemed to be afraid of me. Before the separation, Shane had been very attached to me and we had gone everywhere together. He was a daddy's boy, but must have been traumatized by our separation.It took him a long time to trust me again and to even ride alone with me in the car. Meanwhile, with my brother's help, we were able to find a lovely apartment to rent in Clearwater.

The following Monday, I reported to work at Sperry Microwave's facility. The four men I worked with in Cherry Hill had arrived on time, as well. The SNEP contract team consisted of about 50 people. A few were SEACOR employees, subcontracted to Sperry, but the rest were Sperry employees. In fact, our five-person team was the only one that was 100% SEACOR personnel. Everyone worked in a large room with five-foot cubicle separator panels to provide some privacy amongst the various curricula development teams.

On the first workday, after the introductions and orientation, our team commenced work and picked up where we had left off in Cherry Hill. I enjoyed the SNEP project and working with the team to build curricula materials. Occasionally, the SEACOR president would even visit Sperry to meet with the executives and discuss our work progress. He would see me and usher me aside and quietly ask me how things were going, and I would always be honest, which he appreciated. He would encourage me and the other five to do our best, which we did.

Although my career with SEACOR continued to go well, I would soon face a health crisis within my family. In May of 1979, my beloved wife became very ill and I took her to the hospital. Her symptoms included headaches, unquenchable thirst, a continual need to urinate, and very moody behavior. They ran tests and determined she was a type I diabetic, requiring insulin. Her blood sugar was over 700. The normal range for an adult is from 80 to 120. If she hadn't gotten medical help, her organs would have gradually stopped functioning from diabetic ketoacidosis (DKA), and she would have died within a month. Type I diabetes, also referred to as juvenile diabetes, is a genetic disease passed down through the bloodline. It was diabetic ketoacidosis that had taken her brother, David, and their mother had also been diagnosed as a type I diabetic after his death.

Darlene was admitted into the hospital for a few days. During that time, they taught us how to monitor her blood sugar and administer insulin via syringes. The doctor showed us how to fill and measure the insulin within the syringe, and I held the syringe near her skin while looking at her face. Darlene had been crying during this time, dealing with the sudden realization of knowing that she was type 1 diabetic. I stuck her with the syringe, and she flinched, causing me to remove it quickly before depressing the plunger. This time she didn't move, and I was able to inject the insulin and withdraw the needle. I discarded the syringe, and we held each other for several moments. We cried together in the hospital emergency room because we realized life would no longer be the same. Diabetes is a debilitating illness and would take its toll on Darlene's body and emotions for the rest of her life. However, it never adversely affected her spirit or our love and devotion to each other.

* * *

By late November 1979, the SNEP project was transitioning into another phase. The curricula for all the Saudi ship systems and equipment were almost complete, and the next phase was for Sperry to send instructors to Saudi Arabia to teach the subject matter to their naval officers and enlisted personnel. There was no way I was going to go there, sothe only other choice, I thought, would be to quit and find another job. Thankfully, God had other plans for me. SEACOR's president contacted me and asked if I would like to return to Cherry Hill to manage a new U.S. Navy contract that SEACOR had been recently awarded. He offered me a substantial pay raise and agreed to pay all moving expenses. After discussing the details with Darlene, we accepted the new position.

We returned to Cherry Hill and rented a condominium apartment in a high-rise building. Our apartment was on the 14th floor and had three bedrooms and a nice sized living room and kitchen. The most attractive feature for the kids was the elevator, as they loved operating the controls. Though my children were enjoying themselves, every time I got on the elevator, anxiety set in. It reminded me of my childhood days when I had gotten stuck on an elevator with my mother, reinvigorating my claustrophobia, though I managed to hide it well. Beyond that, it was a beautiful place for our family to live.

My streak of good fortune continued in my career with SEACOR. On Monday, when I reported to work , the president met with me in his office. He was sitting with his back against the large window, and the blinds were open, allowing the morning sun to pour into his office and shine brightly in my eyes. I wondered later if he did this act intentionally to see how I would react to the uncomfortable setting. I never forgot this tactic and used it myself many times later, especially when I interviewed prospective employees. He handed me the new Navy contract and said he wanted me to manage it. He admitted they hadn't gotten any work from it yet and was anxious for me to get started in order to bring in some revenue. He promoted me to program manager and gave me a private office. Before I left his office, he called in another man, who was a vice president. He introduced us and said he would be my boss. The V.P. then informed me that I would have complete freedom to manage the contract and he just wanted me to provide him with monthly status reports of both technical and financial data. I agreed and left the office feeling on top of the world. I had no idea at that time what this new contract statement of work entailed, but I believed if I studied and worked hard, I would be able to prove to them that I was the right man for this important job.

* * *

On December 17, 1981, my father died of lung cancer. He was only 61-years-old. Mom, only 56, was now a widow. I left Darlene and the kids and flew home for a week. The viewing was at Saint Anthony Catholic Church and my five brothers and I were the pallbearers of his casket. I was happy mom had the support from all nine of her children; we cried and comforted each other for the entire week. It was so cold — around 15 degrees — that they had to wait until the ground thawed to bury dad. A few months later, in the middle of February, I received a $9,000 check from my dad's life insurance company. Before he had died, he had designated all nine kids as the beneficiaries, and mom wasn't included. Without hesitation, we each signed the checks over to mom. I wondered if dad did that intentionally to test our love for mom. He was a wise man, taken far too young.

Four years before my dad's death in August 1977, we had received a notice in the mail that Darlene's dad, W.F. Parks had died from a tragic accident on the job in Lakeland, Florida. He, too, was only 61 years old, and had been electrocuted when he inadvertently touched live wires while replacing a light bulb fixture. He fell 12 feet off the platform to the shop floor. With the written notice of his death was also a check for $5,000 — Darlene's portion of his life insurance. In contrast to my later grief, Darlene had felt no emotion concerning the death of her father. She hadn't even attended his funeral, because she hadn't received the notification of his death until long after he had died. Although she had forgiven him for abusing her, they had never communicated or reconciled their relationship.

* * *

In January of 1982, we moved to Medford, NJ and rented a single-story house in the Sherwood Forest subdivision. It was a beautiful four-bedroom ranch with open architecture and an over-sized fireplace between the kitchen and the living room area. The backyard was completely wooded with wild blueberry bushes growing everywhere, and the kids came to love picking blueberries in the summer and fall. Those that they didn't eat, Darlene would use to make pancakes and muffins. During the cold winter months, we used the fireplace often to help keep us warm. I would chop wood outback and Joe would help me carry the kindling wood inside.

One winter night, it snowed several inches, and we used the fireplace to knock the chill off. The next morning, the fire was out and the coals appeared to be cold, but, around noon, Darlene called me at work and frantically yelled that the house was on fire and I needed to rush home right away. I tried to get clarification, but she hung up. It took me around 30 minutes to get home, and I expected the fire department to be there with the house in flames. I was hoping Darlene and the kids had gotten out safely. When I arrived and pulled into the driveway, however, everything looked normal from the outside. There was no evidence of smoke or fire anywhere that I could see.

When I entered, Darlene was a nervous wreck. She took me to the laundry room door past the fireplace and opened it to show me the damage. On the wall, just above the floor trim, was a charred six-inch area in the wallpaper. She told me that, earlier, she had emptied the fireplace's soot into a brown paper bag and placed it in the laundry room, which was adjacent to the back door. When she opened the laundry room door at lunchtime, the sudden rush of air had caused the bag filled with embers to burst into flames. She managed to get the back door opened and kicked the burning bag out into the snow, extinguishing the fire. I was extremely relieved and later patched the charred area with a piece of similar wallpaper, wiping away the evidence of the fire completely.

Meanwhile, I became a workaholic at SEACOR. I thought that I needed to continually prove to my boss and the president that I was the best program manager they had. I had no experience with government contracts and had to work overtime to make sure I understood them. At night while at home, I would isolate myself in a separate room and study the contract to comprehend the statement of work thoroughly and become familiar with all the associated contract clauses, Federal Acquisition Regulations (FAR), and terms and conditions. To move up the ladder of success at SEACOR, I thought I needed a bachelor's degree and possibly a master's and even doctorate. I was determined to continue my formal education, so I enrolled at Rutgers University at the Camden, New Jersey campus. Unfortunately, I did not check with my beloved wife to see if she would support this decision, which ended up being a big mistake that I came to regret. After meeting with a counselor, I chose to pursue a Bachelor of Science Degree in Management, for which I needed around 50 credit hours. I enrolled in the night school and scheduled my courses to get the degree in less than three years. A BS degree was my goal, but it was not God's plan, nor was it my wife's desire.

13
BORN AGAIN

John 3:3 (NASB) "Jesus answered and said to him,
'Truly, truly, I say to you, unless one is born again,
he cannot see the kingdom of God.'"

After a year in Sherwood Forest, we decided that we wanted to put down roots and buy a house, and, in March 1982, I asked my mother for a no-interest loan of $5,000 to buy a house, to which she agreed. We then contacted a realtor who showed us several homes in the area. On June 11, 1982 we purchased a charming brick 2-story four-bedroom house on Linda Avenue in Blackwood, NJ. It was located around 10 miles south of SEACOR, just off the Blackhorse Pike (SR-168). Of course, with a street named after my beloved bride, we knew this was THE home for us. The best part was it was reasonably priced and within our budget.

Darlene was very out-going, friendly, and loved people. By autumn, all three of our kids were in public school. After I left for work and the kids caught the bus to school, Darlene would have coffee with the other housewives in the neighborhood, including two women named Anne and Hazel. Facing the street, Hazel lived on our left, and Anne lived across the street and was an ardent Jehovah's Witness. Before we had arrived in the neighborhood, she had been trying to convert Hazel for some time, but Hazel had remained noncommittal. Like Darlene, she was also a smoker, which impeded joining the JW. During 1982, though, the three of them bonded, taking long walks together, shopping, and talking about everything from their kids and husbands to religion and God.

Darlene told them about our experience with the JWs in which we had been involved for around two years. She said they had been very judgmental, especially of smokers and those who worked in the military-industrial complex. We were guilty of both crimes and told to quit, which we refused, and they eventually gave up on recruiting us. Anne tried to convince Darlene to give the JWs another chance and provided her with JW books to read, as she was determined to prove that they were not all like that. It wasn't long before Anne began visiting Darlene with a couple of JW women to discuss their faith. Darlene would avoid smoking in their presence because she didn't want to offend them, and listened politely and asked questions. When she discussed the JW subject with me, I was not interested. Between my devotion to my work and night classes at Rutgers, I had little time for the JW religion. Little did we know, God's plan for our life was about to be unveiled.

* * *

Carol Bretz, our neighbor on the right, was a devout Christian. At the time, I considered her a "Jesus Freak." Whenever I came home from work or school, I would often see Carol in the yard, celebrating something with her kids and others. It looked like a birthday party. At other times, I would see her outside with other women studying the Bible. Periodically, she would come over and talk to Darlene in the house or the yard about Jesus. Unlike the JWs, she never criticized or judged Darlene about being a smoker. She demonstrated love without expecting anything in return. There were a few other Christian women on our street, who Carol met with regularly for Bible study, including Mary, Joyce, and Pat. They were all involved in the street ministry Carol started in South Philadelphia. Unbeknownst to us, from the moment we had moved in, they had all been praying for us continually and asking God to save us.

One day, Carol related to Darlene the story in the Bible about Lazarus and the rich man. She pointed out how the rich man went to hell, while Lazarus went into the arms of Abraham in heaven. Darlene didn't believe in hell at that time because of the JW influence in our life and was so troubled by what Carol had shared, that she excused herself and went back into the house. Carol continued to pray for us daily and to witness to Darlene at every opportunity that God presented. When the Lord revealed to Carol there was a demonic presence over our household, she also prayed for God to break the demonic hold. When she felt a release in her spirit, she believed by faith that it was finally done.

During that same week, Anne and two JW women stopped by to visit with Darlene. These visits were becoming more frequent and they had begun to pressure Darlene to quit smoking. They explained she couldn't be saved unless she gave it up, which visibly upset her and drove her to tears. When God revealed their spiritual emptiness, my wife immediately ordered them out of our house and off of our property. They resisted at first, until Darlene threatened to call the police, after which they left for good and never returned.

After they left, Carol, who had been praying, was moved by God to come over and visit with Darlene. When Darlene answered the door, Carol saw that she had been crying and asked her what was wrong. Darlene told her that Anne and the two JW women had said that she wouldn't be saved unless she quit smoking cigarettes. Carol was not surprised by this incident. She had been ministering to Anne for years and had witnessed the spiritual bondage that Anne was under. Carol told her she did not have to change anything: God would accept her exactly as she was. She showed her Bible scriptures to support her argument, then lovingly asked Darlene if she wanted to pray together and ask Jesus to forgive her for all her sins and to come live in her heart as Savior and Lord. Without hesitation, Darlene said, "yes," and they prayed.

In that little corner of the earth in our home on Linda Avenue on the afternoon of November 11, 1983, Carol led Darlene in the sinner's prayer. Immediately, Jesus came to reside in my beloved wife's heart forever and she was born again into new life. God spoke the following words through Carol to Darlene:

"I have baptized you in the Holy Ghost and with fire. I have called you, and I am going to use you mightily. I will heal your hurts and wipe away all your tears. I love you. You have cried unto me, and I have answered you, and all your family will come into the kingdom."

Darlene was excited and couldn't wait to share the good news with me. She asked Carol to write down the prayer so she could pray it with the kids and me. On fire with her passion for the living God, she didn't want to wait another day. Carol was quite surprised by Darlene's exuberance, and gave her a Bible, suggesting that she read scripture and ask God to give her wisdom and understanding. She was like a sponge and couldn't wait to soak up the Word of God.

When I came home from work that day, Darlene told me what had happened. I was upset with Anne and the other Jehovah Witnesses for how they mistreated my wife, and didn't understand what Darlene meant when she said that she was now "Born Again" by praying the sinner's prayer with Carol. I had thought we were good Christians already and wondered what had changed. Still, despite my confusion, I had to admit that my wife looked happy, like nothing would bother her. She seemed to be at peace.

A couple of days later, on a Saturday, Carol returned to our house and asked Darlene if she wanted to go to the Philadelphia Convention Center to attend the Kenneth Copeland Crusade. I was sitting on the couch behind Darlene when she turned to look at me. I shrugged my shoulders as if to say, I don't care.

Darlene audibly heard one word within herself: "Go." It was so powerful she couldn't say no. Although the voice was audible to Darlene, I didn't hear anything.

Then the Lord said, "Go" to her again. She turned back to Carol and said, "Yes, I want to go." It was as if Darlene didn't have a choice.

Years later, I learned in a biblical Hebrew class that Darlene and I took at the Messianic Bible Institute Church in Orlando that there is a Hebrew word, (Shama - spelled phonetically), which literally means to hear intelligently, often with implication of attention and obedience. For example, when God first spoke to Abram (Genesis 12:1), He told him to leave with his family and move to Canaan. Even though this was the first time Abram had heard God speak aloud, he listened and obeyed God and immediately did what

He had ordered him to do. Likewise, Darlene audibly heard and immediately obeyed what God had told her to do. Shama! She didn't question the source of the voice, as she was now a child of God and believed Jesus was her Savior and Lord. She had the faith of a mustard seed, and she acted on it.

Obeying God's instructions is how my beloved wife functioned as a new believer for the rest of her life. Did she sin and miss the mark at times? Of course, as we all do. However, Darlene wanted to hear and obey God, and that was her worship, her passion, and her calling. God equipped, tested, and promoted her for the rest of her life and I came along for the ride. Little did I know, God wanted me personally, as well. I was a slower learner, but I did eventually learn.

When Darlene returned from the Kenneth Copeland event late that night, I was very upset because, in my opinion, she got back too late. However, when she entered the house, I looked intently at her face before I spoke to her and the word that came to mind was RADIANT, though it was one I hardly used. She was glowing and I didn't know why and was afraid to ask. She didn't respond to my rude comments about her so-called tardiness. She just went into the bedroom, changed, and went to bed. I did the same, though I was troubled.

For the next several days, every chance my wife got, she would isolate herself and study the Bible for hours. Day and night, she fed on the Word of God, taking breaks only to nap, care for the kids, feed the family, and take care of our home. She believed the Bible was the true and unerring Word of God. She saw herself as a student in class with the Holy Spirit as her teacher, counselor, and comforter. With pens, highlighters, and a notebook, she took notes as He taught so she wouldn't forget. She highlighted verses He showed her and made notes in the margins for further study and application. She was determined to capture all that He revealed because the Word of God was living and like gold and precious jewels to her. It wasn't static but dynamic and real and applicable to everyday life on Earth. She wanted to learn all that the Spirit revealed. Never had she ever experienced scripture in this fresh and vibrant and practical manner, and she had an unquenchable thirst to hear and obey God.

Meanwhile, I didn't understand what had happened to my wife to cause her to change so radically. My snarky comments and criticisms didn't seem to bother her anymore. She would just smile at me and give a gentle reply or listen and not comment. Still, despite my confusion and misgivings, I liked the change in her behavior that I saw.

Finally, on November 19, I approached her and asked her what had happened. She told me Carol had prayed with her to receive Jesus in her heart, and she had been "born again" and filled with the Holy Spirit. She said she had felt totally alive and at peace. She said Carol could come over and pray for the kids and me to receive Jesus, too. I started to fuss and to resist her suggestion. I could think of many excuses for why this was not practical or normal. We weren't in a church and Carol wasn't a real pastor. I reminded her that I was raised Catholic and knew Jesus, but Darlene argued that knowing Him was not the same as having a personal relationship with Him. I didn't know what she meant by that, but she told me Carol would explain everything if I just let her come over to pray with the children and me. I looked at my beloved wife intently and saw deep love in her eyes for me. I also witnessed her peace and joy during the past eight days and realized that I wanted to have that as well. I quickly relented and rounded up the kids.

Darlene called Carol, who contacted Mary, and both came over to our house that afternoon to pray with us. Carol explained what it meant to be born again and how Jesus communicated that truth to Nicodemus, a Jewish leader. Carol said I needed to ask Jesus to forgive me for all of my sins and to invite Him to live in my heart, and, by faith, I would receive Christ and His salvation. She also stated that she would pray with us to be baptized and filled with the Holy Spirit, as the followers of Christ were baptized in the Spirit in the upper room. While my wife stood next to me and prayed quietly, I agreed for Carol to pray with the kids and me. Before she started to pray with me, she told me once I am born again, my life will never be the same again. She said we would continue to experience trials and tribulations in this life, but as a child of God, we would have unlimited access to the Father, and He would protect us and answer our prayers in His way and His time.

In our living room in broad daylight, I closed my eyes and held my arms out in front of me with my palms up in a posture of surrender. Carol and Mary stood in front of me and prayed. I prayed the sinner's prayer aloud and believed in my heart that Jesus could save me as He saved my wife eight days before. When I finished praying, I did not feel any different, but Carol told me salvation is by faith, not by feelings. They then prayed with each of our three children, one at a time. Afterward, we all prayed together and asked God to fill us with the Holy Spirit, and we received the baptism by faith.

On the same day, Pat, another friend of Carol's and fellow believer, spoke the following words of God over Darlene:

"All past hurts are healed. I know what you have gone through, my child. I love you. You will walk in light – My light. You will rise up and be mighty for Me. Your family will rise up and call you blessed. You are special and very dear to Me. I love you. God instructs you, Darlene, daughter of the Most High, to read Proverbs 31 and Psalms 91."

The next day was Sunday, and Carol invited us to attend her church, Lambs Road Assembly of God, for the evening service. A guest evangelist, Richard Myers, was going to preach. We went to the church that night and found that it was packed. We sat in the third row from the front and, during the service, the evangelist stopped preaching and looked around at the crowd.

He said, "Someone here has to make a business decision. Who is it? Come up here."

I felt like someone had pushed me out of my seat. Rather than walk down the aisle, I managed to step over the two chairs in front of me with people in them and stood in front of the evangelist. He was a small man in stature, but he was standing on a high platform. He looked down at me and started speaking prophetic words directly to me. When he finished, he touched my head, and I fell, not from any push, but because I couldn't stand under the power of God. After a moment, I returned to my seat. Fortunately, one of Carol's friends recorded the prophecy, and I played it later to make sure I had heard it correctly and to commit it to memory.

The prophecy was that God was going to take me from promotion to promotion to promotion. Although I had no idea what it meant at that time, I was about to find out in a couple of weeks. The prophecy would continue to manifest itself during the rest of my life.

Darlene, Joe, Steve, Alita and Shane - 1984.

14
MIRACLES

Mark 16:20 (NASB) "And they went out and preached everywhere, while the Lord worked with them, and confirmed the word by the signs that followed. And they promptly reported all these instructions to Peter and his companions. And after that, Jesus Himself sent out through them from east to west the sacred and imperishable proclamation of eternal salvation."

We decided to get plugged in right away at a local Christian church fellowship with other believers to learn how to live as Christians. Carol suggested Living Waters Christian Fellowship (LWCF), a vibrant and growing church in the community. The next Sunday, we attended their service. We were blown away by the love demonstrated by the people we met, including the senior pastor, Dan, and his wife. The preaching was upbeat yet powerful and biblically based. The live band played contemporary Christian music, tailored to the younger believers like us. We came to attend church every Sunday, as well as on Wednesday nights and for other special events. The sermons were all taped and we took copies home to listen and study the Word as a family, growing in our knowledge and wisdom.

We also had Bible study at home often, where we would listen to teaching and testimony tapes and pray and seek answers from God. We would usually start with a prayer followed by praise and worship music, then we would read passages from scripture and discuss the Word. During those sessions, I would relax and try to take it all in. However, many times, I would doze off, and Darlene would wake me up and tell me to stand if I was tired. I wouldn't stand, but I would try to pay attention, only to drift off again. She finally decided to allow me to rest, giving it to God and asking Him to speak to me while I slept. I must admit, I didn't set a good example for the children when I napped. Darlene, on the other hand, seemed to get energized during Bible study. She drank the Word like it was living water, which it was. During praise and worship time, she would dance around the room, praising God and singing aloud His praises in both English and God's language. Our children would sometimes join in with her. She danced with reckless abandon in honor, respect, and deep love for Jesus, the King of Kings.

Darlene was especially keen on what God's Word had to say about physical healing from sickness and disease. Although she had diabetes, she expected God to heal her. Diabetes disease adversely affects most bodily functions, including vision. Darlene's eyesight was poor, especially when her blood sugar readings were too high, and she wore prescription glasses to help her see objects more clearly in the distance. One day, we were standing out in front of our house, and Darlene was looking down Linda Avenue at one of the parked cars that was a block away. She did not have her glasses with her, and asked me to look at a license plate number and tell her if I could read it. I said I could and she then read aloud the numbers and letters on the plate and asked me if she was correct. I told her she had gotten them all right, and I was amazed. She then said she believed God had healed her of diabetes and she didn't need to take insulin injections anymore, but doubt gripped my soul. I suggested she continue taking the shots, just to be sure, but she was adamant and rejected my advice. I was concerned, and I spoke to Carol about this matter. Afterward, Carol approached Darlene and suggested she still take insulin when needed.

Darlene went four days without insulin injections and felt physically well. During those four days, she did not check her blood sugar. She stood on God's scriptures that promised physical healing from all sickness and disease. During this time, I worried each day she was off insulin. On the fourth day, between Carol and me reminding her to be careful, we convinced her to check her blood sugar and to take a shot if required. On that day, Darlene had noticed she could not read that license plate without her glasses. When she ended up taking her blood sugar reading, her levels were high. She was distraught and said it was unbelief that caused her body to revert to being sick. Still, even though Darlene was disappointed, she learned to persevere in God's Word and trust God would make a way in His time.

Another example of Darlene's discipline, when it came to walking-the-walk as a Christian, was in eating food. She would only eat enough to sustain her body. She only put enough on her plate that would satisfy a child. She ate her meal slowly savoring its flavor. It never mattered if the meal cooled to room temperature. Then, before she was filled, she would push the plate away. At times she would say, "I do not live by bread alone, but by every word that proceeds out of the mouth of God." She never wanted food to be more important than the spiritual food of the living Word of God. She was a great example to the kids and me. I was blessed beyond measure and knew it.

Carol believed God wanted Darlene to reach out to the lost beyond the church building. Under the spiritual covering of Lambs Road Assemblies of God, Carol decided to organize a group of female prayer warriors, mostly from our neighborhood, to evangelize on the streets of South Philadelphia. She invited Darlene to join them in the street ministry, and Darlene, anxious to participate, welcomed the opportunity to be used by God. The first time the ladies went to South Philadelphia, they met in the John Chambers Memorial Presbyterian church. There, they planned to show a movie, entitled A Thief in the Night. Before they started the film, Darlene and the other women went outside and started evangelizing to anyone who would listen. Darlene noticed several young kids, who looked like tough street kids, and approached them to share the Word of God with them. Instead of browbeating them to repent and change their ways, she encouraged them and told them they were loved by God just as they were. She said they were special to God and gifted and invited them into the church to watch the movie. They all accepted her invitation. Others came in, as well, off the street following the ladies' invitation.

Perhaps as many as 60 people were there that night and, after the film, Carol preached a message of salvation and love and hope. Through the anointing of the Holy Spirit, Carol, Darlene, and the other women leaders led everyone to repent of their sins and accept Jesus Christ into their hearts. Around 60 people's lives were radically transformed that night in South Philadelphia, and Carol and the other ladies were amazed at the power of God. They were also so excited to witness Darlene's courage and passion for sharing the Gospel. She was only a young Christian, yet she was so bold and sold-out to the Gospel.

* * *

As a first follower of Jesus, Darlene didn't care what people thought of her when she evangelized. She shared the Word of God everywhere and with everyone she met. She had a simple faith and, if God said it, she believed it. Also, she was a great encourager. She believed everyone had gifts given to them by God and it was up to them to discover and use them for the Kingdom of God. She taught and encouraged our children to read the Bible, pray, and seek God's answers on all life's problems. Soon after accepting Christ, our oldest son was reprimanded at school for singing to Jesus in the school's bathroom. A teacher found and escorted him to the guidance counselor's office. The school counselor, Dr. John David Bateman, however, was a Christian who had heard about Joe. He told him if he ever wanted to sing about Jesus, that he could sing in his office. John David also attended LWCF church. Even in a public school, God provided spiritual support to my son. Who said they took prayer out of school? Not there!

In late November 1983, I received a call at work from a stranger named Herb. He was a businessman in Fredericksburg, VA who had worked for a company in New York that manufactured fractional-size motion control products used in military equipment. He wanted to break into the Philadelphia Navy market and asked me if I would introduce him to my Navy customer at the Philadelphia Naval Base. I saw no conflict of interest with our company, SEACOR, so I said I would be happy to help. On Friday, he was scheduled to meet with me in my office. It had snowed heavily during Thursday night and, come Friday morning, there was about eight inches of snow on the ground, and the freeway was a mess. I managed to go to work and didn't expect to hear from Herb because of the bad weather. Around 1:00 pm, however, the receptionist called me and said I had a visitor upfront. When I greeted him, I was shocked that he had driven over 200 miles to meet with me despite the heavy snow. I noticed that there was a silver bird lapel pin on his suit jacket.

"What is that?" I asked, pointing to the lapel pin.

He said, "It's a dove."

I asked, "What does it mean?"

He said, "It means that I'm a Christian."

"A Christian? Praise God," I said. "Come on back to my office. We need to talk."

He wanted to talk about business and I wanted to talk about Jesus, so we ended up talking about both. I felt very comfortable with Herb because he was genuine and talked freely about his faith. He was one of the first Christian businessmen I had met after coming to Christ. After I took Herb to meet my customer, we parted ways, and he drove back home. I didn't know it then, but he would play a significant role in God's plan for me in the business world.

The year before I became a Christian, SEACOR was acquired by Day & Zimmermann, Inc. (D&Z). Their headquarters was at 1818 Market Street in downtown Philadelphia and was privately owned by one man, named Spike Yoh. D&Z had numerous wholly owned subsidiaries that specialized in engineering and technical services for the military. D&Z's annual revenue was over $400 million in 1982. After the SEACOR acquisition, Bob Carr retired and the D&Z CEO hired a retired Army General, Jack Apperson, to take his place.

On December 22, 1983, after lunch, all employees were asked to assemble in the warehouse area, which was the largest room. SEACOR had around 150 employees, and the new president wanted to talk to all of us before the holidays. He announced the company had a great financial year. He planned to implement a bonus program immediately for those employees who had excelled in their jobs. He called me up front and announced publicly that I had been chosen as the top employee of the year. He handed me an envelope that contained a personal letter from him and a check for $2,500. I couldn't believe I had received a Christmas bonus. The company had never done that before, and I wondered, why me? I was only a program manager and, surely, others were more deserving than me. Then I remembered the prophecy spoken over me by the evangelist, Richard Myers. God was going to take me from promotion to promotion to promotion to promotion. After pondering this event, I knew it wasn't a coincidence, and it was part of God's plan for my life. Darlene and I rejoiced and thanked God when I got home because we had been living paycheck-to-paycheck. Receiving this bonus helped us pay off some credit card debt and buy the kids Christmas gifts.

In early January 1984 when I returned from lunch, I noticed several hard-cover business books on my desk with a yellow sticky note that read as follows,

Read these books this weekend and see me on Monday.
Jack, SEACOR President

The business books included The One Minute Manager and Search of Excellence. I read as much as I was able and reported to the president when I arrived to work the following Monday. He told me D&Z, the parent company, was starting a new program for rising stars within the companies they owned. It was referred to as the Corporate Officer Orientation Program (COOP). The president wanted me to attend the first COOP session as SEACOR's representative. He said that once I completed the four-month COOP, I would return to SEACOR and be promoted to vice president with a pay raise. I was again shocked by the fulfillment of God's prophetic Word in my life in such a short time.

COOP allowed me to talk with each D&Z board member one-at-a-time for a minimum of four hours, to learn about their job and their vision for D&Z. Every other week, I met with a different D&Z board member and talked to them about their role. I learned a lot about the corporate executives and the parent company from that experience, and one thing that stood out to me was that these were genuine people, not stiff white-collar phonies pretending to be smart. These executives were positive people who shared their vision of success and were honest and frank about relevant business issues and their vision of growth. They were also highly motivated and positive about the company's future.

In the fourth month of the COOP, my final session was with Spike Yoh, the Chairman of the Board and the CEO of D&Z. His office was a huge corner office that occupied a quarter of the top floor of a high-rise office building in downtown Philadelphia. Half of the office had full-length windows from floor to ceiling and, when the blinds were open, it displayed a clear and beautiful view of Center City Philadelphia. The office furniture was unique and of contemporary design. Instead of a traditional executive desk and credenza, there was a large wooden table with a couple of high back chairs that served as his desk. In the center, there was another table with several chairs around the perimeter to serve as a working area or for small meetings with other executives. This office layout scheme was straightforward and practical and ideal for an active and confident CEO who wanted to have his employees feel comfortable when meeting with him.

Upon entry, he came over, smiled, and proudly shook my hand, congratulating me for being selected in the COOP. We sat down at the large table in the center of his office, upon which were two 12" stacks of file folders containing documents, one on each end. We sat opposite each other, the documents serving as bookends between us. The CEO was very informal with me and wanted me to relax and be myself. His secretary brought us some coffee on a tray and poured each of us a cup. He asked me to tell him about myself. I don't remember what I said, but I got the impression from his body language he already knew some things about me from SEACOR's president. We also talked about the other D&Z board member executives I had met over the past few months and what I learned from them about the company and its mission.

Soon, he disclosed to me that he was dealing with two major challenges. He reached to his left and slid one of the towering stacks of file folders to the center between us. He said this stack of documents is one of the challenges and it represents SEACOR. When he had acquired SEACOR a year ago, he stated he had been unaware of the company's pressing problems. Namely, there were problems with certain personnel in a SEACOR field office on the Gulf Coast. It was alleged there were timesheet mischarges. The issue had even risen to the level of a potential FBI investigation. It was still unresolved, a year after D&Z's acquisition. Though I was somewhat familiar with the problems, having heard about them from other employees in the field, I hadn't known the details because it had been none of my business, and it didn't affect our work at Cherry Hill.

He then asked me how I would handle the SEACOR problem. I gave him a big-picture answer, which he seemed to consider. I suggested that he visit the Gulf Coast office and meet with the disgruntled employee to better understand the problems in the company. He asked me a few more questions about SEACOR, and then the meeting ended. I thanked him for his time and the privilege of meeting with him, I left and returned to SEACOR. I was troubled by this meeting and wondered if the problem would impact SEACOR's business growth, but I was also confident that the D&Z CEO would get to the bottom of the issues and resolve them in a timely way.

The next day I met with SEACOR's president. I debriefed him on my COOP experience, especially the meeting with the D&Z CEO. The president seemed very much aware of the internal issues and thanked me for being a valued employee. He told me he was promoting me to vice president, effective immediately.

While things were going exceptionally well for me on my job, Darlene was continuing to have significant challenges that affected her teeth and gums. She was always in pain, and her teeth were constantly hurting her. Growing up in poverty, Darlene had never received any dental care because her mom hadn't been able to afford it. When I first took her to the dentist after we were married, the dentist indicated the work required was so extensive that he felt she needed to see an orthodontist. We quickly found a reputable orthodontist and made an appointment. After examining her teeth and gums and studying the x-rays, the orthodontist summarized her findings with us. She told us Darlene had significant bone loss around her front teeth. It would be necessary to pull her front teeth and drill new ones in, assuming there would be enough bone left to anchor the replacements. She also explained she had to reconstruct most of the other teeth. It would be a major effort, but not impossible to accomplish. The main impediment was cost. It would cost a lot of money, which we didn't have.

Regardless, I tried to encourage Darlene to have the surgery, but she refused. The orthodontist stated the only other option to eliminate the pain would be to remove all of her teeth, though she was clearly against this option and told us so emphatically. A week or so later, Darlene thought about it and decided she wanted all of her teeth removed so the pain would stop. She did not want to go through the long and painful process of fitting new teeth into fragile bones that may or may not secure them firmly. I pleaded with my wife to reconsider, but she refused to budge. Finally, the orthodontist relented and agreed to accommodate my wife's request.

The in-patient surgery was performed in January 1984, and my wife's teeth were all removed. She was only 32-years-old and still very beautiful, inside and out. For six weeks, she went without any teeth to allow her gums to heal. She didn't stay isolated in the house during this time, however. She was the same as before, outgoing, pleasant, and a good wife and mother. She told me one night right after surgery she had a dream of Jesus giving her His teeth while on the cross. This revelation gave her peace, comfort, and confidence. When she interfaced with people, they never noticed she had no teeth. She could even eat anything without teeth, including steak and corn on the cob. It was truly amazing, and the proof was in the pudding. She was becoming a woman of great faith.

When it came time to get her a set of dentures, I found a dentist in our neighborhood who specialized in making false teeth and had reasonable prices. After the initial appointment, he made her a set for $300, which was within our budget. When we went to pick them up, Darlene came out of the back room with them in her mouth. When I asked her how they felt, she nodded instead of answering me verbally. I repeated my question, and she smiled. When I saw her new dentures, they looked like mice teeth because they were too small for her face. She tried to talk to me but couldn't because the dentures would move in her mouth. When we got home, I was so upset with the shoddy workmanship, that I took the set of dentures, put them in a sealable plastic sandwich bag, and returned them that evening to the dentist. I told him to keep his dentures and that I wasn't going to pay for them because they didn't look right or fit properly. He didn't argue with me and never tried to collect.

The next day Darlene asked me to pray with her for another dentist that could provide her with a set of dentures that looked great and fit correctly. She believed God would give us the name of the dentist He wanted us to use. Although I was skeptical, Darlene never doubted because she believed God was real and would communicate His will to her. We held hands and prayed together. After we prayed, we had a moment of silence, and we waited on the Lord. All at once, Darlene spoke up and said she believed God had given her the name of a dentist. She asked me to get the phone book, which I did. Darlene then asked me to look in the yellow pages under dentists for the name "Dr. Minari." She even spelled it for me. I flipped through the yellow pages, and there listed in the dentist section was the name Dr. Minari. His office was in Haddonfield, New Jersey, which was only 15 minutes away. Without hesitation, I called and made an appointment for Darlene. What were the odds that Darlene would know the name "Minari" was in the phone book, much less listed in the dentist section? It was truly God through the Holy Spirit who had revealed the dentist He wanted Darlene to use.

Within a week, we set up an appointment to see Dr. Minari. When we arrived, we learned he not only practiced dentistry but also taught dentistry at the University of Pennsylvania Dental School. He

126

was considered an expert in the field of dentures and teeth reconstruction. Again, God showed us that he only gives His best answers to His children in a practical way.

After examining my wife's mouth, he came out with her to talk to both of us in the waiting room. He was very upbeat and stated he wished he had pictures of my wife's mouth before she had her original teeth removed. He said he would love to show his students the before and after photos of my wife's mouth. He was also convinced he could make her a great set of dentures she would love and that would fit perfectly in her mouth. When I asked how much it would cost, he said around $2,000. I was surprised when I heard the price because I had no idea how we would pay for them. Still, God had told my wife the name of the dentist, and I believed He would also show us how we were going to pay for the dentures. Before we left, I asked the receptionist to go ahead, place the order for the dentures, and let us know when they arrived.

Outside in the parking lot, Darlene and I talked, and that's when I told her I didn't have the money. She convinced me to pray with her right then. Standing there in the cold January weather, we held hands and prayed together, asking Father God to show us how we would pay. When we completed our prayer, she paused and asked me how much money we were getting back in our income tax returns. I thought for a moment and told her it would be around $2,200. She said, "There's our money for the dentures" and we laughed at how God had answered our prayer again right away. Those dentures turned out to be an excellent investment. Not only did they fit well, but they also lasted for 33 years. The average annual cost was $61.00. It wasn't until 2017 that Darlene had to finally replace them with another set.

* * *

In the Spring of 1984, SEACOR's executive secretary to the president asked me to come to the president's office. She said the president was in the SEACOR Washington, DC office and he wanted to talk to me on the phone. I sat in his chair and took the call. He told me that he had just fired the vice president who ran the SEACOR Washington office and he wanted me to take his place and run the operation. I told him I was enrolled at Rutgers University at night, getting my BS Degree, and had around 18 credit hours to go. I asked him if he could wait until I finished my degree. The president knew I was a Christian, and he was, as well. Rather than answer my question, he suggested I pray and discuss it with my wife over the weekend and let him know my decision on Monday.

That weekend my wife and I prayed together and asked God if we were to move to the Washington, DC area. Darlene was at peace regarding the opportunity and believed we were to take the position. I struggled with this decision, because I knew the DC operation was over my head. I was only 33 years old with an AA Degree and felt I wasn't qualified to run the DC office. Several of the employees were engineers. One person had a Ph.D., and another was a lobbyist with years of experience on Capitol Hill. The man who had been fired was a retired Navy captain with many years of real-life experience. In comparison, I was a young man with no pedigree. I knew I was the wrong guy for the position, but didn't God also know that? What was there to pray about?

While driving somewhere alone in Philadelphia that weekend, I talked and argued with God about this opportunity. I told Him about my weaknesses and my lack of education. In my heart, God reminded me of Moses and how he complained he stuttered and wasn't capable of leading the chosen people out of slavery. God also reminded me how He had anointed Aaron, Moses' brother, as a priest to walk alongside and assist him. God explained He didn't want me to get my college degree. He said If I were highly educated, I would show people my biography or resume and take credit for all the success and promotions in business He was blessing us with. I knew Father God was correct and I needed to obey Him. When I got home, I shared that conversation with my beloved, and she concurred with God. In the years that followed, I never finished my undergraduate degree. I realized then that I had to trust God and believe He was my provider. He was the one that would continue to take me from promotion to promotion in business and in life itself. In my weakness, He was my strength. On Monday, I accepted the promotion, and the president asked me to move in the Summer to the DC area. I withdrew from Rutgers University and told them I would not finish the Bachelor of Science degree.

* * *

Darlene was on fire to spread the Word of God and wanted to get directly involved in ministry activities. The pastor at LWCF church was organizing a mission team to go to Kenya and Darlene believed God wanted her to go. Initially, I was okay with this, but it wasn't long before I started to resist her request for practical reasons. She ended up not going because of my resistance, but it didn't stop God from sending her in the spirit. Over the years, she would awaken at night and kneel by the bed praying for those whom God revealed to her. Many were Kenyans, whom she prayed for as God showed her. She would usually write the words God gave her on paper and refer to them often in prayer. This Word was confirmed on July 1, 1984, during prayer with our neighbor, Carol. She spoke the following words of the Lord to Darlene:

"I, the Lord thy God, am sending you forth to lands far and near to root and give growth, some to harvest and some to cultivate. Your work will be hard and physically trying to your body. Your vines are very strong and loaded with much fruit, and they're in heavy bloom. A large harvest you shall reap, says the Lord of Hosts. You are just one of many laborers, I am sending in power and might to a people whose cries have reached all the way into heaven. You shall cultivate and nurture the way for more to follow. I, the Lord of the harvest, am pouring my glory out as never before unto my people, for the harvest is ripe."

* * *

In July, we hired a moving company and packed up and moved to Northern Virginia. We initially got a three-bedroom apartment in Crystal City, Arlington, VA, which was a quarter mile from the office. We enrolled our children in the Arlington County public schools, and I was given a company car, a 1979 Cadillac Deville. I was anxious to get my first day of work started, but I knew I needed to cover the day in prayer. Darlene and I prayed together before I left for work, which gave me an extra boost of confidence and trust in God's plan on this new journey.

There were less than 15 employees in the SEACOR Crystal City office. Most of them were professional and very cordial and respectful to me when I arrived. The only exception was the lobbyist. After introducing himself and telling me how important he was to the company, he leaned close to me. He quietly said he had helped to get rid of the last vice president and that I would be next if I ever crossed him. He then half-jokingly said he would push me through one of the windows. The office was on the 11th floor. I didn't know if this guy was serious or not, but his words stayed with me the whole day. Although disturbed, I met and talked with each employee, including two engineers who were not Americans. One was from England and the other was from Turkey, and they both seemed to have a good attitude with a positive outlook for the business.

When I left work later that day and returned to our apartment, I was an emotional wreck. I told my wife I couldn't do this job. I shared the lobbyist's remarks and threat with Darlene, and she said we needed to pray and ask God to show me the way. The next day, I had a meeting with everyone and shared my vision and plans for the office. Everyone but the lobbyist bought in. I also met with the two engineers and asked them to help me to better understand what needed to be done to help solve problems and grow the business, and both were very supportive. During that year, I was never able to win over the lobbyist, but it didn't matter. Even without his support, the DC operation became a remarkably productive and successful operation for the company.

About a month into living in Arlington, we decided to put down roots and look for a house to rent farther south of the beltway. Darlene and I prayed God would show us the right place He wanted us to live. During our private prayer time, Darlene told me about a vision God gave her and said the house we were to rent would have a small lake in view nearby with a canoe in the water. She also said there would be a crumbled aluminum Coca-Cola® can in the yard. We connected with a realtor, and she took us to see houses for rent in the Prince William County area. We went to a few places that were okay but not ideal. She then took us to a house located in the Mont-clair subdivision. When we arrived and exited the car, I started to follow the realtor towards the house. Darlene stopped in her tracks. looked around, and immediately called me to come to her. I asked her what she needed and she told me to look out at the lake. I stared at the water, but I didn't see anything unusual. She asked me if I saw the canoe, and I nodded. Then she asked me to look at the ground and pointed down to a discarded empty Coca-Cola® can that lay in the yard nearby. She reminded me that this was the house God wanted us to rent, and I pointed out that we hadn't even looked at it yet. We entered together and, as soon as we entered, I was gripped with a spirit of negativity. I didn't understand why I felt that way — the house was stunning, with large rooms and extra amenities. Darlene loved it, but I remained negative during the walkthrough. When we finished and exited, I asked the realtor about the monthly rent and she stated it was $800 per month. I told Darlene we couldn't afford that amount and rejected the place despite my wife's request and confirmation from God.

The realtor took us to one more house that was located off Hoadly Road. It was nice and only rented for $700 per month. I talked my wife into accepting it and, although she was disappointed, she agreed. We signed a year lease and moved in, but I realized that it was a mistake I would regret. We did not have much peace in that house, and later found out why: the landlord who had lived there previously had had multiple affairs with other women. I then real-ized I should have listened to God through my wife. Unfortunately, I repeated this rebellious behavior many more times in our marriage and, each time, we paid the price. I kept trusting worldly reason over spiritual revelation, which was a grave mistake.

* * *

We wanted to make sure we continued to raise our children in the church and joined a local Church of God located a couple of miles from our house. We made friends there and got active in prayer and other ministries. One Sunday morning after church service, Darlene and I saw a young woman crying outside. We asked her what was wrong, and she said God had recently healed her of brain cancer. The tumor was in a part of her brain that had made it impossible for doctors to remove safely, and she said she had taken healing scriptures from the Bible, enlarged them on a copier, and taped the scriptures all over the house, including in the bathroom. She read them aloud all day every day. Over time, the tumor had moved from the center of her brain to the base of her brain, its new location allowing the surgeon to surgically remove it without damaging her brain. It was a miracle. Darlene and I were amazed by her active faith, and hearing her testimony of her miracle boosted our faith to continue to trust God for Darlene's total healing.

We continued going to our new church and getting involved. Then one Sunday, on March 25, 1985, my wife received the following Word of knowledge from God to share with the congregation.

"Thus, saith The Lord. My children have forsaken me, their first love. For in the days gone by, I have spoken and performed many miracles in your assemblies, and yet, now, you slumber and do not seek my voice or seek or ask me into your presence. My day is upon you, and yes, many, many shall I find asleep on their post and be ashamed on my day. My children have grown tired of eating and are now dieting, and for what you eat daily amounts only to a few morsels of food, and you have become weak from lack of food, and many are asleep. My Word is your food, and I say, eat and grow fat on my Word. For not only will your spirits grow fat, but my Words will become medicine to your bones and marrow and become strong to outrun all evil in your midst. Elijah ate manna prepared by my angels and grew in strength from that meat, 40 days, and 40 nights. So shall my words, your manna performs in you. I do not desire my children to diet, but I do desire all my children to eat of me daily and to grow fat on my Words. Hearken and understand my Words."

After Darlene delivered this Word, many received it, responded positively, and concurred it was from the heart of God.

We kept in touch with Carol and a few other Christian believers in New Jersey. John David Bateman, who was now ordained by pastor Dan of LWCF, contacted us and said he was coming down to our area to minister. The old Baptist church that he was going to preach at was only 14 miles from our house and we decided to hear him preach that Sunday night. It ended up being an unbelievable evening of praise and worship. Revival broke out amongst the congregation and the power of the Holy Spirit was very evident. Many people were baptized in the Holy Spirit, and others were slain in the Spirit as they received prayer. Darlene led a procession of worshippers around the church, praising God and praying for revival. John David Bateman prophesied over Darlene the following words from God:

"God had anointed Darlene as a Prophet and Teacher of the Word of God. He said that God would pour forth through Darlene, touching the lives of all those who came near her. Many lives would be changed and set free. Darlene would give answers to questions that have not yet been asked."

It was a night to remember with how God moved so powerfully among his people. Darlene was called and anointed as a prophet and teacher in the body of Christ. And, though no pastor officially designated her or assigned her this calling, scriptures show God, Himself, appointed Saint Paul as an Apostle. John David prophesied it, and as her husband and helpmate, I was sure of it. She didn't care what other Christians thought about her calling. Only what God said mattered to her. Three years later, I visited pastor John David Bateman at his home in New Jersey and he made it official by issuing Darlene a ministerial license under his Christian denomination.

* * *

It wasn't long before Darlene organized a children's Bible study in our house. She created a children's Bible curriculum, made flyers, and went around the neighborhood, handing them out. It would be held every Friday afternoon when the kids got home from school. Besides our three children, other children regularly attended. Over time, Darlene led all of these kids to pray and to receive Jesus into their hearts as Lord and Savior. She also prayed with them to be baptized in the Holy Spirit. She recorded their names and pictures in a personal prayer log and prayed for them and their families regularly. She truly was a faithful prayer warrior and teacher of the Word.

Meanwhile, God had plans to move us again and provide me with another promotion at my job. SEACOR had satellite offices near major naval bases and shipyards across the USA, but not one in Orlando. I knew from marketing research that we could capture new business from the Naval Training Systems Center (NTSC) in Orlando if we had a full-time marketing presence there. The mission would be to identify and assess the competition and submit a comprehensive technical and price proposal when NTSC issued the solicitation. I estimated the market potential for the logistics work at NTSC to be $3M over three years. There was an incumbent contractor, but I thought SEACOR could beat them once we identified their weaknesses. I discussed this opportunity at every marketing meeting we had at SEACOR headquarters and even identified an experienced candidate, who was also a friend of mine, who would be ideal for this position.

One day in the Spring of 1985, I arranged a meeting with the president to meet my proposed candidate for the Orlando position. During the meeting, the president listened carefully to my argument about the need to market in Orlando and the value of having an experienced candidate on-site to bring it to fruition for the company. After presenting my evidence to the president, he finally spoke up and said he knew me personally and professionally. He also said he believed my Orlando proposal was valid. However, he said to ensure we had the best chance to capture this new logistics business with NTSC, he wanted to send me to Orlando. He mentioned there would be a place in SEACOR for the proposed candidate, as well, and we could discuss the details later. He told me to think about the Orlando opportunity and let him know my thoughts later. He then abruptly stood up, thanked us for meeting with him, and politely escorted us out.

I was blown away and somewhat embarrassed by the president's response. Once outside, I apologized to my friend and told him I was completely taken aback by his answer. My friend said he understood and had no hard feelings. That evening I discussed this potential move to Orlando with my beloved wife. She was open to the move if God provided us favor and direction. Together we prayed and read Ezekiel 2:1-10 and 3:1-12. In prayer, we received the following words from Jesus:

"Your paths shall be my paths, for I, your Lord, am leading you and paving your paths. Yes, the devil does tempt my children to turn and run on different paths than the paths I have chosen for them. I am sending you on a new phase of your journey, and you must not question but obey my Spirit. For He knows my will and shall reveal all to you before it comes to be. I shall deliver you at the door, but not at the door you once thought, but a new door shall you stand before."

I met with the president shortly after that and told him we were willing to move to Orlando. We had only been living and working in the DC area for a year, but, that summer of 1985, we contracted a moving company, packed up again, and drove the family to Orlando. We stayed at a hotel the first night in town. There, we met an elderly lady from Australia named Molly, who seemed troubled over some personal matters. The more we talked with her privately, the more she opened to us. My wife told her we were Christians and asked her if we could pray for her, to which agreed. During the prayer, Molly started crying and Darlene hugged her. Afterward, she asked her if she was a Christian, and she said she was not, which prompted Darlene to share the Gospel with her. Before long, Darlene asked her if she wanted to receive Jesus into her heart. Molly gave her consent and she led her in the sinner's prayer and, by her faith, Christ Jesus entered in. Darlene then asked me to give her the Bible I had with me. It was brand new and I had just gotten it and, even though I didn't want to part with it, Molly needed it more than me. She told us she had never read the Bible before and Darlene saw this as a perfect opportunity to bless a new Christian with the best gift, His living Word. Later, I repented for being selfish.

LINDA FORTNER
Prophet and Teacher

Leading Disciples Forward
Outreach Ministry

Phone: 703-
Cell: 703-
Fax: 703-

Dale City, VA 22193
E-mail: ldfortner@
www.geocities.com/sweetvoiceldf/index.html

15
LEADING DISCIPLES FORWARD

Isaiah 54:13 (NASB) "All your sons will be taught of the LORD; And the well-being of your sons will be great."

We found a beautiful single-family, four-bedroom house to rent in Casselberry, Florida, a suburb of Orlando. It was in the Howell Estates subdivision right off Red Bug Lake Road. The closest non-denominational, Spirit-filled Christian church was the Messianic Bible Institute, which was only a mile from our house. We loved this small assembly, mainly because 24 of the members were Messianic Jewish believers. The pastor also showed an affinity to God's chosen people by recognizing Jewish feast days and Christian holy days. He also taught a two-year Bible study course on the Old Testament and the original ancient Hebrew. My wife and I enrolled and attended classes at night, where the pastor was an incredible teacher and preacher of the Bible.

One day in church, my wife noticed a foot cast on Marnie, a 12-year-old girl, who was a friend of our daughter, Alita. During the service, she quietly went over and asked her if she wanted her to pray to God for her foot to heal. She willingly accepted her prayer. Darlene laid hands on the cast and asked God to heal her foot, and, after a minute, she ended the prayer and told the girl to believe by faith that God had answered her prayer for healing. Later that day, the girl asked her father to remove the cast, explaining what had happened in church. He resisted at first, as she hadn't had the cast on for very long, before finally giving in and cutting it off due to her insistence. He told her that if she needed another cast, her mother would have to take her to the hospital. However, once the cast was removed, she tested her foot right away and did not feel any pain. She declared aloud to her father that Jesus had healed her foot, then came over to our house to share the good news. Darlene wasn't surprised because she expected God to honor His Word, especially since she had heard God say to pray and believe during that service.

It wasn't long before Darlene restarted teaching children's Bible study classes in our home. This time I could be more involved since I would be working for SEACOR from home. We purchased some electronic equipment that gave Darlene the ability to tape each class, and our kids passed the word to their friends at school. By September 1985, classes reconvened.

Every Friday, when the kids got off the school bus, several would accompany our children to our home for an hour of Bible study. Darlene was very organized. She prepared the lessons in advance and studied and prayed for God to anoint her and the kids. Upon arrival, she warmly greeted all of the children and gave them the lesson for that day. She would assemble them in the living room in a circle and either pray or ask one of them to lead the prayer, before giving each child a Bible and having them refer to the scriptures for that class. Following the reading, she would choose a Christian children's song to sing and have all the kids join in, and then she'd share a story about Jesus about which they'd ask questions . A closing prayer would be spoken aloud by her or someone else in the class, and, as they left, Darlene would always offer them snacks and a drink, which they gladly accepted.

The kids loved the Bible studies. Most who attended were between the ages of seven to 13 years old and did not attend church but were very open to prayer and learning about the love of God. Darlene always encouraged the children and told them that they were special and God loved them. At times, the kids would share problems they were having at school or home, and Darlene would pray with them. During that school year, all the kids who attended accepted Jesus into their hearts. One of the youngest kids, who was Jewish, wanted to be saved and baptized in water. Darlene met with his mother and told her of his desire. She allowed my wife to pray with him and baptize him in their pool. By the end of 1985, 12 young souls were won to Christ and filled with the Holy Spirit. Some of them received water baptisms, as well. Darlene continued teaching the children Bible classes every Friday afternoon through 1986, where 10 more children accepted Jesus into their hearts.

* * *

Darlene was an incredible prayer warrior who kept her spiritual ear close to God's heart. In one instance, Darlene learned that someone in our neighborhood had lost their job and was struggling to pay their bills. She prayed, and God led her to go door-to-door and ask other neighbors to donate food or cash to help them out. Most were very generous and willing to give, though a few found it odd that Darlene was doing this on her own initiative. I'm sure God was quite pleased with His daughter.

On another occasion, as she drove down Red Bug Lake Road to a doctor's appointment, God spoke to her and told her to pull over and stop the car. He then showed her a woman sitting by herself at a picnic table near a small lake. God told Darlene to go over and tell her that God sent her over to pray for her. Darlene obeyed God, and the woman burst out crying and said she was just talking to God about her problems. She asked Darlene to pray for her. Her husband, who was in the lake swimming, heard his wife crying and came out to see what the matter was. He thought Darlene had made his wife upset. He calmed down when his wife told him Darlene was sent by God to pray for her.

God used Darlene to help heal our family, as well. During prayer time on Christmas eve 1985, the Lord revealed to Darlene a vision about our youngest son, Shane. He was only nine years old and had a non-cancerous tumor in his bladder. God instructed her to trust Him and turn her faith over to Him, and He would be her strength and helper in this time of need. On January 3, 1986, we met with the doctor before Shane's surgery and prayed with him. The doctor removed the tumor with no problems, and Shane healed quickly. My wife's faith was growing more and more each day in the Word of God.

* * *

In September 1985, my marketing effort in Orlando paid dividends. SEACOR won the follow-on 3-year logistics contract with NTSC Orlando, to which I gave God all the credit. I opened an office for SEACOR in Casselberry and immediately hired the 21 people I had recently interviewed and selected for the 3-year contract. Unfortunately, the incumbent contractor who had lost to us in the competition was quite upset with the loss and tried to sabotage us before we got started. When the government customer at NTSC requested the incumbent contractor turn in the application software developed during their logistics work for the past three years, they refused, even though it was funded totally by the government, and the government did not have the leverage to force them to comply. We seemed to be at an impasse. How could SEACOR do the work expected without the use of the existing application software? I told my software engineer, a foreign national with dual citizenship of Algeria and France, that for SEACOR to be successful, he would have to reverse engineer the software application program for our new logistics contract. He said he could do it, but it would take around 90 days.

At contract award, I had to submit the resumes of all 21 employees for government review and approval, before starting work on the logistics contract. The initial kick-off meeting was to follow shortly. Before the meeting, I heard through the grapevine that the key government technical representative was not going to approve my software engineer to work on the new contract because he was a foreign national, which I thought shouldn't have mattered, since the contract was unclassified. As I prepared for the meeting, I prayed silently for wisdom and favor for the company and all our employees. During the meeting, I explained to the government representatives that we had to reverse engineer the logistics application software program since the previous contractor had refused to return it to the government after SEACOR's contract award. I asked them to give us 90 days. If the government didn't approve of our new logistics application software product, then I would replace my software engineer.

We took a break and allowed the government representatives to meet independently and discuss our proposal. When we rejoined them, they unanimously agreed to allow us to proceed with our 90-day plan. Later, when I was home with my family, I told Darlene the good news and we thanked God for answering my prayer. Before the three months were up, my engineer completed the application software program, and it received government approval. He was brilliant, thanks to God.

My secretary, Mati, was also a perfect choice as my office administrator. She was a devout Christian, happily married, and had a young son. Having previously lived and worked in New York City, she was used to high-pressure jobs requiring her to multi-task. I was a very demanding boss with my employees and myself. I expected the employees to do their best work every day, be honest and forthright when they made mistakes, and correct their errors promptly. Some of the employees were Christian, which was terrific. Mati prayed for my wife and me often, and we reciprocated.

* * *

It didn't matter what time of day or what she was doing, if someone asked Darlene to pray, she would pray, right then and there, most of the time. She expected God to answer her prayers and made sure they were deliberate, specific, and based on the living Word in the Bible. At times, we prayed together for each other, our kids, the church, people we knew, finances, and anything else that entered our minds during prayer. She was never in a hurry to finish praying, and only when she felt God was done, would she stop. I was not as patient as her, but I learned over time to wait. If I prayed with unbelief, she would stop me immediately and correct the prayer. To Darlene, prayer was the key to unlock the mysteries of the kingdom of God on Earth, as it is in Heaven. After prayer, she would write down the date, the time, the prayer, and the reply from God, and file it away for reference later. She also wrote down her dreams, visions, teachings, sayings, poems, short stories, prophecies, words of knowledge, and other things that God had shared with her from the time she was saved. She was unbelievable, and I was truly blessed to have her as my bride.

At 12:05 am on October 26, 1985, Darlene and I were in prayer enquiring about a book that I felt God was leading me to write. We were asking Him for wisdom. God spoke the following words to us:

"My words are a sword of fire. As you speak My words, they shall break asunder all evil which bind your finances. For no chains are strong enough to outdo the power of My Words. As you write and speak and give my Words in this book, multitudes shall be set free. And as you give out, it shall be met back unto you. And deliverance shall be yours."

After God spoke to us, I received the number 75 in my mind, and at first, I thought it meant a generation. The more I pondered and prayed, though, I sensed it meant $7 + 5 = 12$. Seven represents a perfect book by the Holy Spirit's guidance. Five is the 5-fold ministry, as my beloved wife described in the book. The number 12 means the book will be complete when it is finished.

On January 15, 1986, I had a vivid dream during the night, and it was very detailed about the book I was to write. I wrote the dream down and shared it with my beloved, and she prayed and provided interpretation.

Steve's Dream about The Book on January 15, 1986

I, Steve Fortner, had a dream last night. I entered a very narrow yet tall building of approximately 100 floors to return a book to the library on the 100th floor. The building resembled the Washington Monument in stature. When I first entered the lobby, I noticed there were people milling around, laughing and carrying on in normal conversation. I also stared at the elevator directly across the way and became scared and nervous when I realized I had to take it up to the 100th floor. The elevator door then opened, and people got

142

off. They were laughing, joking, and just having a good time as they departed. I was anxious. The elevator looked too small; only three or four people could fit inside at the most. I was also afraid it would fall before it reached the top floor. However, I had to return the book. I then saw two people get on it. If I didn't get on that elevator right then and there, I knew I would have to wait until it came back down again. It only opened on the 1st and the 100th floor.

Just before the doors closed, I hurried onto the elevator and thanked them for holding it open for me. I laughed nervously and tried to hide my anxiety on the way up. I remember asking them about the safety features, and they told me it was old but perfectly safe and not to worry. The elevator raised slowly, and, after several minutes, we finally reached the 100th floor. The elevator door opened, and I saw a steep staircase directly in front of me that went to the top, where the library was. I saw a woman librarian at the top, hurrying to get finished with her work. She had sweat on her face from rushing around. Directly in front of me were the ten steep steps leading to the top. There was no platform to step off from the elevator. If I took a step out, I would be on the first step of the staircase, which had handrails on both sides covered in a brilliant white fabric, like laced cotton. After hesitating for a few moments to grasp the picture, I immediately got off the elevator and started to climb the staircase. I noticed the other two people, women, I think, stayed on the elevator talking to each other casually. I also felt good and safe when I left the elevator. However, I remember being concerned about the buildings swaying in the wind at that level. Someone, possibly the librarian, said it was safe to come up.

When I got to the top of the steep staircase, after holding both handrails firmly all the way up, the librarian, still rushing around, was glad and relieved to see I made it before closing time. As a matter of fact, I was her last customer. She took my book, filed it on the shelf, grabbed her sweater, and descended the staircase to leave work. I also followed her and entered the elevator, which was still there waiting for us. As the doors closed, I asked the two people who stayed on the elevator if it descended quickly. They said it did descend rapidly, but it was safe. Almost immediately after their comment, the elevator dropped rapidly towards the first floor. So fast, indeed, it took my breath away. Halfway down, it slowed a little then dropped quickly again. I tried to brace myself during the dissent, but it still scared me and took my breath away. The three people with me did not seem to be affected by the rapid descent. Just before arriving at the first-floor lobby, I woke up. Even though I didn't reach the first floor in my dream, I knew I had made it safely back.

Interpretation: through Darlene on January 16, 1986:

The narrowness of the building means God's road is narrow, and few find it.

The 100 floors of the building mean completing it will result in a 100-fold return.

The book represents the book that Steve is to write about Darlene and that it was finally finished.

The Library represents that all things come from God and shall return unto God. A library represents a place full of knowledge that you can go to, but you must return what you have been given to receive the right to take anything else out.

The anxiety of the elevator was God showing Steve there is fear within him, and he must learn to trust God and have full confidence in God and himself as a child of God.

The people in the elevator speaking to Steve and reminding him not to worry, represented God's people through prophecy, speaking God's private Word to Steve not to worry, for worry is from the devil and not God.

The elevator ascending represents God raising Steve from promotion to promotion to promotion, which were words first prophesied over Steve from the Lord through the evangelist and pastor John David Bateman, reminding him it is God who promotes, not man.

The staircase represents the final stage and Steve having to decide between finishing his task of returning the book and fighting the fear of the steep staircase and conquering his fear or deciding to never go up the stairs to return the book for fear of the narrowness and steepness of the stairs. In the dream, God showed Steve overcame his fears and completed the book and received a 100-fold return from God.

* * *

During the years, God would nudge me by the Holy Spirit and give me unusual signs the book needed to be written, but I continued to procrastinate. Later that month, I had to visit Pensacola, Florida on business and decided to take an evening flight. It was a stormy evening when we took off from Orlando on a small two-engine propeller aircraft. I hated flying, and the fact we were bouncing all over the sky made it even scarier. I was sitting next to an elderly man, who had the window seat, and he had a manuscript in his lap and a red pen out for marking it up. I was so nervous I began to read the manuscript and noticed the name of God in several sentences. I finally asked the gentleman what he was doing, and he stopped and looked at me and said he was editing a friend's manuscript. He said he was a senior editor for Christianity Today magazine, and he also taught at King's College in Canada. I told him about my dream of writing a book. He handed me his business card and invited me to send him the manuscript when I completed it and he would edit it for me if I desired. I was blown away because it was another confirmation from God.

On another occasion, as I was lying in bed on my back resting, I imagined myself with a large purple colored fountain pen. It was the size of my arm. The cap was off and attached to the back, exposing the golden tip, which dripped dark blue ink. The huge pen was resting on my entire right arm as I lay in bed and the ink was dripping from the tip through my fingers and onto the bedroom floor. As I looked down, I noticed that there was quite a lot of ink spilled on the floor. God showed me that His pen was ready for me to begin the book project and it was filled to overflowing with ink. With these signs from God, how could I put off this work when I knew He wanted me to get started? Still, I delayed beginning my book, anyway, because I felt I had time to write it later when I wasn't so busy with work.

* * *

During many times in my life, as I looked at what happened around the world, I was thankful for God's grace and blessings over my family. I was also grateful during the times that God would cause me to slow down and pray during the tragedies taking place in others' lives. On January 28, 1986, the U.S. Space Shuttle Challenger exploded minutes after launch at Cape Canaveral, killing all astronauts aboard. I remember coming home for lunch that day and hearing the news report on the radio. I stood in my driveway and looked east and prayed for their souls.

On February 1, 1986, during prayer with my wife, God spoke once more about my need to write the book, and He even gave me the title: "My Blessed Bride." I was to write it in love and compassion. Still, I continued to hear and not obey. Either God stopped talking about the book, or I didn't hear Him discuss it anymore. Nevertheless, it never left the back of my mind, and I always knew I had to write it one day.

16
OFF THE BEATEN PATH

1 Peter 5:6-7 (NASB) "Therefore humble yourselves under the mighty hand of God, that He may exalt you at the proper time, casting all your anxiety on Him, because He cares for you."

The SEACOR Navy contract was going so well in Orlando, Darlene and I decided to put down roots and look for a house in the area to buy. In the summer of 1986, we bought a house in Geneva, FL, and moved from the Howell Estates subdivision in Casselberry. Geneva was located between Sanford and Mims off State Route 46, and our house was on Rest Haven Road. It was a dirt road cut into a very secluded and highly wooded area surrounded by lakes. The house, built in 1965, was a 3-bedroom, 2-bath, single-story with a partial brick-face in front. It was water-front property, located right on a small lake. There were only around eight other houses spread out on this road, tucked in amongst all the palm trees and vegetation. We were approximately 20 miles from SEACOR, and there was usually not much traffic in this rural area. I told my friends we lived in the middle of deer hunting woods. Wildlife was everywhere, including venomous snakes, alligators, raccoons, egrets, and giant woodpeckers, to name a few.

In our backyard, there was a small 5'x10' slip that extended out onto the lake, where we could stand and look out at the beauty of God's creation. During the sunrise and sunset, a family of large snapping turtles would swim over, expecting us to feed them, which we usually did. One day, Alita cooked her first meal for dinner, which was spaghetti and meat sauce. She was so proud of her accomplishment, and, like a good mom and dad, we tried to eat her meal, but it was so bland and unsavory we asked her if we could give our dinners to the turtles. She thought it was a good idea, and we all got our plates and went out to the slip. A few minutes later, the family of snapping turtles swam over, and we dumped the spaghetti into the shallow water. Immediately, the turtles began biting and snapping at the food so voraciously trying to eat and keep other turtles from getting their stash. It was quite a scene to behold.

We would also admire the flock of egrets as they would rise from the treetops in the early hours and soar over our small lake to Lake Harney, a much larger lake a quarter of a mile away. By sunset, the flock of egrets would faithfully return to their nests in the treetops. The trees were across from our house on the far shore, and the egrets would huddle together, screaming out at the darkening sky. Another time, while Darlene and I were standing on the slip, talking, she noticed a pair of water moccasins in the water to our right. She calmly asked me to get the manual hedge cutters, which I did. She took them from me and casually leaned over and cut each snake in half without fear or hesitation. These types of snakes were aggressive, and she didn't want to take any chance of us or the kids getting bit.

On another day, we were getting in the car to go to church, when I saw a coral snake in the grass in front of me. My wife and kids had already walked by it without incident and got in the car. I took a wide berth around the snake, not wanting to disturb it. Sometimes snakes would fall from a palm tree without warning. I guess they were trying to eat the bird eggs and would lose their grip on the palm tree fronds.

Then, there was David, who we named and considered our personal alligator in our lake. At times, he would surface when we would be out canoeing. I would poke him with the canoe paddle to keep him away. When my youngest son, Shane, was with me in the canoe, he would freak out whenever David appeared. To warm himself, David would leave the lake and lay in the road or another dry, sunny section. We had to be careful when we took walks down the road because we never knew where he might be hiding.

* * *

A couple of my SEACOR employees went to a vibrant Christian church called New Life Christian Fellowship in Titusville, FL. It was only 20 miles east of Geneva near the Indian River, across from Cape Canaveral. It was a relatively new assembly pastored by a young man named Larry, whose vision was to teach the kingdom of God in a non-judgmental way that spoke dignity and esteem to every person. It was a Spirit-filled fellowship that believed God's kingdom is not something you do but a lifestyle you join. We decided to visit and, soon after that, joined the assembly.

Even though we were in a good church and a decent neighborhood, life in the world was starting to affect me negatively. It was subtle at first, but Darlene could see my priorities were not in the correct order. I didn't realize it, but my job was still more important than God and my family. In February 1986, God gave me a word through Darlene. She said the following:

"Steven, the Lord spoke to you in New Jersey and said to get your priorities right. Now in your job (world), God is teaching you discipline and the ranks of command and how to honor and obey the laws of business. Not your way or to go around but to go through each level. This is His way of teaching you how to get your priorities right."

1, God
2. Family
3. Job
4. Calling
5. Congregation (body of Christ)

On May 1, 1986, during Darlene's prayer time, God spoke to her again about me. She wrote it down and gave it to me to read and ponder.

"My son, I gave you my love. I shed abroad in your heart, my love. Not as the world gives love but divine love from above.

Perfect and unselfish is my love. As I have given you, so you, my son, are to give. Give, not take, but give. For I have given you all, you need to accomplish all I have asked of you. I have given you the measure of faith you need, all authority, my Son Jesus' name, my precious Spirit, ministering angels, my Holy Word, access into the holy of holies at all times, and all the fruits of the Spirit to walk and be clothed in. Every need supplied and so much more. Yes, more, my son, you don't even know is within your wells! So, find a hurt, find a need, find one who is in trouble, and give my love out to a dying world. Be my troubleshooter and shoot the devil down and set my people free by giving all of yourself to others in love as I gave my Son, Jesus Christ, to you in love unto death. For I love you very much. For there is no greater love than to die for one another. Let fear and doubt be no part of you, for you are a holy vessel, my child. Remember my Word, 'The arm of the Lord is my strength and my joy.' Stretch forth your arm and take my hand. For I will never leave or forsake you. I have never left your side. I love you, saith The Lord of Hosts."

On May 27, 1986, God spoke yet again through my beloved wife. Again, she wrote it down and gave it to me when I got home from work.

"Energy equals power, thus saith The Lord. My son, when energy is given to any object, it produces, as it was made to work. Now, if something within us is not working right, the energy or power does not stop going forth, but causes it to overpower itself and burn up or blow up or short circuit. This also happens to my children who are not standing on my words or led by my Spirit. You must release the power from on high, which I have endowed you with toward positive goals, and you will see productive action come to be in your life and on your job. Every leader has a certain objective. He prepares his battle of attack, and neither does he go to the left or the right, but straight forward to battle. In all battles, you must have defense strategies and pull back to not be defeated. But a leader never loses his first objective. He goes forth with another attack until victory has been achieved. My son, I love you, and I am your strength, and my power is within you. Channel my power in my ways and statutes and trust I, your Lord, and all else shall come to be. Do not grow weary. But pull back and plan your attack and be led forward by my Spirit, to not become weary and burned out, to die by the enemy, by confusion, and darkness, saith The Lord."

Darlene referenced the following scriptures:

Deut. 8: 17-18; 14:2; II Sam. 22: 31-37; Luke 10: 19-20.

During this time in Geneva, there were many more words from God spoken to Darlene, me, and the kids. The world was having a negative effect on the kids and me. Darlene remained faithful and prayerful and recorded much of what God said and shared the words with us, hoping we would hear and obey. At that time, my children were growing up into their own unique personalities and going down their own paths in life.

Joe was 14 and very smart in school. As a young teenager, he was somewhat rebellious and difficult to handle. He was also into a game, Dungeons and Dragons, which his mom and I warned him to avoid because of its dark theme. Joe was also becoming a loner and a schemer. Once, on a school fundraiser, he decided to raise the price of the candy bars and sell them around the neighborhood, keeping the extra profit for himself. He also stole $10 from a neighborhood boy and denied it to the boy's mother and us when she confronted him at our home. Later that day, he owned up to the theft, and we had him return the money.

Meanwhile, at 12, Alita had her physical challenges. She had been a juvenile diabetic for three years. Going through puberty caused hormonal changes that affected her blood sugar, causing her levels to go from extreme highs to extreme lows. We had a difficult time managing her blood sugar levels. One day at breakfast, she had a seizure and passed out. I immediately called 9-1-1 but could hardly explain the emergency on the phone due to my anxiety and worry. Our youngest son, Shane, who was 10, dropped to his knees nearby and prayed for his sister, while I was on the phone. Darlene was also praying and caring for Alita as she lay on the floor. Thankfully, the ambulance arrived in time and treated her for low blood sugar. She fully recovered within a few minutes.

* * *

God not only spoke through Darlene to encourage and direct our family, but He also used other Christians to speak His Word into our lives. For instance, John David Bateman, a pastor in New Jersey, contacted us by phone in October 1986 and shared a word for Darlene that the Lord had given him.

"Breaking out! You're about to spring forth. Stay in prayer. You must stand in God's presence. Be quick to receive, and then you must give it out. For no sooner you give to others, God will give more to you to say. You must then be ready and alert to give out without delay."

In late March, John David contacted us again with another word from God for Darlene.

"Until I come, devote yourself to the reading of my Holy Scriptures, preaching, and teaching. Do not forget your gift, which was given to you through a prophetic message. Be diligent in these matters. Give yourself wholly to them. Watch your life and doctrine closely. Persevere in them, because if you do, you will save both yourself and your listeners, saith the Lord of Hosts."

Mati, my administrative secretary at work, also urged me to honor my beloved.

Here are two words she received from the Father for me in the fall of 1987.

"Thus saith the Lord: Love your wife for who she is and don't apologize for her. She is a rare and beautiful person I, the Lord, have selected for you, and she is your equal. God gives Darlene His words over you to create a balance. God loves Darlene, and God loves you. However, you feel superior to her because of your education, career, and knowledge. The Lord has balanced your marriage by giving her your same skills (education and knowledge) but in His Word. Whereas, yours is in your career. This way, you must rely on Darlene. The Lord wants to humble you."

Deut. 10:2 – "Thus saith the Lord: You must give glory to the one who loves you and carries My Word. She, too, is my temple. Honor her as she does honor to you, my son. I, The Lord, gave you My Words for you to read and for you to know. You have taken them, marveled at its truths, but did not fully understand that you must live them for the Lord's glory. Your house is the temple of God. It is there where you must start. I, The Lord thy God, have many wonderful and glorious things for you. You must listen to my ordinances. (Deut. 11). Keep close to you the words I have given you concerning my daughter, Darlene. Write them and carry them with you."

When I would receive these words from God, I would ponder them and be thankful for God's correction and guidance in my life. However, it wasn't long before I forgot them and reverted to my old ways of living with the cares of the world and my career as my real focus and not His Word.

* * *

Darlene was always open to anyone asking her to pray and to share the word of God. One night at 9:30 pm, on April 19, 1988, Mati called Darlene and shared a word she received from the Father for her.

"Thus, saith the Lord: My child, know first that I love you and hear your pleas. Know also that the time has not come for what you ask. Follow your heart, for I am there. Walk out in faith and know that you do not walk alone, for I have been with you, teaching you and giving you purification. The final test is the one I'm giving you now. Walk out to do my bidding. Do not be afraid, for I will be there for you and with you."

155

Ten days later, Mati had a word of knowledge for my beloved wife.

"Corner of the table – God wants you in the center."

She was instructed to read John 12:26 by The Lord.

* * *

On July 28, 1988, Pastor John David Bateman officially licensed my beloved to preach and teach the Gospel under his ministry, which was Open Door Community Fellowship Outreach Ministries of New Jersey, Inc. He presented her with a ministry license made out to "Linda Darlene Fortner." The word spoken to Darlene by pastor Bateman from the Lord was as follows:

"Thus, saith The Lord: I have found you faithful. I have found you prepared and ready. I have made ready your paths, and I have opened your gate. This ministry license, which I am giving you, will open doors, which would otherwise not open and give you entrance to preach and teach my Kingdom. The time for you to go is now. This is your last lap of your journey."

Darlene was humbled and very honored to be credentialed by Pastor John David Bateman. Through 1988, she also continued holding children's Bible study. She led two more children in the neighborhood to Christ on August 14, 1988. They were also baptized in the Holy Spirit.

Overall, during the three years we lived in Florida, Darlene remained focused on God's Word for guidance as a wife and mother. She also relied on the Holy Spirit to hone her spiritual gifts of a prophet and teacher of the Word. Despite the evidence of God's anointing of my beloved wife through many signs and wonders, I became more ambitious and attracted to the opportunities the world presented. My wife and children took second fiddle. I was on the road to failure both professionally and spiritually and didn't even know it. As a Christian with a praying, loving, and faithful wife, I should have repented sooner rather than later, to avoid the consequences to come down the road. It was only a matter of time before my spiritual trouble manifested itself in the natural realm.

O.D.C.

Certificate of License

THIS IS TO CERTIFY

Linda Darlene Fortner

who has given evidence that God has called him into

THE GOSPEL MINISTRY

was Licensed to preach the Gospel as he may have opportunity, and to exercise his gifts in the work of the Ministry

by **Open Door Community Fellowship Outreach Ministries of New Jersey Inc.**

on the _____ 28th _____ day of _____ JULY _____ , 19 88

_____ Clerk _____ Pastor

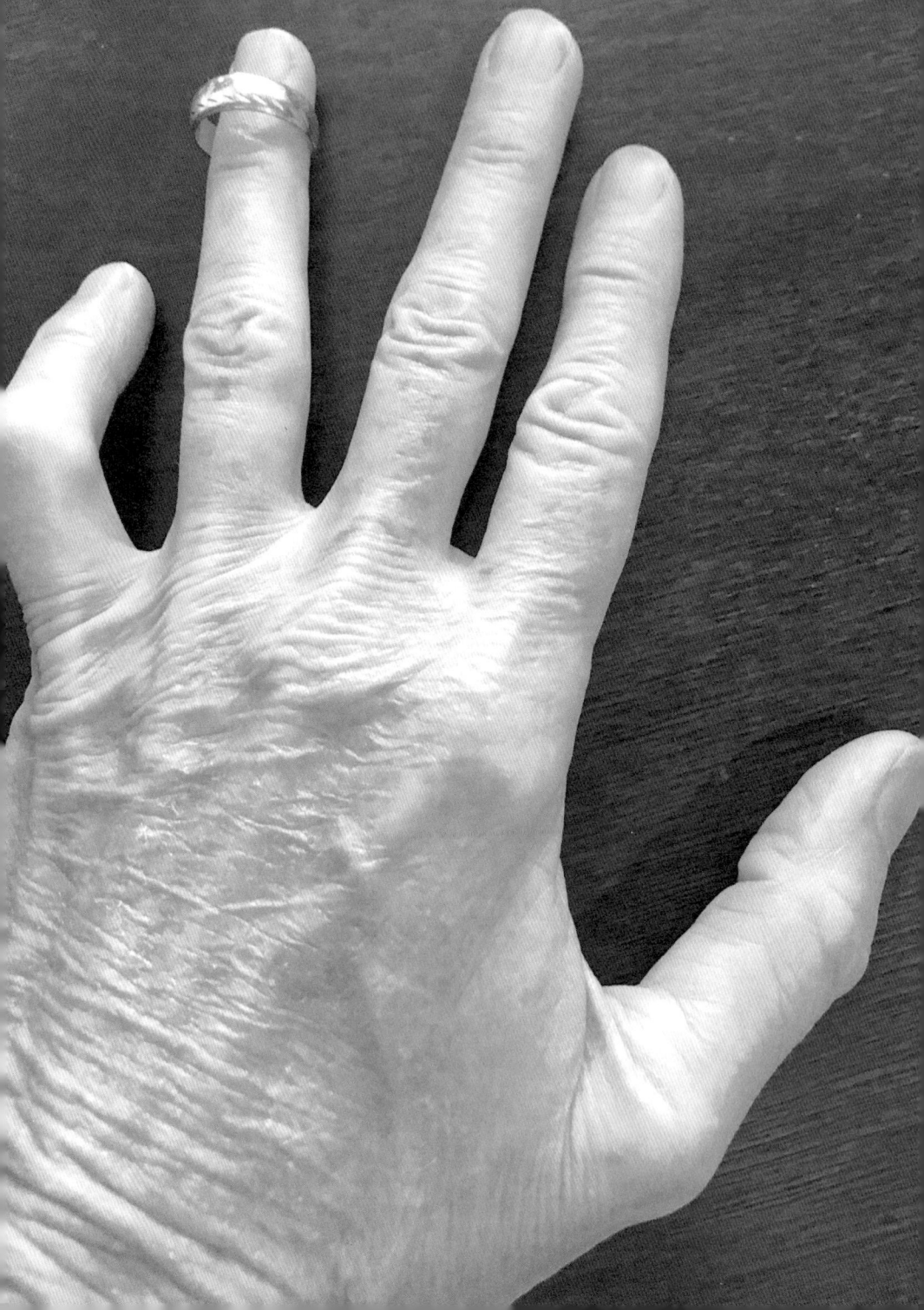

17
DIVORCE

Psalm 51:1 (NASB) "Be gracious to me, O God, according to Your loving kindness; According to the greatness of Your compassion blot out my transgressions."

Many times, we don't realize our own worst enemy is looking back at us in the mirror, our imminent destruction usually driven by pride and ego. At NTSC Orlando, one day, I ran into a contractor friend, named Lee, who I hadn't seen for a couple of years. Lee used to work for one of our competitors, but he told me he was no longer working in the naval defense contracting world. He was now an executive in a small high-technology business in downtown Cocoa, FL called IMAGENeT. It was a penny stock, publicly traded firm that he said was expanding and looking for a CEO to market its high-tech products and services. Though it sounded interesting to me, I was very content as a vice president at SEACOR.

In the late summer of 1988, NTSC re-competed our contract. We submitted our proposal and hoped and prayed we would win it for another three years, as it was the only work we had with the Navy in Orlando. If we lost the follow-on contract, we would be out of business and probably forced to lay off everyone and close the office. More than likely, SEACOR's president would also want me to return to headquarters in New Jersey.

Unfortunately, the worst came to pass and we lost the contract to the company we had beaten three years earlier. I was traveling for business when I got the call from our NTSC government customer. Before I could return to work, the NTSC technical representative hurried to our office and demanded we turn over the logistics software application program that we had developed under contract. SEACOR's software engineer called me and I told him to release it officially. When I returned, I talked to each employee individually and gave them permission to look for another job as soon as possible. I also suggested that they contact the awardee to see if there were any openings. Many left soon after that.

Mati planned to return home and become a housewife, but I asked her to stay with me until I could find out what the president wanted me to do with the Orlando office, and she agreed. I called the president and gave him the bad news, but he told me not to worry about my career, as I would always have a job at SEACOR head-quarters. He directed me to take my time and close the operation if there was no other near-term Navy business we could capture. There wasn't.

Darlene and I prayed together and believed God wanted me to stay at SEACOR. I had no fear of losing my job or position in the company, and we thought He wanted us to return to New Jersey, where we had become believers and were baptized in the Holy Spirit. Darlene would also be able to reconnect with Carol Bretz, who was now officially ordained as a pastor and had a congregation that met in South Philadelphia. Their primary mission was ministering to the lost and hurting on the street. Our future was set, and all I had to do was to obey God's Word.

Within a week or two, however, I received a call from my contractor friend at IMAGENeT. He said that he had heard we had lost the follow-on logistics contract at NTSC. He told me that the CEO position was still open for me if I wanted it, and the company would match the pay I had received at SEACOR. The icing on the cake was when he offered me 2,000,000 shares of the company's common stock if I accepted the job. I hesitated for a moment and then I told him that I would have to think about it.

I shared that conversation about the new job offer with Darlene at home and with Mati at work. Both prayed for me separately, and both warned me God did not want me to take the job. I knew they were right and I shouldn't take the job because God told me, as well, but pride and ambition got in the way. I started thinking about being a CEO of a publicly traded penny-stock high-tech company with a lot of stock, and how I would oversee the operation and be responsible for its growth.

A week after the job offer, I decided to visit IMAGENeT in Cocoa to see the operation myself and to meet the employees. What harm, after all, would that do? When I stopped by, I was shocked to learn there were only three other employees working there, besides Lee. Two were software engineers and the third was administrative. I also learned that there was one more person in the building with his own private office. He was a lawyer, as well as the founder and principal investor in IMAGENeT. Although he owned 51% of the company's stock, he was not operationally involved and wanted someone else to be the CEO.

At the end of the tour, I was very impressed with the technology and the potential I envisioned there to be in marketing and selling their services. Lee was pleased to hear my interest, but I reiterated I wasn't considering the position since I was pleased in my present career at SEACOR. However, I also told him, if anything changed at SEACOR, I would let him know. The seed of ambition had already been planted in my soul. I left that day thinking about the opportunity and how I could be successful at IMAGENeT if given a chance.

When I returned home, I told my wife about the tour and my thoughts about the company's future. She saw by my facial expression and positive viewpoints on IMAGENeT that I was tempted to take the job. She asked me point blank if I was going to quit SEACOR and take the job with IMAGENeT, so to ease her mind and to get her off my back, I gave her a direct answer of "no."

That following Sunday, we went to church as we always did. Afterward, we went home, had lunch together as a family, and shared some quality time. It was a typical day, but, Sunday evening, all of that changed when the telephone rang. It was Lee. He went into a sales pitch and asked me if I would accept the offer to be CEO of IMAGENeT. I hesitated and looked into the living room to see where my wife was. I extended the phone cord as far as it would stretch into the kitchen and I stooped down low to the floor. I whispered to Lee that I would accept the offer, but I had to confirm it with my wife. Lee was ecstatic and took my answer as a definite "yes. As I hung up the phone, I started to feel a knot in my stomach, as I knew I had to face the music and tell Darlene. Much to my chagrin, she already knew what had happened by the look on my face and my behavior on the phone call. She said I was going to have to give SEACOR plenty of notice since I was leaving the company. I started to feel better because it seemed like my wife was on board with my decision, though, in reality, she wasn't at all.

On Monday, I told Mati about my decision, and she was very disappointed in me. She reminded me God hadn't wanted me to take the job and asked me what my wife thought about my decision. I told her that Darlene supported it, even though she didn't believe it was the right one. I called SEACOR's president that week and advised him of my decision to resign, then sent him a resignation letter, as well. I had worked for SEACOR for nine years, and it had been a great company that gave me tremendous opportunities for growth.

Most importantly, we had become born-again Christians through the SEACOR-New Jersey job connection. In November 1983, God had promised me through an evangelist that I would receive promotion, to promotion to promotion. What, now, had changed? God still spoke to me in prayer to stay the course at SEACOR and to trust Him for our future. He had also confirmed this word through my beloved wife and Mati. Yet, I listened to another voice within my mind that countered God's Spirit. It was a voice of vanity and reason. It had an insatiable appetite to prove its worthiness and value through action and works. It wasn't patient, nor was it dependent on spiritual guidance from God through faith. In a way, it was strange accepting this new position as a CEO. In the world's eyes, it would appear to have been a promotion, but, in God's eyes, it was a demotion and a step out of His will. I would learn what that meant very soon.

Meanwhile, we had to move again so I could be closer to IMAGENeT. This time, we were moving east to Brevard County, which was near the church we had attended in Titusville. I was going to contact a realtor and have them market and sell our house, but Darlene suggested that, instead of doing it that way, we should pray and ask God to bring a buyer. I reminded her that we lived on a dead-end dirt road with less than ten houses and no through-traffic. Of course, she was aware of those facts, but she was also aware of God's power and what the Bible says about faith and prayer. I finally agreed we could try to sell it ourselves without an agent. We didn't put a "For Sale" sign in the yard or tell any of the neighbors of our intent to sell. As a backup plan, however, I decided to place an advertisement in the Orlando Sentinel Newspaper, which would run only on Sunday. It cost around $48. I did not tell my wife I ran it.

We prayed together in faith, asking God to bring a buyer for our house. The next day, I had forgotten about our prayer and was watching TV in the living room. Darlene was also sitting in the living room, looking out the picture window towards the road. As she sat there, she was praying and asking God to bring a person to buy our house. After a while, I asked her what she was doing. She responded and said she was waiting for a buyer for our home. I'm not sure how long she sat there, but eventually, an old pickup truck drove slowly down the road and stopped in front of our house. Darlene immediately got up and went outside to the truck. I looked out the door window and saw her talking to a woman, who was the driver. After several minutes, the woman exited the truck and walked with my wife towards our house. They were talking together and laughing about something.

I opened the door for them and Darlene escorted her into the house. I introduced myself, and then Darlene gave the woman a tour of our home. No more than 10 minutes later, they had finished the tour and the woman told us she would talk to her husband and hopefully come back this evening for him to also see the property. We shook hands and thanked her for coming, and she left. I looked at my wife with complete surprise.

"What just happened?" I asked.

She said, when she went to the truck, the woman asked her if she knew where the house that was for sale was located. My wife told her there was a house near the main entrance of Rest Haven Road that was for sale, and she must have missed it on her way down the road. She then told her we were also selling our house and asked her if she would like to see it.

Later that evening, the woman returned with her husband. He also toured our house with his wife and liked what he saw. I told them our price and, without hesitation, they said they would like to buy it. We prepared a contract and signed it that night. The following day, Sunday, my advertisement ran in the newspaper. I wasted $48 by not trusting God.

In October, we packed up and moved to Rockledge about 20 miles east of Geneva. We rented an affordable 3-bedroom apartment at the Red Roof Inn on a month-to-month lease, and enrolled the kids in the local public schools. Joe was 16 and a junior at Rockledge High School, and Shane and Alita were enrolled at Rockledge Middle School. Alita was in the 8th grade and Shane was in the 6th. Joe got his first real job at Wendy's Restaurant, which was around two miles away, and rode his bike to and from work. Joe loved working and wasn't afraid to work hard to prove his worth.

All the while, we looked around for a home to buy while we rented. It wasn't long before we found a beautiful Florida ranch style house on Fairway Lane for sale. The elderly couple that was selling the house had built a new home on the adjacent lot to live and retire, and we felt, if they were going to live next door to us, that was a good sign of the quality of the home for sale.

We contacted a realtor and did a walkthrough. The inside was also very nice. The living room and den featured double-door version pocket doors, which were sliding doors that, when fully opened, disappeared into a compartment in the adjacent wall. The living room and den could be totally and easily isolated from the rest of the house when the pocket doors were closed. Additionally, the windowsills were all constructed of marble or granite material and looked quite attractive. The den featured built-in, dark mahogany bookcases from floor to ceiling. And in the backyard, there were two Valencia orange trees full of fruit and a plantain plant. We decided to buy the home and moved in about three months later.

* * *

IMAGENeT was in downtown Cocoa, two miles north of our home and a block away from the state employment office. The single-story brick building had huge black lettering on the front, facing the main highway, which spelled out the name IMAGENeT. Overall, the company name projected an image of quality and high technology.

Upon entrance, my office was directly opposite the door in the front corner. Though it was rather small, office size didn't matter to me as long as I could move around freely and have a spare table to sit at when I had informal side meetings. My office also had a large whiteboard across from my desk attached to the wall. I loved being able to write and illustrate on the board, as it enabled me to visualize problems and brainstorm solutions more easily. Even though I was the CEO, my job was primarily to market and generate new business, and, since there were only a few employees, I didn't have any financial or operational responsibilities.

Lee was designated as vice president, and he handled all payroll, finances, and administrative matters. The two software engineers worked in a large open area. One office that was discreetly tucked away in the corner of the building, where Perry, the majority stockholder, worked. He had his own private entrance to the street. Perry was rarely in his office when I first started. Over time as I struggled on the job, he would appear more often and participate in our marketing and finance meetings.

My first day on the job was quite exciting, and I spent a lot of time trying to learn the technology. After a week or two, I believed we could market and sell this unique engineering technology service to the marketplace. Any company or government entity that produced engineering drawings by hand could use our service to digitize the data into an AutoCAD electronic database to archive, or to manipulate and change. The problem I saw was that the market was mostly unaware this economical digital conversion process existed.

When I started with the company, I didn't realize it had very few purchase orders for our services. Most of the orders were one-off in nature and generated very little revenue for the company. It seemed we were always doing samples, free-of-charge, to prove our capabilities, which I found odd. Since the company had been in existence for several years with this technology, why didn't we have a steady backlog of orders by now?

My marketing mission was to convince potential customers we offered state-of-the-art drawing conversion from manual drawings to an electronic AutoCAD file format in a timely and most economical way. In short, for the next 15 months, my marketing and sales mission turned out to be a "mission impossible." I didn't know it then, even though I had figured out that the technology was overrated. Regardless I remained enthusiastic, ready, willing, and able to spread the gospel of IMAGENeT to any prospect who would listen.

It didn't take long for reality to set in. Despite my intensive marketing efforts, I couldn't even seem to get to first base with potential customers. I made numerous marketing cold calls, attended trade shows and ran ads in trade magazines, and met with prospects and existing customers to show off our products. I even offered to digitize one of their drawings to prove the technology. After a few months of marketing, we managed to get a few customers to try out the technology, and they seemed very pleased. One A&E firm from Baltimore sent us an old drawing of a Marriott Hotel in downtown Baltimore. Another customer that tested our service was AMTRAK Philadelphia office. They sent us an original drawing of a railroad bridge that was completed in ink on linen and signed by a draftsman on January 31, 1913. It was a historical record and we mailed it back to AMTRAK without attempting a scan for fear it would destroy the drawing.

I could clearly see that IMAGENeT wasn't making much revenue, and I wondered how long Perry would allow us to operate in the red. I suggested to Lee that we have monthly board meetings with Perry in attendance so that we could update him on our marketing efforts, as well as our operation and financial issues. Each month, the three of us would meet in my office and discuss near-term and long-term business goals. In the first six months, the meetings were productive and supported by Perry. If we didn't have enough income for payroll or operational cost that month, he would contribute additional funds from his account, as needed, into the Company's checking account. At times, IMAGENeT would receive enough revenue to have a positive cash flow for a month or two. Still, other times, we were scrambling just to stay afloat.

It was frustrating when we would meet and have to ask Perry for money to pay the bills and to help with payroll. The attorney would intimate at times that Lee and I may have to sacrifice and waive our salary if there weren't enough funds to operate. He also hinted that he might only contribute enough to cover his secretary and the two engineers. That statement was a clear yellow flag warning and it bothered me a great deal. I could not make ends meet at home without a full paycheck each time. Regardless, I remained focused and optimistic that, over time, I would prove to him I could successfully market the company's products and services. I had always been successful in the past, so why wouldn't my success continue? I was so blinded by ambition at that time that I kept pushing past the fact that I was acting outside of God's will by working for this company in the first place. I failed to realize my success, personal and business, depended on God's favor and being in God's will and not by my knowledge or experience.

While I was wrestling with God about not being in the right place, God showed Darlene just how pleased He was with her obedience to Him. On December 21, 1988, at 1:00 am during Darlene's prayer time, God told her she was in the right place personally and spiritually with Him:

- He brought me here. It is by His will I am in His straight place. It is in that fact; I will rejoice.
- He will keep me here in His life and give me grace as His child.
- He will make the trial a blessing, teaching me the lessons He intends for me to learn and to work in me the grace He meant to bestow.
- In His good time, He can bring me out again how and when He knows.
- Thus, I am hereby God's appointment and in His keeping and under His training for His time.

I was falling further away from hearing the heartbeat of God, and my relationship with Darlene had grown strained because I had disobeyed God. On February 15, 1989, Darlene handed me a couple of pieces of paper that had numerous scripture references and words from God for me she had received during prayer that day. They were clearly a warning to me. He said my heart was not right with Him.

"My son, I, the Lord, know your past, present, and future, and your capabilities and needs. I alone can open and close all doors, I and none other. I gave not the 10 Commandments for my benefit or as a whip, but for man's well-being. I demand true obedience from my children, says the Lord of Hosts."

I was always receptive when Darlene or Mati received prophetic words from God, but they still went in one ear and out the other. Although they were warnings, I didn't heed them, and I went on my way and forgot them.

On May 12, 1989, Darlene received a word from the Lord for herself. The subject was "A Higher Standard of Beauty."

"Don't be concerned about the outward beauty that depends on the jewelry, or beautiful clothes, or hair arrangement. Be beautiful inside, in your hearts, with the lasting charm of a gentle and quiet spirit, which is so precious to God."

I Peter 3: 3-4

"Everyone has turned away. All have gone wrong. No one anywhere has kept on doing what is right, not one. Their talk is foul and filthy like the stench from an open grave. Their tongues are loaded with lies. Everyone has turned away. Everything they say has in it the sting and poison of deadly snakes. Their mouths are full of cursing and bitterness. They are quick to kill, hating anyone who disagrees with them. Blessed and to be envied are those whose sins are forgiven and put out of sight. Yes, forgive and let the love of God reign within."

Darlene attended to what God said, and His words caused her to be more diligent and aware of His presence. But, even after the word of God came through Darlene, I continued to go to work at IMAGENeT. Little did I know, God was about to give me a way to get back on the right path with Him and my future.

One day, at work, a man dressed in a nice suit entered the building and came directly to my office door. He knocked lightly, and I invited him in. He stepped inside and reached into his inner suit jacket, pulling out a wallet with a badge. He said he was a revenue officer with the IRS and wanted to meet with the person who signed the individual payroll checks. I told him that my vice president of finance signed all the checks. I then asked Lee to come over.

When Lee arrived, the revenue officer stated that the IRS records showed that IMAGENeT had never paid payroll taxes since its inception five years earlier. He also noted that the company had never filed the necessary paperwork. Lee mentioned he should discuss these matters with IMAGENeT's principal owner. Fortunately, Perry was in his office and available to meet. Lee escorted the IRS revenue officer to the lawyer's office. During their meeting, I wondered if the IRS was going to shut IMAGENeT down for tax evasion, but I later learned that Perry had convinced him to allow IMAGENeT to make tax payments over time. This additional IRS cost would exacerbate our cash flow problem, and was another sign I needed to quit that I still did not heed. I talked to Darlene about this incident, and she saw it as a red flag, as well. Yet, I was still spiritually blind and holding out for the best.

* * *

By June, our children were on summer break. Joe was now 17 and worked full time for Wendy's. He was doing so well that he was promoted to shift manager. He was very ambitious and hard-working, and it wasn't long before management transferred him to another store located in Cocoa. It was still only a few miles away from home, but I hated it when he worked night shifts, because I was worried about his safety, especially since he was riding a bicycle at night.

Alita was 14 and had started to become interested in boys and dating. She wanted to go out on her first date and told us about a boy she liked. She invited him over to meet us one day, and the four of us sat at the kitchen table together and talked. He introduced himself and said he was 17, which was noticeably more than a few years older than our daughter. He had a pickup truck with over-sized wheels, which Alita liked, and he asked us if he could take our daughter to an early dinner at a local restaurant nearby. He promised to bring her home right after they ate.

Our daughter was very young and had never dated anyone before to our knowledge. My gut instinct was not to trust this guy. He reminded me of Eddie Haskel, from the TV series, Leave it to Beaver. He even sounded and looked a lot like Eddie. I asked him several pointed questions, such as, where do you live? What does your father do for a living? What are your plans for the future? Where exactly do you plan to take my daughter to eat? Alita kept trying to run interference for him by interrupting me. However, he willingly answered them all to the best of his ability as an 18-year-old kid.

I then felt it really wasn't any harm for two kids to get some-thing to eat, and besides, what could happen? I thought, maybe, I should follow them secretly in my car to make sure there were no bad intentions. However, I changed my mind and allowed her to go with him for dinner. That was a mistake.

Later I realized I should have secretly followed them that evening. A couple of months later, we found out Alita was pregnant with "Eddie's" child. I couldn't believe it. I was angry at myself for allowing her to date and in shock that our 14-year-old daughter was with child. I spontaneously hopped on my 10-speed bike and rode several miles away, praying to God for peace and good health for my daughter, Alita, and my unborn grandchild. When I returned home, Darlene and I and Alita, hugged and prayed and cried. At no time did we consider an abortion. It was an unborn child, and we were going to have a new baby in our family. Being pregnant, Alita was not permitted to attend high school in the fall because of their rules, so she had to be homeschooled, so we hired a tutor for that task.

Along with the new pressures at home, my job continued to take on challenges. Work was becoming less and less appealing to me every day. I saw the writing on the wall of impending doom. We couldn't make any money. During our monthly board meetings, I continually had to ask Perry to help us make payroll, and he was getting tired of contributing and starting to hold back payroll from Lee and me.

Due to the lack of income, I was unable to pay the bills at home and often didn't have enough money for groceries. One day, as I returned home from work, I noticed Darlene was having a yard sale. She was selling some of our nice household goods to help us make ends meet. Our Wurlitzer spinet upright piano was one of the items sold. We had originally paid over $900 for it, brand new, and she sold it for around $200. She also sold a few other treasured items, which bothered me. I asked her why she was selling our stuff, and she said we needed money to pay the bills and buy food. She also said I needed to contribute to the yard sale. So, I went and got my ice skates and two hard-back books on the history of the American Civil War. I figured I wouldn't need ice skates in Florida, and the books only cost me $5.00 at a yard sale years ago. I was embarrassed that my wife had to help support the family, since that was my job. I even had to borrow money from our son, Joe, to pay some bills. Joe was very supportive and a great source of encouragement.

He was always on board with me and wasn't selfish about his own money. Still, we had numerous credit cards, and they were maxed out. We could barely pay the minimum amount each month. It was a horrible way to live, and I was blind to a solution.

At work, I reached out to many former business associates around the country to tell them what I was doing. I explained the benefits of contracting IMAGENeT for their engineering drawing conversion requirements. Most were not interested but politely listened anyway. If I was able, I would turn the conversation around and explore any job opportunities they may have or know about, which matched my experience. Unfortunately, no one had any suggestions and no doors of opportunity opened. No ideas were forthcoming from any of my friends or former business associates, either. It was as if I was permanently stuck in quicksand and no one would help. I made my bed, and I had to lay in it.

* * *

After a year at IMAGENeT, we were barely getting enough work to survive. Our board meetings were painful because the future looked so dim, and we all knew it. Even Lee was feeling stress over the lack of work. I decided to visit the local Florida state employment office one day, which was a block away from the office. I wandered in after lunchtime and walked up to the receptionist. I felt like a fish out of water. I was wearing a nice suit and most everyone else there wore jeans and a tee-shirt. The lady who greeted me asked me to complete an application, which I did, and then I waited in the lobby until a counselor called my name.

Once called, I went over and sat next to his desk. He read my application and scanned job openings on his computer to see if any jobs listed matched my experience. After a couple of minutes, he came across a technical writer job in Orlando. He turned towards me and asked if I had any technical writing experience. I said I had written quite a few technical proposals over the last ten years, so he printed the job description and handed it to me and suggested I contact the Orlando company and try to arrange for a job interview. I thanked him for his help and left. Upon return to the office, I put the job opportunity in the upper right-hand desk drawer and went back to work.

That evening, I discussed my visit to the employment office with my wife, and he seemed pleased I was looking for work because we needed the money. The next day at work, I decided to follow up on the job opportunity. I pulled the slip of paper from my desk drawer and called the Orlando company. The person who placed the help wanted advertisement took my call. After introducing myself, I told him a little about my experiences and indicated that I would like to hear more about the technical writer job position that was open. He gave me a summary of what the job entailed and said it was only part-time. It sounded interesting and something I was sure I could do off-hours

Then, he asked me to tell him about my experience in the technical writing field. After going over my background and experience, he wanted to know what I was presently doing. I told him I was the CEO of a small high-tech firm in Cocoa that specialized in converting engineering drawings into an AutoCAD format via a raster scanner and an electronic vector conversion process. He seemed impressed and asked me why I would want to do part-time tech writing work. I told him I hadn't been able to successfully market the company's services since I'd been hired as CEO over a year ago. I also told him I couldn't understand why, since I had a proven track record of business development success before IMAGENeT.

Out of the blue, he asked, "Are you a Christian?"

I said, "Yes, I'm a Christian."

He said, "It sounds like you are out of God's will. As a Christian, you know what you have to do."

I said, "What?"

He said, "You've got to quit."

I said, "Quit?"

He said, "Yes. God will not answer your prayers until you repent."

I replied, "I don't think I have the faith to quit before God opens up another opportunity."

He said he would pray for me. I thanked him for his time and hung up. I tossed the paper back in the drawer and went back to work. All that day, I couldn't get his words out of my mind.

Then on New Year's Day 1990, Darlene received a word of knowledge from God during prayer.

"I have heard your soul cry out unto me and have seen your tears. Weep no longer. For, I, The Lord, am your Provider and Deliverer. I shall deliver you from all your fears. I have sent my Angel to encamp around you, and the Angel of the Lord, whom I have sent shall deliver you. You shall be blessed and have no want, for you have taken refuge in, I, your Lord and God. I, the Lord, hear you, for my ears are opened to your cry, so know and be at peace, child. For I shall deliver you out of all your troubles. I have ordered your steps. You shall not be utterly cast down. For I shall uphold you with my hand. I shall not forsake you. Nor shall you beg for bread. I shall deliver you from the wicked one. For you trust only in I, your Lord, and I shall be your strength in your times of trouble."

On the morning of January 26, 1990, my wife's 38th birthday, it started like every other IMAGENeT workday. I rose early, took a shower, shaved, ate breakfast, spit-shined my dress shoes, slipped on a nice button-down shirt with a tie, put on a suit, and headed off to work. On the way, I noticed my wedding band was missing off my ring finger. I didn't remember taking it off. I hadn't taken it off since we had gotten married, and it bothered me that it was missing.

Then I heard a voice say within my heart say these words: "I'm divorcing you!"

I was immediately shocked by what I heard, and I pleaded with God not to give up on me. I told him I would quit IMAGENeT that day if He would give me a sign, just like He did for Gideon. I begged him not to divorce me. I asked Him to forgive me, and I would quit if only He would show me a sign at work, so I would know that's what He clearly wanted me to do.

I heard nothing else from God. I was on edge, feeling like I was going to Hell. I felt like my life was meaningless, and it was over. Upon arrival at work, I went to my office and tried to compose myself and think about the plans for that day. I knew we were scheduled to have a board meeting later that morning with Lee and Perry. I prayed and asked God to show me a sign, either before or during the meeting, about my need to quit the job immediately. I was so rattled and fearful of what God had said to me. I didn't want to screw this up because I felt this was my last chance to hear and obey Him.

At 11:00 am, we convened a meeting in my office. Perry stood up and used the whiteboard to list IMAGENeT expenses and income for the period. When he finished listing the items, it showed that expenses greatly exceeded expected income. At that moment, God nudged me inside my heart and I felt this was His sign.

Without hesitation, I got up from my chair and announced to both men I was resigning from the company, effective immediately. They thought I was kidding at first. I told them I was serious and that I was going home. I mentioned I would return over the weekend to collect the rest of my items. As I exited the building, I felt a ton of bricks falling off my shoulders, and I began to praise and thank God aloud for giving me a sign. Once in the car, I continued to pray, sing, and cry, thanking God, and asking Him to forgive me for being so rebellious.

When I arrived home, I felt like a lot of weight was lifted from my soul. I walked in, and my wife was waiting for me in the kitchen.

I said, "Happy Birthday, Dar! I quit IMAGENeT today!"

She said, "I know. God told me you would."

I laughed, cried, hugged, and kissed my beloved bride, and told her how sorry I was for not obeying God. She gave me a lot of grace. That weekend I read the four gospels and prayed and thanked God for His mercy and grace and for a beloved Godly wife who was faithful and stayed with me through the wilderness. The following Monday, we prayed and asked God to open the doors of opportunity for our family to start a new journey together, this time in God's will.

18
A New Beginning

Ephesians 5:25 (NASB) "Husbands, love your wives, just as Christ also loved the church and gave Himself up for her."

The 15 months of wandering in the wilderness for being out of God's will were finally over. IMAGENeT was now behind us, and what lay ahead, only God knew. From the time I was 18 years old, I had always had a job and worked hard, and now I had none. I only had my beloved wife and children to stand by my side at that moment. Darlene kept encouraging me to pray and seek God's will for direction. He had never left us or forsaken us, that much I knew, and why would He abandon us now? Reading scriptures that weekend assured me God would honor His word and open new doors of opportunity.

Early the next week, after spending time in prayer, the name of John Lopes came to mind. I hadn't spoken to him in many years. The last I had heard, he worked for Bell Textron. When I had worked at SEACOR in New Jersey, we had collaborated on a business opportunity between our two companies in support of a new military aircraft known as the V22 Osprey. Boeing was the prime contractor of the airframe, and Bell was the manufacturer of the powertrain. Back then, I had proposed that SEACOR subcontract to Bell Textron to develop the V22 training materials in support of the military. SEACOR hadn't won the contract, but John and I had forged a good business relationship and promised to keep our eyes out for other mutually beneficial business opportunities in the future.

I decided to call his old work number at Bell Textron in Texas. Fortunately, the person who answered knew John and stated

Opposite: Top ~ Darlene. Bottom ~ Shane, Joe, Alita and Charity.

he had left the company a few years back and moved to Mobile, Alabama to work for TESCO, an 8(a) company. An 8(a) company is a designation of a minority business enterprise. At least 51% of the common stock must be owned, operated, and controlled by an American citizen of a minority classification. Under the Small Business Act, minority-owned 8(a) designated small businesses could receive direct contracts from the federal government without competing with other firms for the business. In this way, the government attempted to help minority businesses grow and prosper in the marketplace.

After a little more research, I found TESCO's phone number and called it. When the receptionist answered, I asked for John Lopes, but she informed me he was out of the office and would return my call upon his return. While I had to wait for his return call, my mind was racing with doubt. Would he call? Would he remember me? I mean, it had been several years since we had talked, and had we never really worked together on any project. We had only discussed an opportunity that never came to fruition. I tried to remain calm and tell myself to trust God and pray.

The next day, John called me at home; his demeanor was very warm, friendly and familiar. It was as if we were friends, even though we hardly knew each other, and it had been several years since we had last talked about business. During our conversation, he brought me up to date on his business life. He said that, when he left Bell a few years back, he had decided to partner with a young man whom he had worked with at Bell to form a new business in Mobile. He said his business partner was 11% American Indian heritage. Their business plan had been to split the ownership of a new company between them, 51% - 49%, with his partner being the majority stockholder. Before they pursued government business, they applied for minority status through the Small Business Administration (SBA), hoping to be certified by the federal government as an 8(a) minority-owned small business. Sure enough, after the SBA reviewed the application, the Government approved TESCO as a minority-owned small business under Section 8(a) of the Small Business Act.

I could hardly believe someone who was only 11% American Indian heritage could be considered a minority by the federal government. He pointed out that, for the next nine years, TESCO would be able to market and obtain contracts directly from federal government agencies throughout the USA without having to compete for them. It sounded like a golden opportunity to me.

John indicated TESCO had recently been awarded a multimillion-dollar contract with the Naval Sea Systems Command (NAVSEA) training support branch in the Washington Navy Yard. It had been several months since the contract award, but there had been no delivery orders issued by the government customer. John said he and his business partner, who was president, were very frustrated and didn't understand the root of the problem. The program manager, who the vice president had hired to run the new contract in the TESCO Alexandria, was making excuses for the lack of work. On paper, the program manager was well qualified and had the necessary experience, education, and familiarity with the specific NAVSEA training organization, but he wasn't producing results.

I told John I was very familiar with the NAVSEA training support group. I explained to him that, when I had worked for SEACOR for nine years, the NAVSEA training support branch was one of my key customers and that SEACOR had acquired millions of dollars of orders during my tenure. SEACOR had an excellent reputation with NAVSEA in those days. From John's reaction to my comments, I could sense the wheels turning within his mind. He reasoned that, if he could only get me to come to Washington, DC to analyze the problems, TESCO could then fix the issues immediately, resulting in the government flood gates opening and millions of dollars in new work flowing to the company. That was an oversimplification of what I had been thinking. However, it was a big picture view that I had, and I felt John was having the same thoughts, as well, which was confirmed immediately when he then asked about my availability to travel to Washington, DC. I told him I was available at any time, and he said he would talk to the president and call me back soon.

The next morning, John called and said the president would like his vice president of marketing to meet with me the following Monday. I made plans to fly to Washington. The only problem was I didn't have the money to buy a ticket. Our family credit cards were maxed out, and we had no savings and very little money left in our checking account. Darlene and I prayed God would make a way for me to purchase a round trip plane ticket to Washington. By the grace of God, when I made the reservations, the airline approved my credit card, and I was issued a ticket. It would only be a day trip because I couldn't afford to stay overnight in the DC area.

Upon landing in Washington and departing the plane, I spotted a gentleman holding a small sign that said TESCO. We shook hands and greeted each other and headed for his car in the parking lot. On the way to the Washington Navy Yard, he provided me with more details about the new contract statement of work and the company's struggle to get any delivery orders. I listened intently. Before our arrival, he had arranged meetings with key NAVSEA training support personnel to discuss the contract and prospective orders for TESCO. He wanted me to be there as TESCO's consultant, to listen and to take notes.

We parked near the building and entered the NAVSEA Training Support Branch. Most of the government employees in the training support branch worked on the same floor. The entrance was on one end with offices on both sides and an aisle down the middle of the room. At the far end, in the center, was the largest office in the room, where the NAVSEA training support branch program manager. I noticed his door was open. Our meeting was with him.

The TESCO vice president led the way and we walked slowly towards the last office. While we walked, a few government employees rubber-necked from their side offices to see who had entered. Some of them recognized me right away and called out to say hello, and I responded in kind. A few even got up and came out of their offices to say hello and to shake my hand. These spontaneous greetings delayed our progress, but I didn't want to seem rude and rush past familiar customers, so I didn't hurry away. The vice president observed these impromptu encounters with wonder. It wasn't long before the noise level increased to the point where the NAVSEA program manager came out to see what was going on. When he saw me chatting with a few of his people, he walked over to us and said hello and invited us to meet in his office.

He seemed pleasantly surprised to see me with the TESCO vice president. He asked me if I was employed with TESCO. I told him I was only a consultant to provide support to TESCO as required. He looked at the TESCO executive and said candidly that he should hire me right away, which led to a rather awkward moment. He then asked me if I lived in the area, and I told him that I was presently living in Florida. He suddenly perked up and suggested that TESCO needed to open an Orlando, Florida office to support NTSC. He said I could do that for TESCO since I was living in the area. He also mentioned that he had funds available to support the operation and would contract the work through the new TESCO contract.

The TESCO representative spoke up and asked him when TESCO could anticipate some tasks for the Washington DC operation, as he had about 20 people that needed work. The NAVSEA manager said there had been some problems in getting the new TESCO training support contract started. He said he had funding available. He also intimated that the issue was personnel-related, not within the government, but within TESCO, as he had barely seen TESCO's program manager meet with his people to discuss requirements. He said for him to fund projects, it was important for TESCO to be proactive and not wait for the government to contact them with requirements. After an hour, the NAVSEA program manager told us he had another meeting, and we said our good-byes. As we walked away, the last thing I heard was that he looked forward to me joining his team.

The vice president and I left the Washington Navy Yard and went to lunch to discuss what we just heard and learned from our meeting. We now both clearly knew what the problem was and how to solve it. He asked me if I was available to work for his company. Up to that point, I hadn't told him I didn't have a job, so I tried to remain calm and stoic when he asked. I immediately replied I was interested in working for his company full time, and said he had to talk to the president, but he would let me know. He also said he had to fire his new program manager immediately, which I agreed needed to be done, based on what we had heard. I promised to send him my resume when I returned home. We finished lunch, and he took me back to Reagan National Airport. On the way there, he called his program manager and arranged to meet him that afternoon.

God had answered my prayer within a week of my repenting and leaving IMAGENeT for this new path. On the return flight home, I was in Heaven. My mind considered the wonders of God and how He meets all our needs through His riches and glory, if only we trust Him and His Word. I embraced my beloved wife when I got home and gathered the kids around and told them the good news. Although I still had to work out the details with TESCO concerning my salary and benefits, I wasn't worried because I knew God honored His Word and would provide for us and help us to prosper. We were His children.

* * *

John Lopes called me the next day, thrilled that I was joining his company. He said the president wanted to meet me right away to discuss employment details. TESCO agreed to pay for all travel costs, and I caught a flight right away to Mobile. I had a great meeting with the president and John Lopes, his right hand; though I was surprised at how young and inexperienced in business the president appeared to be. It wasn't criticism, only an observation. John, however, was much older than the president and had a great deal of business experience, and I could see he guided the president and was training him on how to run a company. The young man, at that time, needed to oversee the company on paper because of his minority status and the stringent rules governing the SBA's 8(a) program.

The president offered me a $50,000 salary to start with an excellent benefits package. He didn't want me to worry about setting up an Orlando office for the company because that could be taken care of later down the road if required. I would be on the payroll immediately, and they would pay for the move of our household goods to Northern Virginia. The move would occur after we sold our Florida house and acquired a new home in Northern Virginia. We shook hands, and I left Mobile, feeling very excited about this new venture. I couldn't wait to share the great news with my sweetheart.

Besides having to sell our house in Rockledge, Florida, we still had another major challenge we had to address: Alita's pregnancy and the pending birth of her child. Her pregnancy was considered high risk because of her age and health. She was only 15 and diabetic, but, by God's grace and mercy, she weathered the challenges. On March 13, 1990, just before the midnight hour, our beloved 15-year old daughter, due to complications, underwent an emergency C-section and gave birth to a beautiful baby girl. After delivery, Alita started hemorrhaging and pleaded with her mom to care for the baby if she died. Fortunately, Alita fully recovered and named her daughter Charlie LeAnne Fortner, with the name Charlie being chosen from a popular perfume fragrance. My wife was with her during the entire painful labor and birthing process, speaking words of comfort and praying for her continually. Days later, Alita and her baby came home. She was gorgeous and weighed about 8lbs and 7 ounces. She was a bundle of joy and so loved like the others.

The challenge facing Alita, though, as a young teenager raising and caring for an infant, was overwhelming. Darlene was heavily involved in direct support from day one. The rearing of Charlie wasn't going to change until Alita got much older. After all, how could we expect a young girl to raise a child on her own? It was impossible and not practical. We discussed options with Alita, including the option of adoption, but she wasn't keen on that idea. She suggested we take guardianship until she turned 18, then at that time, we could transfer guardianship to her, as Darlene didn't want to have the added responsibility of motherhood unless she was legally the mother. I was open to either option, but I didn't understand the complexities or mindset of motherhood. I was more pragmatic when it came to this subject. Mother and daughter were more emotionally bound.

After a great deal of discussion and prayer among the three of us, Alita finally agreed to allow us to adopt our granddaughter and raise her as our daughter legally. In preparation for this serious decision, my wife and I also discussed changing her first name from Charlie to Charity because Charity symbolized love. Even though Alita didn't think the change was necessary, she went along with it. We completed the adoption of Charity in late spring 1990 in Orlando.

Charity would be raised as one of our children. She would be Alita's daughter in memory and her sister legally. Charity would grow up not knowing until she was 12 years old about her adoption, and we had no idea how these decisions about Charity's adoption would drive a wedge between Alita and her family.

Looking back on this important life changing decision, my wife and I did not fully understand the effect that the adoption and changing of her child's first name would have on Alita. The adoption was one of the most difficult decisions we had ever made in our lives. Changing her name at the same time added to Alita's pain. From her perspective, it was if we were trying to remove the identity of her child permanently from the record.

As I prayed, I received a word from God at 9:30 pm on March 23, 1990. He told me not to fear.

"There are footsteps set up by man that will bring confusion so that I will not know the way. Trust God (total submission), and He will open my ears to hear Him for the steps He wants me to take. Fear not. A new path, if I hear and obey Him, will set me on high. I will be a witness of the Father. I must not let my weakness of wanting to be guided and accepted by man, keep me from hearing His voice. God has stood beside me, and I didn't know it because I was hearing man and not Him. Yet, He has never left my side. God is telling me to submit to Him totally, and I will hear Him and the steps He wants me to take on this new path."

Before we moved back to northern Virginia, the last order of business was to sell our Rockledge house. Darlene wanted to trust

God to bring a buyer and not to contract a realtor, and I remembered how faithful God was with selling our last home in Geneva without advertising or a realtor. I asked myself, why wouldn't He do it again? I agreed with Darlene, but still wanted to have a backup plan, so I advertised in the Orlando Sentinel Newspaper, Sunday edition. I had done this for the Geneva sale and wasted $48, and I was about to lose money again by not totally trusting God. I still hadn't learned my lesson. I lacked faith and was double-minded.

James 1:6-8 (NKJV) "But let him ask in faith, with no doubting, for he who doubts is like a wave of the sea driven and tossed by the wind. For let, not that man suppose that he will receive anything from the Lord; he is a double-minded man, unstable in all his ways."

I stopped by the realtor's office on my way home one day and asked the agent if I could have one of their blank contract templates to keep. He asked me why and I told him we were selling our house ourselves without an agent. He gave me a template, and I left. Later that afternoon, the agent who originally represented us when we bought our Rockledge house, called me at home. He said he had a young couple that may be interested in seeing our house. I told him we were selling it ourselves without a realtor, but he said he didn't expect any commission and wanted to do this as a favor to this couple. He also knew Darlene and I were Christians, and so was he. This couple he represented was also believers, so he had a spiritual motivation, which was unique. I agreed to allow him to show our house that evening. The realtor brought the husband and wife over to see our house. After the walkthrough, they made us an offer, which we accepted, and we signed the contract I had on hand. The following Sunday, my advertisement ran in the newspaper.

As we made plans to move, I traveled to Virginia in advance. I found a lovely four-bedroom, two-story house in Dale City, but found we couldn't afford the monthly mortgage payments, as we didn't have enough money for the down payment. Our realtor worked a deal with a private investor to pay the $5,000 down payment and, in return, they would be on the deed as a co-investor. We signed a separate loan agreement with them with a fair interest rate.

* * *

Although we planned the move to Dale City in late June, two of our children would not be coming with us. Joe was graduating from high school in June and decided to join the Navy right away. He would stay with my brother, Michael, and his family in Orlando until he could enter boot camp there. He had taken a year of JROTC in his senior year of high school and enjoyed it. I was very proud of Joe for following in my footsteps by joining the Navy. Alita had announced that she wanted to stay with a guy she had met, which bothered her mom and me. We told her she absolutely could not stay with him and, as a minor, she didn't have a choice. Unfortunately, she disobeyed us and ran with him, anyway. I did not know where they went and, although I was angry, we continued to make plans for our move up north.

We decided Darlene, Charity, and Shane would take the Amtrak to northern Virginia, and I arranged to have Darlene's car on that train with her. Once Darlene and the kids arrived at the Occoquan train station, which was less than 10 miles from Dale City, she would drive to our new house. I planned to drive our family car to Virginia, with or without Alita.

Everything worked like clockwork on the day the train left with three of my loved ones. The only mishap occurred with the family car. On the day I was to leave Florida, the engine developed a serious oil leak and overheated and broke down. I needed a new engine. It took a week and cost over $1,300. While I waited for my car to be repaired, I called Alita's cell number, and she answered. We had a chance to meet and discuss her present circumstances and her future options. She told me she didn't have any plans and was living day-to-day. Once my car was repaired and ready, I met with Alita again and convinced her to go with me to Virginia for a new start in life. Thankfully, she agreed, and we left Florida on good terms together. I realized later that the car breakdown was the Lord's will, as it gave me time to talk to Alita and convince her to come with me.

As Romans 8:28 (NKJV) states: "And we know that all things work together for good to those that love God, to those who are the called according to His purpose.

On the road trip to Virginia, I got a call from my brother, Mike. He told me Joe was getting a medical type of discharge from the Navy boot camp in Orlando, and I couldn't believe what I was hearing. I thought the Navy was railroading my son out of the service unjustly, and I called my congressman's office and asked them to investigate the matter. My brother took him in to live with his family. While there, my son told his uncle and aunt what had transpired during his boot camp period. He had been medically diagnosed with scoliosis. They tried to encourage him as best they could and to keep him hopeful about his future.

Darlene was still unpacking boxes when Alita and I finally arrived a few days later. She was pleasantly surprised to see Alita with me. I didn't tell her I was bringing her up.

The Dale City house featured two-stories, with a red brick-faced front and a single-car garage. It had four bedrooms and was in a nice neighborhood. The backyard was relatively flat with a privacy fence that came in handy as Charity grew older. We had a couple of sapling trees in the front and one in the backyard. The house also had a small, partially finished basement.

Darlene and I had to adapt to our new way of living. She embraced motherhood with a passion, and I embraced my new job much the same. Alita and Shane were trying to find their way forward with having to make friends all over again. We enrolled Alita in Osburn Park High School and enrolled Shane in Coles Middle School. Later that summer, Joe decided to catch a bus from Orlando and move to our Dale City home and live with us again. By September, we were all, once again, living under one roof with Charity, who was six months old and growing fast.

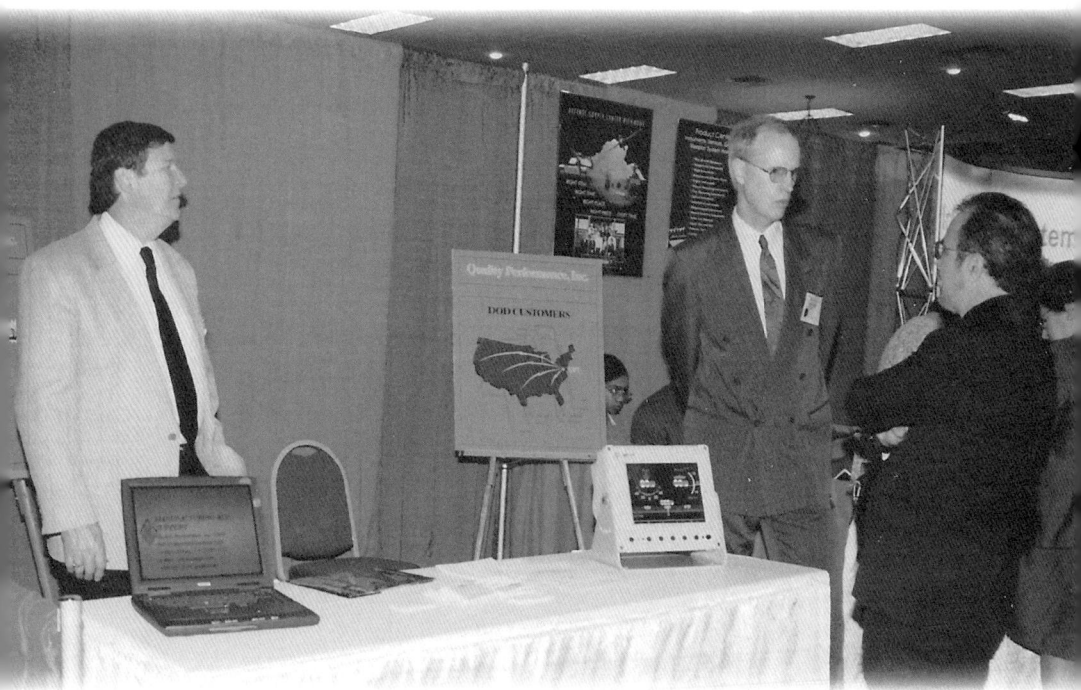

Herb McDermott and Steve Fortner

19
FROM PROMOTION TO PROMOTION

Ecclesiastes 4:9-12 (NASB) "Two are better
than one because they have a good return for their
labor. For if either of them falls, the one will lift up
his companion. But woe to the one who falls when
there is not another to lift him up. Furthermore,
if two lie down together they keep warm, but how
can one be warm alone? And if one can overpower
him who is alone, two can resist him. A cord of
three strands is not quickly torn apart."

I started work at TESCO's Alexandria's office in July 1990, and discovered right away that the cost of living in Virginia was more than Florida. We continued to struggle financially to make ends meet even though I was making a decent salary. I couldn't go back and ask TESCO's president for a pay raise, due to the higher cost of living, so I had to find another way. Darlene and I prayed and asked God to meet our needs by His riches and glory. Little did I realize then that God's answer to our prayers was going to be beyond anything we could ever hope for or imagine.

It wasn't long before I reconnected with Herb, who I had initially met in late November 1983 at SEACOR. He was the first Christian businessman who I had openly shared my "born again" experience with at work in my office. He was also very open about his faith. Instantly, God created a spiritual bond between us that would lay dormant for seven years. He was still working for the same company, Vernitron, from his Fredericksburg home office. Fredericksburg was about an hour's drive from my house, and we had lunch together to catch up... During lunch, I mentioned I wasn't making enough money from my new company to get ahead or pay tithes. We had a lot of credit card debt, and we were only paying the minimum required each month. Because of the financial strain, we weren't tithing 10% of our income, either. We did support various charities and gave to the local church we attended, but, still, it was after the bills were paid and groceries were bought.

Almost casually, Herb mentioned perhaps I could consult for his company as a sales representative at the Defense Logistics Agency (DLA) in Richmond. He mentioned Vernitron Corporation consisted of three divisions: Vernitech, Magtech, and Precision Components. They all manufactured motion control devices, like fractional-horsepower AC and DC motors for military equipment and systems used by warfighters in the field and fleet. Their largest government customers were the four DLA facilities in the USA. They were in Richmond, Virginia; Columbus, Ohio; Dayton, Ohio; and Philadelphia, Pennsylvania. The annual DOD budget for each DLA was over $1B.

The DLA Richmond was the primary customer for most of Vernitech's motion control products. The parts would be purchased by the DLA and stored in their huge warehouses until needed by warfighters in the field for repair of systems or equipment. Each DLA functioned like a large distributor of military spare parts for the Army, Navy, Air Force, and Marine Corps.

Herb's primary job was to manage all the Vernitron sales representatives in the Atlantic region, including all states on the East Coast. He told me their current sales rep for DLA Richmond was an underachiever and should be fired. He also suggested I visit the Vernitech New York office with him and make a proposal to the general manager, as he thought that I could do a better job and bring in more business for the company. I told him I would be very interested in talking to the Vernitech general manager about my capabilities and experience, and he gave me some Vernitron corporate literature and product specification sheets to read so I could familiarize myself with the company and its military products. He said he would call Vernitech and plant a seed of interest for me to replace the deadbeat sales rep. We finished lunch and parted, promising to keep in touch. For the next several days, I anxiously awaited his reply.

Darlene and I rejoiced over the news of the opportunity God had presented to us. It was very enticing to me: as a sales representative, I would have to function as both an engineering technician and as a salesman. Technical knowledge would be needed to communicate with the DLA engineers, and my gift of salesmanship would help me to influence the DLA buyers. The added fact that I was a Christian gave me an additional advantage of spiritual wisdom, which comes from God through the Holy Spirit. I found out quickly that Godly wisdom was the key to success in everything, including business and finances, with the other key to success being continual prayer with God. Agreeing with my wife in prayer daily would enable us to hear and obey more fully. Darlene and I recognized God was answering our prayers, and, in turn, we thanked Him, even before the solution was manifested in the natural realm.

Herb called a few days later to inform me that the Vernitech general manager wanted to meet me and discuss how I could help the Vernitech division obtain more business at the DLA in Richmond. He said I could ride up to the Long Island office with him, and he would do the introduction; after that, it would be up to me to convince him to give me a chance. He told me not to worry about the travel cost because he would cover it, which was extremely helpful, as I didn't have any money to spare.

On the drive up to New York, we got to know each other a lot better and became comfortable discussing just about anything, especially spiritual matters. I liked having another businessman around that felt free to talk about Jesus and how He is alive in their life. Herb was seven years older than me and happily married and with children. He had been a Christian a few years longer than I had, and seemed grounded in God's Word, especially in regards to tithing. He explained that his wife had heard a tithing message at a Bible study and had impressed upon him the need for them to start tithing. They weren't tithing at that time, so he researched the Bible and saw that God required tithing 10% of your income. When Herb had reviewed the family budget, he had discovered that they were spending money on allergy shots for their one daughter, and cigarettes and alcohol for him and his wife. In prayer, Herb asked God if He would deliver them from all three expenditures, so he could commit to tithing. God had miraculously answered Herb's prayer. His daughter had been delivered of her need for regular allergy shots, and he and his wife had quit drinking liquor and smoking cigarettes immediately. From then on, they tithed. I was impressed with his obedience to the Word of God.

It took about five hours to drive to Long Island, New York. As we walked toward the Vernitech office, I felt confident God would give me favor with the general manager. The initial meeting was a success, with the general manager offering me a consulting contract with a monthly stipend of $1,000. In return, I committed to visiting DLA Richmond regularly as Vernitech's sales representative and would report monthly progress to Herb. On that day, my annual income jumped from $50,000 to $62,000. I reminded myself of God's prophetic Word when I was saved.

"Everything needs to be done in the light," was a constant echo in my mind. TESCO hired me as a full-time employee, and, if I was going to consult for Vernitech, I would need TESCO's approval. To complicate the matter, TESCO was under new ownership, as my old friend, John Lopes, and his business partner had sold the company to two businessmen. The new TESCO president was a retired Navy Captain who was originally from Washington, DC and would split his time between the Mobile headquarters and the Alexandria office where I worked. His business partner worked mostly in the Mobile office.

At the first opportunity, I discussed the Vernitron consulting arrangement with him. I told him I would only need a couple of days a month, maybe more initially, and assured him that there would be no conflict of interest. He didn't seem bothered but wanted to discuss it with his business partner. Shortly after, I met with his counterpart, who took a more critical view of the matter, but realized he couldn't stop me from the consulting work.

* * *

1990 was a turning point in my business life and a year of preparation for war in the Middle East. In the summer, Iraq invaded Kuwait. The Department of Defense referred to that period of preparation, when our troops were planning to invade Kuwait and Iraq to conquer the terrorists, as Desert Shield. A year later, in 1991, Desert Storm began, with our military going on the offensive and driving the enemy back to Baghdad. It was also the year that QPI went on the offensive.

During this time, Vernitech was approved by the DLA value engineering to manufacture 48 additional spare parts that were not in their original product line, as Desert Storm provided a new market demand for military spare parts. . Vernitech's two other sister divisions, Magtech and Precision Components, also contacted me and wanted me to represent their products at the DLAs, as well. I was offered an additional $1,000 a month to support the other two divisions, which I accepted.

Herb and I agreed it was time to incorporate QPI. We met in his Fredericksburg home office and prayed together, asking God to lead and guide us as we created an organization chart. On the piece of paper, we showed God as the president and both of us as His servants. We recognized this spiritual structure would not be acceptable in the secular world. However, as Christians, we were committed to putting God first in the new business and to seek His will before we acted. We also agreed to pray together at work on all major issues involving our business.

On July 11, 1993, I was laid off from TESCO. The president handed me a letter he had been carrying around for more than a week. He said he didn't want to let me go, but budgets were tight. I was in shock, as I didn't see it coming. I thanked him for all he did for me at TESCO, collected my personal things, and left. I called Herb and told him the news. My mind was spinning, and I was trying to figure out what to do. Fortunately, I did nothing but go home and spend a lot of time with Darlene in prayer and discussing the problem.

It's important to understand while I was busy at work daily, my wife would spend hours at home reading and studying God's word on many topics, including tithing. She understood God's command that we were to give a minimum of 10% of our income as our tithe. If God said it in His Word, Darlene believed it and acted on it. Her challenge was always trying to get me to agree with her. We had plenty of examples in our life of God-honoring His Word. Tithing, she knew, should be no exception.

When I arrived home that evening after being laid off at TESCO, Darlene and I sat down and created a family budget. We listed all of our monthly expenses, which added up to $6,284.66, including 100% social security and Medicare tax payments. $706.47 of our monthly expenditures went to pay the minimum amount on our credit cards. Next, we projected what we expected for our monthly income. I estimated QPI could provide me $5,000 a month. Therefore, I would need to supplement my QPI income with another $2,000 income from another source. My wife then wrote in ink below the total amount: "Tithing - $700.00". We agreed in prayer to pay the $700 tithes first and then pay all household expenses second. We also asked God for the additional $2,000 monthly income needed to balance the budget, laying our hands on the budget and thanking God for being our provider and meeting all our needs.

The next business day, I sensed I needed to call RDSI, a small high-tech company in Alexandria that specialized in electronic warfare technology. I knew the owner, but I hadn't talked to him in years. I arranged a meeting and brought him up to date on my life and explained the mission of QPI. I mentioned that I was unencumbered and able to fully market his company's product and services to the military market. He said he was willing to contract me for six months to see what new business prospects I could identify, and I signed an agreement with him that day for $2,000 a month. When the six-month trial period was over, he chose not to extend the term, and the contract ended.

During those six months, however, QPI had acquired more clients, and our revenue had increased. Best of all, we were able to increase my QPI monthly income to $7,000. Darlene and I thanked God for nudging me in the Spirit six months earlier to contact RDSI for consulting services. I also thanked our Lord for leading us to begin tithing 10% of our income. At this time, I began to put God first, then Darlene and the children, then my company. In doing so, I saw God bless my life in a colossal way.

* * *

Another major event for QPI took place in 1993. Herb traveled to England on behalf of Vernitron and met with key engineers at Aeronautical & General Instruments Ltd (AGI). AGI was one of Vernitron's key customers for their "torqsyn" motion control devices. While there, he learned AGI manufactured navigation aids for ships and submarines for navies worldwide. He told them about QPI and our desire to represent them in the USA. When Herb returned, we met and discussed the possibility of QPI being their exclusive representative in the USA.

In the spring of 1993, we met with an AGI executive in the Ritz Carlton Hotel in Washington, DC, and signed an exclusive agency agreement. The agreement gave us the authority to market AGI's naval marine products to customers throughout the USA. It would take us six years before we finally broke into the U.S. Navy market for AGI, but we persevered and never gave up. We also prayed regularly at work and believed God would open the door for AGI in the U.S. Navy. The icing on the cake occurred in March 2002 when the Navy awarded the QPI/AGI team a contract with potential value of $94M over five years. The contract was to design and develop a solid state meteorological wind measurement system, called Moriah Wind System. I knew deep inside, God had given us a miracle. I remembered God's word to me back in November 1983 when I was born again. I will take you from promotion to promotion, to promotion.

20
SPIRITUAL WARFARE

Ephesians 6:12 (NASB) "For our struggle is not against
flesh and blood, but against the rulers, against the powers,
against the world forces of this darkness, against the spiritual
forces of wickedness in the heavenly places."

Diabetes is a terrible disease that wreaked havoc on Darlene's body through the years, but it never could her soul or spirit. By this time, diabetes had taken a toll on Darlene's eyesight and ability to walk, and was slowly destroying her nerve functions in her extremities. Unfortunately, there is no cure, and it is a debilitating disease that eventually affects every organ in the body. Darlene was meticulous about reading her blood sugar levels several times a day and taking insulin as required. She recorded all of her readings to show her doctor at each office visit, which was quarterly, as she wanted to prove she was taking care of herself as well as she was able. At the doctor's office, her A1C levels would be checked, which would show how well her blood sugar levels had been over the past three months. The goal was an A1C of less than 7%. Darlene was so proud of herself when her A1C was in the 7-7.5% range, though she was never below 7% that I can recall. It's almost impossible for a person with diabetes to achieve less than 7%.

Besides taking insulin, a diabetic must maintain a nutritional diet, get adequate sleep, and perform physical exercise. Her planned daily diet was no breakfast, a small lunch at 11:00 am and a balanced dinner at 4:00 pm. Occasionally, she would have a snack at bedtime. Darlene was also a night owl, finding quality time with the Lord when everyone else was asleep, before crashing somewhere around midnight to 1:00 am. She would awaken by 9:00 am for

Opposite: Darlene and Steve in Dale City house - 1999.

her blood sugar reading and shot if required. She couldn't do much exercise besides walking around the house, as any stress or physical pain would negatively affect her blood sugar, causing it to rise and possibly requiring more insulin to maintain a normal level.

Her entire adult life was a balancing act with her body, trying to get it to obey her will. Darlene read and studied God's Word daily. She read scriptures and faithfully confessed God's healing word over her body. She would continually tell it she did not live by bread alone but by the Word of God, and she would demand it to align itself with the Bible and be healed by Jesus stripes. She did what was required to manage her blood sugar, but she always spoke the healing Word over her body. When she would get down on herself at times, she would remind herself that His word is true, and if the healing wasn't manifested until she was raptured with the saints to meet Jesus in the air, then so be it.

By the grace of God, through the 1990s, diabetes didn't hamper her ministerial activities much. She still could drive her little 1989 red Honda CRX hatchback around town with Charity secured in the back, visiting with her friends in Dale City. She continued to love people and enjoy sharing God's Word with them in a practical way. She made friends easily with everyone she met, from a busboy at a restaurant, to a hairstylist, to an automobile service manager. No one was a stranger to my blessed bride, and I loved that about her.

As I mentioned earlier, another beautiful quality of my beloved bride was she was a good listener. She told me she was a true Floridian, never in a hurry to leave a conversation or need unfinished. People, especially our children, loved to talk to her because Darlene never interrupted and she wholeheartedly attended to their topic of discussion. Only when it was appropriate did Darlene seek to respond. Many times, she would mention a scripture verse if she sensed the subject required God's help. If it was a trivial or secular matter, she would just listen and offer advice or comment as appropriate to edify, comfort, or exhort the individual. Most people tend to have a short attention span, and, if they listen at all, it is only half-heartedly and for a short period. It is just a reflection of modern times, since there are so many more distractions today that compete for our attention. Darlene was special in that way and so many others.

She prayed continually in the spirit, always trying to be led by the Holy Spirit wherever she went and with whomever she met. She would pray for many people she got to know in Dale City, and, later, when she saw them again, she would ask them if God had answered their prayer. She wanted to follow up with them because she believed God's Word, where it states that "...whatever you ask the Father in my name (as My representative), He will give you." John 16:23 (Amplified Version)

* * *

In 1995, Shane graduated from high school and continued living at home. He was a big help to his mom and didn't mind spending time with her and assisting her with her daily routine and doctor appointments while I was at work. That same year, Charity started kindergarten, and Shane also assisted with her as needed. I loved that Shane and his mom bonded so well together. With Shane's help, Darlene was able to keep up her routine of going out in public periodically to visit her friends, see how they were doing, and pray and encourage them to walk in faith. She always left them with the belief that God loved them just as they were.

Also, in 1995, while Alita was working for a lobbyist on Capitol Hill, she fell in love with a man she had met there and soon moved in with him. Later that year, she became pregnant with their child. On April 15, 1996 she gave birth to a beautiful baby girl and named her Alisha Marie. The relationship between Alita and the father, unfortunately, didn't last for many reasons, including physical and verbal abuse. It wasn't long before Alita and her daughter moved in with us. Alita allowed the father to visit his child, but, one day, he took the baby and never returned her. Costly court battles ensued over the years, but he managed to retain custody.

Alita moved on with her life and, in 1997, met William Gilliom, who was five years her senior, and fell in love again. William had two young children, William Gilliom III (7) and Kimberly (6) from a previous marriage. He shared joint custody of the children with his ex-wife. This time, the relationship Alita had with William was built not only on love, but also friendship and mutual respect. It wasn't long before she moved in with him. My wife continually prayed that they would commit to marriage, and, fifteen years later, God answered her prayer when they were married on September 1, 2012, at Colonial Beach, Virginia. The Christian ceremony was conducted by a pastor friend.

Alisha remained in her father's custody until she became pregnant at 17. The father of the unborn child was Jeff, a pastor's kid. Alisha got into an argument with her father over the pregnancy and left for good as a result, moving back in with her mother, Alita. When Alita broke the news of the pregnancy to Jeff's parents via a phone call, they actually suggested that she should have an abortion. Alita, stunned by this uncaring remark, told them that she would never consider it. Several months later, Jayden was born, a healthy boy, on June 14, 2014.

* * *

My mom had only been 56 when dad had died in December 1981. She seemed content to live as a widow over the next 15 years, staying mostly with my sister, Carolyn's family. She eventually purchased a small cottage house in Latonia, which was a suburb of Covington, where she lived alone. The house was next door to my sister, Mary's house. Mary spent a lot of quality time with mom doing various things around the house and always took her to Mass at Holy Cross, the local Catholic church. One day, out of the blue, mom made the following comment to Mary, "Is this all there is?" After getting clarification from mom, Mary realized that mom wondered if God had another man for her to marry or was she meant to live out her life as a widow. Mary prayed with mom that God would answer her prayer. Within a couple weeks God answered their prayer.

Father Barnes, senior pastor at Holy Cross introduced mom to Lou Martin, a single gentleman six months her junior. Soon, Lou asked Mary permission to date mom. It wasn't long before they fell in love and wanted to marry. Before giving them the "Fortner Children Blessing" from all nine of the kids, we held a family council in their living room with Lou and mom in attendance. It was a little testy in the beginning, but by the end of the meeting we all agreed to the wedding and welcomed Lou into the family.

In 1996, at 71 years of age, mom and Lou decided to get married at Holy Cross Catholic church. The wedding was conducted by Father Barnes. I sang at mom's wedding. One of the songs I sang was "Holy Ground." Mom loved to sing as well. During the wedding, she suddenly left Lou at the altar and came over to me, expecting to sing with me. I motioned for her to go back to Lou, which she did. We knew then that mom was showing early signs of dementia.

In November 2005, Lou died from complications from diabetes. Five months later, on March 19, 2006, my mom passed away peacefully of Alzheimer's disease. She was almost 81. I was able to hurry home before she died to visit her in hospice. Though she was unconscious by then, I took the opportunity to pray with her and my siblings. Each of us had our private times with her to say our goodbyes. One of the last things I did was to sing to my mom "Ave Maria," a song that she had loved all her life. As I sang it quietly next to her ear, I detected that she heard the music because her face was relaxed and she seemed to embrace the song. Singing to my mom reminded me of all the good times we had had together with our family when I was growing up, and how special my mom was to us all.

* * *

In 1999, at 27 years of age, our oldest son, Joe, wanted to start a business in Lima, Peru. He was self-taught and fluent in Spanish and he wanted to set up a training facility in Lima to teach the locals how to speak English in order to better their lives. I helped

Joe write a business plan and funded his trip. And, though I thought that it was an impossible task, I didn't want to deny his dream. He ended up spending three years in Lima, living off their economy, which was extremely challenging. My wife and I kept in touch with him and continually prayed for his safety, security, and well-being. He returned in 2002 and then, eight years later, he went back for another year to give it a second try. The business was never profitable financially, but he personally touched many lives while there and helped many people make a living in small ways.

God truly blessed our son through his outreach to others in need. One of the women Joe had met during his travels was Carmen, who was originally from Mexico and, at 18, had crossed the border and travelled to Chicago to live with her aunt. She had lived in this sanctuary city for almost 11 years when she met Joe. Soon, they fell in love and were married on May 31, 2014. Today, they live in Montgomery, Alabama where hardly anyone speaks Spanish. God must have a sense of humor.

* * *

In the late 1990's, I bought Darlene her first personal computer and printer for the home. She took an interest in learning about the Internet and how she could use it for God's work. With the help of Geek Squad and other computer wizards, by the year 2000, she managed to establish a web page that she used to communicate the love of God. She especially loved learning about Israel and God's chosen people, which she shared on her page. Her main web page was set up with an introduction and salutation. Additional pages were links to other sites she loved, such as ministries, kids, favorite sites, music, and poems. The main page read as follows:

"SHALOM

Baruch Ha Shem Adonai Yeshua Ha Mashiach!
Blessed be the name of the Lord Jesus Christ!

I believe in everyone being allowed to be themselves and expressing their own views. For we are all special and unique, and each of us has very special gifts to share with each other. I don't believe in judging anyone. That job belongs to my Lord Jesus Christ.

First, let me tell you a little about myself. My life totally changed on November 11, 1983, when I received the Holy Ghost baptism and rededicated my life to Jesus Christ as my Lord and Savior. I can say I am loved and accepted for just who I am by the Lord. He taught me what true agape love is and how to love everyone for themselves and not to judge others. He also taught me how to be a God pleaser and not a man-pleaser. I am a wife of 29 years of marriage with a terrific husband and four wonderful children, which my Lord has blessed me with. I want this page to bless and inspire all who visit. May the links I provide help you in your daily walk with the Lord and in your life walk in general, as they have for me in my life. I want everyone to feel free to express their views on any topic and share any links they feel I could use to better the site. Please send me any links you find helpful or informative. I want you and me to enjoy our links together and get to know each other. The owners of each link page are totally responsible for all contents found on their pages. I would like us all to remember what II Timothy 2:15 states, 'Study to show thyself approved unto God, a workman that needs not to be ashamed, rightly dividing the word of truth.'

GOD LOVES EACH AND EVERY ONE OF US VERY MUCH, AND HE WILL NEVER LEAVE US OR FORSAKE US!"

Unfortunately, with the emergence of newer and more user-friendly web sites, the Geocities website became obsolete, and Darlene's web page disappeared with it.

Darlene also designed and printed business cards to give to people she met who needed prayer or had other needs. She named her ministry "Leading Disciples Forward." The first letter of each of the three words was L-D-F, her initials: Linda Darlene Fortner. On the card, it noted the ministry was an outreach ministry and that she was a prophet and teacher. She wasn't afraid to step out and share the gospel with everyone she met. She would ask them if they knew Christ as their savior or if they needed prayer for anything. If they did need prayer, she would pray with them right then and there, never missing an opportunity to share God's love and word.

She also rarely judged anyone for bad behavior. She saw it as a symptom of a problem. When she got an opportunity to address an issue, she would ask questions and listen and pray during their response. Then, being led by the Holy Spirit, she would pray for them in a specific area God showed her. I remember one occasion where Darlene shared with me how God had led her to minister to her hairdresser. She had been going there for years. One day, Darlene was the only client in the salon when her hairdresser asked Darlene to pray for her. She stated the issue, and they prayed together. During prayer, the Holy Spirit revealed to my wife the root cause of the problem, but when my wife shared with her what God had revealed to her, her friend was caught off-guard and denied it. Despite the awkward situation, Darlene didn't say any more about it.

A few months later, Darlene made a hair appointment with her friend. Upon arrival at the salon, the hairdresser took her aside into her office and admitted what Darlene shared through the Spirit during prayer was right. Darlene told her she wasn't judging her and only sharing what God had revealed. She reminded her friend God loved her and wanted the best for her.

My beloved wife loved the simple things in life, like holding hands, listening to music, or enjoying a fresh cup of coffee, which she would never drink without having a cigarette, as well. Those two habits went together, like ham and cheese, and she couldn't have one without the other, though she really didn't indulge in either one. Her coffee would mostly sit idle in her cup until it was cold enough for her to take a few sips, then she'd only drink a few ounces before it was at room temperature, at which point she would pour out the contents and get a fresh hot cup of coffee and start the process all over again.

Every cup required her to light up a cigarette. She would take a puff or two and place it in the ashtray, and it would remain there until she was able to taste her coffee. It would usually be extinguished by then, and she would have to relight it and take another puff. She had smoked since she was 12 years old, and told me many times she wasn't going to quit smoking unless God took it away. She often reminded me that God delivered her of fear and other frailties and could deliver her of smoking. We had both smoked when we first met, but I had quit cold turkey on that bet with my father. From then on, I hated the smell and would complain to her about the bad habit, but it did no good. I tried to bite my tongue and not criticize her for the smoking habit. It was one of the few worldly pleasures she could still enjoy. Besides, it wasn't a sin, was it?

"Not what goes into the mouth of a man defiles a man; but what comes out of the mouth, this defiles a man." Matthew 15:11 (NKJV)

I was the healthy person in our marriage. I never had anything wrong with my body. If I had a cold during the year, I would make a fuss so that I could get some sympathy from my family. I remember when we moved to Florida in 1985, I got the flu the first month we were there. I was sitting in a recliner with my feet up and a blanket over me to keep me warm. Darlene prayed for me and told me that God wanted me to get up and praise Him and that He would heal me immediately. I resisted, telling her that I was sick and needed to rest, but she was convinced that God had spoken to her, and pleaded with me to get up and praise Him. I finally relented and got up and started praising the Lord with my hands and arms raised. Within 20 minutes, I felt amazingly well. I was healed through obedience to His word.

Another time, on a flight for a business trip to Huntsville, Alabama in 2000, I felt very uncomfortable in the seat and experienced severe neck pain and headaches in the back of my skull. At the hotel, I met up with my client, who had flown in from San Diego. We decided to relax after dinner, and take a dip in the pool, discuss work, and other stuff. The water didn't soothe me at all, and I finally told him I was going to go to bed early because I didn't feel well. The next morning, I was suddenly awoken by pounding on my hotel room door, but couldn't get out of bed to answer it. My client was there and had gotten the clerk to open the door. I pleaded with him to take me to the ER, which he did.

Once there, I was in horrible pain and started throwing up. The triage nurse immediately requested assistance, and I was rushed into the ER room flat on my back. If I even attempted to raise my head, I would throw up from excruciating pain. All I could think was that I was dying and God was calling me home. In those days, you weren't allowed to use a cell phone in the hospital to make or receive calls. As I lay on my back, staring at the ceiling, a young doctor came in and told me my blood work did not reveal anything wrong with my body's chemistry. He said he was going to have to take some fluid from my lower spine, but I was in so much pain I didn't care. However, I did have one question for him. I looked at him from below and asked, "Are you a Christian?"

The question must have caught him off guard because he hesitated at first, and then he said confidently, "Yes, I'm a Christian."

"Then, you can give me a spinal tap," I replied. I did not feel the needle or the fluid leaving my body.

Sometime later, the doctor returned and said the fluid was clear, which was a good sign. However, he still had no clue what was causing the back of my head and neck to explode with pain. After 12 hours in the ER, the orderly moved me to the infectious disease wing of the hospital. I noticed he was wearing a mask over his mouth and nose as he transported me. I counted the lights in the ceiling while I lay on my back.

Once he lifted me in bed, he hurried out of the room. I was still in my business attire, as no one had bothered to change me into a hospital gown. I felt so alone. The only thing I could do was to pray. Besides the Lord's Prayer, the only other prayer that came to mind was Psalm 23. I said those five verses over and over, and, each time, I personalized the scripture and visualized Jesus lying in bed with me to comfort me and to hold me close. I feared being all alone with no one to help except Jesus. I repeated, "The Lord is my Shepherd. The Lord is my Brother. The Lord is my Healer." Slowly, the fear dissipated and was replaced with the reassurance that Jesus was present with me. I fell asleep in His loving arms.

Several hours went by before a nurse arrived to attempt to insert an IV into my left arm. He tried and missed the vein several times. I finally got fed up and told him to get out and get someone else to do it. He took offense to my bad attitude and harsh words, but I didn't care about protocol or manners at that moment. I felt like I was dying, and I needed help. Finally, some other nurse arrived and managed to start the IV process properly without much effort. Thank God for trained nurses who show compassion and mercy.

When it became apparent I was going to be on my own most of the time, I decided to locate my cell phone and call my wife. It was all I could do to get out of bed. Immediately, my head exploded with pain and I threw up near the toilet. Afterward, I found my phone and fell back into bed and lay totally flat on my back. I held the phone close to my face to see the numbers clearer and dialed my home phone number, and my wife answered. Finally, a lifeline. I told her where I was and that I felt trapped and to pray without ceasing for me to get well. I told her I was supposed to have caught a flight home earlier that day. I also told her what I knew, which wasn't much, and asked her to call my mother and siblings for prayer.

On the fourth day in the hospital, the medical experts still had no idea what was wrong with me. They tested me for everything, including AIDS and meningitis, and nothing was discovered. A CT scan of my brain and upper spine also revealed nothing. A team of doctors and nurses visited me and suggested I get an MRI as a last resort and scheduled it for 6:00 am the next morning. I was gripped with fear when I heard that, mainly because I was claustrophobic. There wasn't anything I could do about it except pray for God to heal me so I could be discharged and not need an MRI. Healing seemed an impossibility at that moment, but I prayed anyway.

Around 11:00 pm, my guardian angel entered the room in the appearance of my older brother, Michael. He had been on travel in Starkville, Mississippi when my wife had called him. He had immediately left and drove six hours out of his way to come to rescue me. He had with him a container of baby lotion and a clean set of clothing for me. He immediately took charge of the situation and commenced to wash me thoroughly from head to toe. He then carefully turned me onto my stomach and climbed on top of the bed, straddling my back. For the next five hours, he deeply massaged my neck and lower skull with baby lotion. He worked continuously without any breaks, all the while praying, singing, and talking to me. I felt such love and compassion during this time. What a great brother!

At 6:00 am, the MRI crew showed up, and I told them I didn't need an MRI, and I wanted to be discharged. The crew listened to me and left the room. Up until that point in time, I hadn't been out of bed in four days. Then, around 8:00 am, a team of doctors and nurses arrived to argue with me to stay and continue the testing, but I refused. The head doctor said they weren't going to support my request for discharge. When I told her I wanted to sign myself out, I had to prove to her I could get up and walk to the door and back, which I did. The pain was excruciating, but the five hours of rubdown my brother gave me helped immensely. Afterward, I signed myself out and the medical team left the room with the release paperwork.

I decided to get dressed in the clothes my brother had brought, and I could hardly believe the clothing he had chosen. The underwear was boxers with images of golf bags on the material. The outerwear included sweatpants and a sweatshirt that were both fire engine red. The sweatpants were too short and only stretched to my ankles, revealing the white gym socks that Mike had also supplied. Still, I honestly didn't care how I looked to the outside world. I just wanted to get home.

Mike drove me to the airport and stayed with me in the terminal. I lay on the carpet at the gate until the flight was called and then laid across all three seats. I had to get a connecting flight in Charlotte. The attendants knew I was ill, so they allowed me to wait until everyone departed, then took me off in a wheelchair. On the return flight to Baltimore, it was crowded and I was unable to lie down. I had a middle seat between two adults. I closed my eyes the entire flight and prayed. Once the plane landed safely and docked at the gate, I got up and lay in the aisle. This action startled the flight attendant, but I told her I was ill and needed help to deplane. A wheelchair was brought and I was escorted off to the exit. Fortunately, Herb, my business partner, and Dave, one of our QPI employees, met me there. I rode in Herb's SUV, lying down in the back, and Dave drove my car back to my house. It was a two-hour drive home. I didn't sleep but prayed and talked to Herb about what I had gone through with my illness.

It took three months before my immune system eradicated the virus or bacteria trying to kill me. During those three months, I was disabled and mostly flat on my back. My family took good care of me while I was on the mend, and Darlene prayed for me constantly. Eventually, I was restored to complete health.

* * *

In 2002, my beloved's body grew weaker and she began to experience more problems after she turned 50. Besides diabetes, which had continued to take its toll on her body, she had periodically started having extreme chest pains. An MRI revealed that she had a couple of tumors in her liver and gallbladder was unusually large. She was admitted to the hospital in October of 2002, and during surgery, a biopsy of both tumors was taken, both of which were thankfully determined to be benign. The surgeon also removed her gallbladder, which was the cause of her extreme chest pain. She was hospitalized again in November due to a low blood sugar situation. Still, despite the physical challenges, she kept a great attitude and fought hard to regain her independence and mobility.

Later, in 2005, her kidneys started to fail. Her creatine levels were high, and the nephrologist tried to prepare us for dialysis treatments, which he believed was inevitable. Through much prayer, thankfully, Darlene never had to go on dialysis. In fact, her doctor was quite surprised when her kidneys improved in functionality through the years. He commented that he had never heard of a patient's kidneys improving and suggested we should continue doing what worked. Of course, we told him God was answering our prayers. Her kidneys were still diseased, but Darlene never had to be on dialysis treatments, which was a major blessing.

* * *

In the midst of my beloved's physical challenges and spiritual battles, in the summer of 2005, we broke ground at Lake Anna for our new waterfront dream house to be built. On that beautiful summer day, my wife and I stood next to a large oak tree on the property and prayed for God to bless our land and future home. I made sure it was going to be handicap accessible and could easily accommodate a wheelchair. I also planned to have an elevator installed in the master bedroom to allow easy access to the finished basement without my wife having to negotiate steps. Sixteen months later, we moved into our new home at Lake Anna. It was November 11, 2006, exactly 23 years after Darlene had received the baptism of the Holy Spirit. What I loved most about our new home was it provided Darlene a place of peace and rest in the country near the lake.

A week after we moved in, our house was burglarized while I was at work and Darlene and Shane were out shopping for items for the house. The burglar stole all of my wife's jewelry and her strongbox filled with cash and valuable papers. More than $100,000 in cash and jewelry was taken in less than 45 minutes. We were devastated. Two detectives came and took fingerprints and assessed the crime scene. They speculated it was someone we trusted and who was familiar with our routine. The person we suspected was a friend of the family. Ironically, many years prior, my wife had led him to receive Christ as his savior. He was never apprehended for the crime, and we never saw him again. Hopefully, God will have mercy on his soul. We knew that material things could be replaced, and what was most important is we forgave him for what he did.

* * *

Around 4:30 am in the spring of 2007, I was jolted from my sleep when I heard my wife screaming in pain. She had fallen out of bed and was on the floor. I got up quickly, called 9-1-1, and checked her blood sugar. Her levels were very low and she was almost comatose. Within five minutes, the paramedics arrived, checked her vitals, stabilized her neck and head, and transported her to the hospital while I followed in my truck. In the ER, Darlene told me what had happened to her. During a low blood sugar episode, she had started having seizures with her body flopping back and forth violently and involuntarily on the bed. She said she knew she was under a spiritual attack from Satan. At some point, she was tossed out of bed, and her head and neck hit the granite top of the nightstand as she fell to the floor. X-rays showed she had fractured her C-1 cervix in two places, but her spinal cord was undamaged.

We were blessed to have one of the best neurosurgeons in Fredericksburg as her doctor. After a CT scan and thorough analysis, he talked to Darlene and me about the situation and the treatment options. He showed us a very detailed scan of my wife's cervix on his computer. He pointed out the two fractures on the C-1 and the possibility of complete paralysis or death if it were to damage the spine. He recommended she get the halo surgery as soon as possible to mitigate the risks. My wife and I were on the same page and told him we were Christians, and we wanted to pray and ask God for healing first. We asked him if we could wait to see how God will miraculously heal the cervix. He did not agree with our suggestion to wait and cautioned us to be extremely careful not to apply any force to the neck's damaged area. He agreed to meet with us in three months to check her healing progress with another CT scan.

During that three-month time, I must admit, we tested God's patience with us. I took Darlene out boating one day, thinking the water was calm. Once out on the lake, the wake from the other boats caused our boat to rock and roll violently for a moment. Thank God my wife was securely seated during that event. Once the boat settled, we motored back to our dock carefully and returned to shore.

At the next office visit, a scan showed the C-1 cervix was slightly better. The doctor still recommended the halo as his preferred surgical remedy, but we stood on God's Word and resisted the halo. We continued to pray and trust God for Darlene's healing. Nine months after the accident, we went back to the neurosurgeon for an X-ray and progress report, but this time he didn't see us. He had his physician assistant meet with us, and she was ecstatic when she came to the lobby, holding the latest X-ray in her hands. She said the X-ray showed that my wife's C-1 cervix was totally healed. We saw her joy and thanked her for the excellent news. We also wanted to thank the neurosurgeon, as well, but he was too busy to see us. Thank God, Papa wasn't too busy to heal my beloved wife.

One other very important factor was evident at the time of my wife's neck injury. The local volunteer fire department was located only a couple of minutes from our house. Before 2007, it was only staffed during the day. At night, the paramedics would be on call at their homes for emergencies. This delay would have been a severe problem for my wife's condition, and she may have even died before they arrived. However, at 4:30 am, the morning of the accident, the local VFD was fully staffed and reached within five minutes. God cares about all the details.

* * *

One of our most beautiful times together was when we took a vacation in the Bahamas. It was indeed the most relaxing and enjoyable period of our marriage. We scheduled it during our anniversary in 2010, which made the vacation even more precious and special. Before that time, we had only gone on one other vacation together, and that was in 2004 on a seven-day cruise to the eastern Caribbean islands.

The Bahamas vacation was totally different and much better because it was land-based. We had three butlers assigned to our suite, who catered to our needs and wants. Of course, my wife was limited in her mobility, so the butlers became our friends, and we spent time talking to them about everything, including our faith. On

214

April 3 (our 39th wedding anniversary), we celebrated by having dinner alone on the beach at sunset. Our host seated us at our private table for two in the sand, and, for the next two hours, our waiter served us delectable portions of food and quality wine. My beloved bride and I fell in love all over again that evening. I have since forgotten what we ate, but I will never forget the aura of our love for each other. When we returned to our suite, there were rose petals on the bed and the floor leading to a hot bubbly bathtub filled with aromatic fragrances. In every corner of the room, we were met with surprises that helped to fill our romantic night together. On the bed were chocolates and strawberries and other delectable treats. Two swans that were created from bath towels sat proudly on each side of the treats, and two white cotton robes lay casually open at the footboard. The vacation of vacations ended too quickly for us.

* * *

Unlike my mother's passing, the events leading up to the death of Darlene's mother were the opposite of peaceful. In the spring of 2010, Geraldine Parks had fallen and broken her hip. She was taken by ambulance to Winter Haven hospital. Once stabilized, she spent two months in a rehabilitation hospital recuperating from the injury. During that time, Gayle and her husband, Jim, visited her often, encouraging her to complete the three-month physical rehab. Unfortunately, Geraldine was stubborn and only did two months, refusing rehab for her lower back. She demanded that Gayle and Jim allow her to move in with them to care for her, but Gayle refused to do so because she was unable to lift or move her mother. Gayle did, however, manage to find a nursing home in the area and convince her mother to live there. Except for Gayle and Jim, Geraldine refused visitation from any of her siblings, children, or friends. She was continually angry and upset about life in general. She verbally abused the medical staff who tried to help her at the nursing facility.

The second week she was there, Gayle received an urgent call from a nurse at the facility who said that she needed to come right away. Keep in mind Gayle and Jim lived in Port Charlotte, which was a couple of hours away from Winter Haven. Her mother's blood sugar that morning was over 600, which meant that she was experiencing diabetic ketoacidosis (DKA). If left untreated, she would die shortly. Geraldine refused to take her insulin and fought the nurses as they tried to intervene. An ambulance was called, and the EMTs struggled to get her to comply. During the transport to the hospital, she had a massive heart attack in the ambulance. Still, the hospital managed to save her life despite her behavior.

Once she was stabilized in ICU, she discharged herself from the hospital and demanded that Gayle take her to a hospice facility nearby, which she did. Gayle and Jim stayed with her all that time with no sleep. After two days, they finally went home to rest. The next day, July 1, 2010, Geraldine took her last breath and passed away. In her last will and testament, she designated Gayle as the sole beneficiary. The total amount of cash, certificate of deposits and equities left for Gayle amounted to more than $130,000. In addition, she was also willed the deed to her small house in Winter Haven. Gayle offered to split the money with her two sisters, but Darlene told Gayle that she didn't want any of the money and for her to keep it. We never knew if Geraldine had a chance to make her peace with God. Per Geraldine's dying wish, Gayle cremated her body and retained her ashes in an urn. There was no memorial service. Darlene and Gayle were content that their mother's struggle in life was finally over.

* * *

We owned a 23' power boat, but it was becoming very difficult to get Darlene aboard for a ride on the lake. We had 60 steps that led down from the backyard to the boathouse. She usually could walk carefully down the steps by taking her time and holding onto the rail. Walking back up the steps, however, was another matter entirely. I had to pick her up and carry her up. Thank God, she weighed less than 100 lbs., or I wouldn't have been able to manage it.

My wife loved the water, especially listening to the sounds of the ripples as they came ashore. She also loved being in a swimming pool. She could lie on a float, close her eyes, and drift in the peace of God all the while meditating on His Word and talking with Papa. As I investigated the cost of acquiring and installing a tram that would transport a wheelchair from our backyard to the boathouse, I discovered that the acquisition cost alone would be over $75k. I then looked into the cost of a 45 foot inground kidney-shaped salt pool. It was only $52k, so I decided to invest in building it., and it was completed in July 2011, just in time for Charity's wedding to Cory, her high school sweetheart.

Charity and Cory lived with us for the first year of their marriage. They had the downstairs all to themselves, and we were thrilled to have them at our home so we could help them as needed. Plus, I wanted to monitor Cory to see how he treated our baby girl. After a year, they decided to move to Greensboro, NC. Upon arrival, Cory got a job as a physical fitness trainer in a local gym, and Charity, who wanted to work with exotic animals, visited an animal rehab facility. They told her that they weren't hiring but that didn't deter her. Daily, for a month or so, she visited the facility even though it wasn't open to the public. Finally, a manager told her that if she really wanted to work there, she would have to prove it by volunteering her time at the facility from 4:00 am to 12:00 pm daily, Monday through Friday, for two months. During that time, she would be trained how to feed and care for the wild animals. Charity was faithful and at the end of the trial period, they interviewed and offered her a job. She did this work until she became pregnant in 2012, at which point she resigned and became a full-time homemaker. Wynter Sofia was born on October 14, 2013, and her sister, Snoe Lillianna, followed three years later on April 26, 2016. They are two beautiful children.

Charity and Cory's marriage ended after five years, but, not long thereafter, Charity met a man named Wallace Thomas, who worked in a Waffle House as the store manager. They dated for a while and, following Charity's divorce, married. Wallace had custody of his daughter, Kiyia, from a previous relationship, who was the same age as Wynter. A year after they were married, Charity gave birth to another little girl, named Autumn Rayne.

* * *

Our life at Lake Anna consisted mostly of doctor office visits. During an office visit to Darlene's primary care physician in October 2011, the nurse practitioner noticed Darlene's oxygen level was dangerously low, in the 80% range. He strongly urged her to go to the hospital emergency room and get further evaluated for low oxygen. Preliminary tests in the hospital indicated she had probably experienced a silent heart attack due to a blockage in the heart. Darlene underwent outpatient surgery and a heart stent was implanted. There were other partial blockages, but they remained untreated since they were less than 50% obstructed. The blockage was probably due to complications from diabetes and smoking.

Diabetic neuropathy increased in Darlene's body, causing numbness in her hands, feet, and legs. In that condition, she could hardly stand without having to hold onto something to balance herself. When she tried to walk, she couldn't feel her feet on the ground, which made her unstable and susceptible to falling. She gradually got to the point where she needed a powered wheelchair to get around in the house, but the neuropathy in her hands made it difficult for her to operate it. Her fingers, like her feet, had a continual tingling sensation that never went away. Sometimes a knuckle would lock up and not open or close. Using the other hand, she would have to manually manipulate the fingers of the affected side to break it free to move. Administering insulin through injections became a big problem when her fingers would not cooperate. Coupling this with the reduced vision due to diabetes, she was unable to read the measurements on a syringe or the labels on pill containers. Darlene had to rely on her loved ones to assist in administering all of her medications, and yet, despite all the physical challenges that had confronted Darlene through her life's journey, she never stopped believing in God's healing power. Her soul and spirit stayed on the Lord.

One day, as I was taking her to Fredericksburg for a doctor appointment, she anxiously told me that she felt as if her bowels were going to release. She struggled with Irritable Bowels Syndrome. We were still in the country and there were no service stations or fast food restaurants nearby. The only place that was close was the local Mine Run Store. I hurried and parked and went inside and asked the clerk if my wife could use the restroom. She said the only restroom available was for employees only. I explained my wife's condition and pleaded with her. She checked with the owner in the back room and told us again that she denied our request. I couldn't believe her response. When I returned to the car, I repeated her answer. I was so angry I felt like burning the place down. Darlene took a different approach. She prayed aloud and asked God to handle it. Within a year after this event, the store closed permanently for business. To this day, it remains closed. Coincidence? I don't think so.

Here are a couple of scriptures to ponder:

Matthew 10:14 reads, "And whoever will not receive you nor hear your words when you depart from that house or city, shake off the dust from your feet." (NKJV)

Matthew 10:41 states, "He who receives a prophet in the name of a prophet shall receive a prophet's reward. And he who receives a righteous man in the name of a righteous man shall receive a righteous man's reward.

21
Labor of Love

1st Corinthians 16: 14 (NASB) "Let all that you do be done in love."

Love Is

Love is Merciful.
Love is Obliging.
Love is Magnificent.
Love is.

by Darlene

Springtime Seems To Blossom When You're Around

When you are weak in body,
I am strong.
When I am weak in spirit,
You come along.

Oneness is the goal.
Selfless is the key.
Love is the answer,
To how I must be.

to Darlene from Steve

As QPI continued to grow, Herb and I discussed selling the company. We felt it was the right thing to do. My wife's health was getting worse, and I wanted to be home more with her. Of course, we prayed and discussed it with our wives first. We all had peace about the matter, so we proceeded to investigate possible suitors. In 2012 we were courted by Valkyrie Enterprises LLC, a small business defense contractor in Virginia Beach. We almost signed a deal in 2014, but in prayer with my wife, I sensed that it was not the right time. I called Valkyrie's owner and explained my position. Naturally, he was surprised and somewhat upset, since he had invested a lot of time and money. Two years later, again, during prayer, I sensed it was the right time to sell. With Herb in agreement, I reached out to Valkyrie again. We negotiated a purchase agreement and on August 4, 2017, we sold QPI to Valkyrie for millions of dollars. I retired to Lake Anna to spend my remaining years on earth with the love of my life, my beloved bride, Darlene.

Darlene was 65 then, and she liked her freedom and tried to maintain as much independence as possible. She could still walk around the house, but she had to be careful to keep her balance. She had a power chair that she would use when necessary. Besides regular insulin injections, she had to take a variety of pills daily. She gave the meds little thought. Her sole focus was to live as full of life as possible.

Despite all the physical challenges, she never stopped reading or studying God's word. She also loved spending time indulging in computer technology because it gave her access to a world of wonder. She would sit in front of her iPad and research or read various articles on many subject areas. When it became difficult to focus and read, she would access audiobooks and dive into another world of fascination and discovery.

The last two years of my beloved's life on earth were challenging, to say the least. In retirement, God enabled me to come alongside and lighten the load. Even those days when the pain was unbearable, we would just hug or pray or do both until she went to sleep, or the pain eased, and she could rest. Along the way on this journey, I never considered what I did to help as anything more than being her husband. She was my wife, in sickness and in health. When she hurt, I hurt, and vice versa. We were one flesh, according to Genesis 2:24, That is why a man leaves his father and mother and is united to his wife, and they become one flesh. (NIV).

Despite all the difficulties she faced, Darlene had small pleasures she enjoyed. On days she felt well enough, we would sit at the kitchen bar across from another. She would have her iPad on scrolling through pages and updating apps. She wanted to make sure all the apps and other software were up to date. She was a little obsessive about it, but I thought it was cute and loved observing her mannerisms and behavior. She always had her coffee and cigarettes with her. Her coffee was in a mug that kept it warm and, if knocked over, wouldn't spill out easily. In the morning, she rarely ate breakfast because her stomach was unsettled then. Her favorite time to eat was around 4:00 pm. It brought me joy to learn how to cook her favorite meals, and I even attempted to get her to try food she didn't care for, like sautéed brussels sprouts. She would say her mother forced her to eat sprouts when she was young, and she didn't like them. I made them different by sautéing and seasoning them with fresh garlic. She hardly recognized the taste and was pleasantly surprised at its unique flavor.

Darlene and I also loved a glass of good wine with our meals occasionally. She believed it helped her digestive system. Our favorite blend was full body, dry, merlot red. She rarely drank white wine. I would insist when I served fish, pork or other white meat, we should drink white wine, but she protested and, of course, I relented. Crushed snow ice was her other drink of choice. The Ninja blender I bought her was the perfect appliance for this drink and she added no flavors to the ice. Using a spoon and wrapping the Ninja single-use container with a paper towel, she would spade the ice chips out gingerly and place them carefully in her mouth, trying not to lose even a sliver of the ice. Perhaps she loved ice so much because she had been anemic for so long in her life.

When she was pregnant with our first child, she had only wanted crushed ice to soothe her cravings. In those days, we were poor and didn't have a blender. I would take three or four ice cubes and lay them side by side in a clean dish towel. I would then roll the towel up and use a mallet to pound the towel until the ice was crushed. Then I would unroll the towel and scrape the ice chips into a glass. This may seem odd, however, it was better and cheaper than having to run out in the middle of the night to buy ice cream and pickles for my pregnant wife.

During Darlene's illnesses, God blessed us daily with some happy moments together. During days of good weather, we would sit outside on the balcony and enjoy each other's company and the view of the lake. The birds would sing and chirp, and she loved their music. I always felt she had a real connection with God's nature. She especially loved watching monarch butterflies and felt God would use them to lead her from danger if necessary.

At times, Darlene would be able to relax in our swimming pool. I would assist her in the pool and make sure she didn't injure herself. She would have to be very careful entering the water since she didn't have good balance and her legs were feeble. Once on the plastic float, she would lay back with her eyes closed and absorb the sun and the peacefulness of the water rocking her gently. She often told me being that close to the water is how she heard God the best. She was able to quiet her mind and body and allow her spirit to listen to the Spirit's inner voice.

Christmas 2017 was a very special time for us. All of our kids, grandkids, and great grandkids visited during the holidays. We took a lot of pictures, shared many stories, and exchanged several gifts. The highlight was when my sweetheart gave rides to the little ones on her power chair throughout the house. It was a wonderful time of celebration with family.

As time progressed, however, Darlene found it harder to do some basic things. Her vision was poor, so she couldn't read the blood glucometer or administer the right amount of insulin dosage into the syringe when her sugar levels were high. Getting in and out of bed was dangerous because she had no sensation in her lower extremities. She used a small footstool to assist, but with limited feelings in her feet, she couldn't always tell if she was safely on the stool. Bathing was also a challenge even though the shower had a bench to sit on. The power chair would get her close to the shower, but she had to be careful when getting in, since she could barely walk. Even when Darlene sat at the kitchen bar with her iPad, coffee, and cigarettes, she was hardly able to control the device any longer and I would need to help her select the app she wanted to use.

Most of the time, I was able to help with all the tasks for which she struggled. However, her body's continual deterioration was wearing on her, not only physically, but also mentally, because she felt she was losing her independence. She did not want to be a burden to her family. By Thanksgiving of 2018, she could not hold a utensil steady enough even to eat food. Even though our daughter, Alita, had bought her some larger flatware to use, it didn't make a difference. Smoking was also no longer possible because she kept dropping the cigarette, and I was afraid the house would catch on fire. I bought her a vape device and put a necklace on it for her to wear around her neck. That way, when she dropped it, she would be able to retrieve it. I even tried scotch taping the vape unit to her index finger, and it worked for a while. Eventually, though, the tape would give way, and the device would fall from her finger and hang down from the chain. We were all very frustrated with this exercise because it seemed futile. We ended up just holding it for her and allowing her to get a few puffs of satisfaction.

* * *

Early one morning on December 4, 2018 I awoke suddenly to Darlene crying. I jumped up quickly and ran into the bathroom. The shower was still going, and she was lying on the floor, unable to get up. She had fallen hard in the shower and injured her neck and head. I lifted her carefully out of the shower, dried her, got her dressed, and took her to Mary Washington Hospital. The Emergency Room physician ordered CT scans of the brain, upper spine, abdomen, and pelvic area. They also x-rayed her chest and did complete blood work. The scans were inconclusive, and the doctors were unable to determine if she had fractured her neck. After consulting with the ER doctor and prescriptions for pain medication, Darlene was discharged, and we went home.

We followed up with her primary care doctor on December 6. Darlene was still in severe pain in her neck and shoulders. Also, she could no longer stand, walk, or use her hands or arms much anymore. She was forced to use a wheelchair to get around. Even though she could still move her arms without the use of her hands, it was pointless. The primary care physician suggested we should get an MRI of the neck. He issued us an order for the MRI and additional medication to help ease the pain. We noticed at home that, occasionally, one of her legs would suddenly kick out involuntarily. She tried to restrain this action but was unable, and it would continue from either leg for an indefinite period. When it occurred, Darlene experienced severe pain down her spinal cord, and it was exacerbated if her leg were to strike anything close by. I tried securing her legs to the wheelchair using a towel, but the pain of resistance was just as severe. She took pain meds, which helped a little, but wore off. Many times, I felt helpless, and all I could do was hold her gently and pray for God to give her release from the agony. At this point, we started making plans to get in-home care to help us with Darlene so she wouldn't fall again.

A week later, on the evening of December 13, she had extreme pain in her neck. I called the ambulance, and they took her to Culpeper Hospital, where they performed an MRI of her upper, middle, and lower spinal canal. The radiologist was unable to read the results clearly, probably because of Darlene's inadvertent reflexive leg movements during the procedure. Around 3:00 am, the ER doctor ordered her transported by ambulance to Virginia Commonwealth University (VCU) Hospital in Richmond. I told my wife I would be there with her at VCU, but she was very sedated at the time and did not remember this.

I followed in my truck but went home first to take a nap because I was exhausted. I didn't think I could make it without a power nap. After a two-hour nap, I continued my drive to VCU. On my way down, I received an urgent call from the Richmond police wanting to know where I was. I told the policeman I went home for a two-hour nap because I was exhausted. He said my wife was freaking out because I wasn't there as I had promised her, and I told him I would be there in an hour and asked him to let her know. I realized then that Darlene was somewhat drugged when we parted at Culpeper Hospital and may not have remembered my exact words.

When I told Alita that I was going home first to take a power nap, she decided to drive two hours to VCU to be with her mom until I got there. She had been there an hour or so when I arrived at the ER, and I immediately saw that Darlene was distraught and agitated and wanted to go home. I tried to calm her with a smile and a warm kiss, but she would not have any of it and made sure I knew she wanted to leave. Coincidentally, the ER Doctor and nurse were in her cubicle when I arrived, and I asked them what they thought about her condition. The doctor mentioned Darlene had an MRI of her lower back, and it showed no abnormalities. He suggested a second MRI of the neck area. My wife spoke up and said she didn't want any more tests, and she wanted to go home. I concurred with my wife's request and asked the doctor to release her. The doctor reluctantly agreed to discharge her and directed the ER nurse to prepare discharge papers. Within an hour, we left VCU and headed home.

Darlene could not be left alone at home and needed 24/7 care. Shane lived with us and he wanted to help. I was so grateful for his request and accepted his offer in love. I remember all those years I worked at QPI; our children were always there to help when needed. Darlene and I were truly blessed with wonderful children.

We now needed to make arrangements so Darlene could be as comfortable as possible, especially at night, when she slept. We decided to use a sofa that was near the master bedroom as Darlene's bed. She was small in stature (only 95 lbs. and 5' 1" tall) and couldn't move due to paralysis. Therefore, we didn't have any concern about her falling off the sofa. She had to be on oxygen full time since she had developed COPD. We placed the oxygen generator near her bed, and she continually took oxygen. We monitored her oxygen saturation levels continuously using a pulse oximeter. During this time, Darlene's oxygen readings were in the 80's and low 90's, which were dangerously low.

The other major problem we continued to have was when Darlene was sitting up or in her power chair, and her legs would involuntarily kick out at random intervals.

We had to make sure there was nothing in the way that she could kick. Unfortunately, her legs would end up bruised and cut, and she would have extreme pain shooting down her spine whenever this reflex occurred.

When Darlene was in her power chair, she could no longer operate the controls or joystick easily. She would accidentally run into things, so I had to manage the controls for her. Using a wheelchair was not possible because it had no support to keep her body upright, so the power chair was a better alternative for transport in the house. In the morning, I would move her in the chair to the kitchen, where we would sit together and have coffee and breakfast. Most of the time, it was just coffee. She would say her pills and insulin injections were her breakfast. I would place her iPad in her view and turn on a movie or TV series she wanted to watch. Usually, it stayed off, and we just talked to each other about life and its challenges and God and His mercy and grace.

During the last two weeks of December, Shane and I worked out a plan to care for her. I would be with Darlene from morning until bedtime. Then, Shane would relieve me and watch her through the night, only if I needed him. During the night, I would lay in bed and listen to make sure she was resting peacefully. Most of the time, Darlene could sleep during part of the night, and I thought I could handle it without Shane's help. Often, she would wake up around 2:00 am and call out my name, and I would hear her because I slept like a cat and was very attuned to her voice. I would ask her to try to go back to sleep, and, if she persisted, I would get up and go out to the sofa and sit with her. Usually, she wanted me to turn her over or to fix her pillow or blankets. Occasionally, she wanted me to sit her up or move her to the power chair, which meant I would have to wake Shane up to watch her or stay up myself and care for her. I was not a night person, so my attitude, sometimes, was not good.

Every night, it was the same routine. She would wake up in the middle of the night and call out to me to help her. One night, I was so tired that I begged her to allow me to go back to sleep, but she persisted and kept calling and asking me to come. She said she wouldn't bother me again once I helped her. I reluctantly got up and went to her. I propped her up next to me on the sofa and held her hoping that would be enough. Yet, she kept asking me to put her in the power chair so she could sit upright. She also wanted me to move the chair for her to the kitchen and position her iPad on the counter so she could watch a TV series. I finally gave in and lifted her into the power chair, attached her seat belt securely, and moved her to the kitchen in front of her iPad, which was on the countertop. I then turned on a "Father Brown" episode on her iPad, made sure she was safe and satisfied, and went back to bed. A couple of hours later, I woke up and went quickly to the kitchen to find my love still sitting in front of her iPad, watching a blank screen. She was quiet, yet I could tell from her facial expression she was in a lot of physical pain. I looked at the iPad and determined all the "Father Brown" episodes had played while I slept. I also noticed a plastic cup was on the floor beside her. I felt so terrible for being so selfish and uncaring for my blessed bride.

"Oh my God," I yelled. "Please forgive me, Dar, for treating you so badly. I'm sorry, sweetheart. I won't leave you again." I held her close and kissed her. She was so forgiving and so understanding. I stayed close to her for the rest of the day and did my best to take care of all her needs.

We had to do everything for her, including feeding, cleaning her, and helping her in the restroom, which was the most trying of all tasks. Occasionally, I would call my sister, Carolyn, a retired hospice nurse, and ask her about certain bodily functions and how to help my wife. We used adult diapers when it became too hard to control or predict when she needed to relieve herself. I learned how to use my legs whenever I had to move Darlene around. However, at times I could feel lower back pain, and Shane also had these challenges. We had to care for all her medical needs, including insulin injections, several times each day.

I was so very in love with her, I could hardly stand seeing her in this condition. Here was a woman who loved God above everything and everyone. He was her Abba Father. She was physically broken but did not blame God. Instead, she looked forward to going home to be with Him. She taught me so much about God's love during our 48 years of marriage. I would tell her what I was doing now was a labor of love, and it wasn't work. I loved her, and I wanted to do all I could to help make her life a little better. All our kids felt the same way and wanted to help mom in any way they could.

On Monday, December 17, I took Darlene to a urologist because she could no longer urinate. Our granddaughter, Kimberly, a nurse, had previously worked for this doctor and recommended him to us. During the visit, the nurse placed a catheter inside Darlene's urethra to drain the bladder. We were hoping it was only a temporary measure, but it turned out to be permanent. From then on, she had another cross to bear, to go along with her diabetes, COPD, heart disease, kidney disease, lack of bowel movements, and paralysis.

On Tuesday, December 18, we met with an orthopedic surgeon in Fredericksburg to discuss the spinal cord trauma and possible causes. He took an x-ray of her cervix in his office and discussed the film with us. He clearly saw the cervix was damaged, and the spinal cord was compressed. He needed more details, so he gave us an order for an MRI to be done ASAP. The soonest Darlene could get the MRI was on January 2.

On Christmas Eve, we received a visit from a nurse who worked for a palliative care company. Soon, Darlene got approved for home nurse care, which was needed at this point. A nurse was assigned to visit our home and provide medical care, two or three times a week. The palliative care nurse was very helpful and kind, and he was also a strong Christian. I loved how he would pray for Darlene before he would leave our home. We also had a lady who would come and wash and clean Darlene on the makeshift sofa bed.

We managed to get an MRI done at Lee's Hill Imaging Center in Fredericksburg on January 2, 2019. For the first time, a radiologist could see the C-4/C-5 and C-5/C-6 cervix had ruptured and were compressing the spinal cord, which caused her continual severe pain and suffering.

On January 8, the orthopedic surgeon did another x-ray in his office of Darlene's upper spinal canal. He explained to us that he needed to decompress Darlene's spinal cord and fuse the cervix's damaged areas. He did not promise us she would be able to walk or use her hands again, but he said she should be relieved of all pain caused by the compressed spine with the surgery. He said surgery should take around 1 ½ to 2 hours and scheduled for January 14 at Mary Washington Hospital in Fredericksburg.

It is important to understand this orthopedic surgeon was a Christian and had a good reputation as an excellent surgeon. We prayed with him in his office that day and shared our belief that God would hear our prayers for healing, and he agreed with us. I was happy my wife showed no fear about the upcoming surgery because she believed God's healing Word.

On the morning of January 14, Shane and I took Darlene to Mary Washington Hospital and registered her for in-patient surgery. It was scheduled for the late morning, and I promised my wife I would stay with her in the hospital full time. I wasn't going to let her go through this alone, and I promised I would be there with her during the five days of recovery. While we waited in the pre-op room, the nurse prepped Darlene for surgery, but there was a brief delay due to an irregular heartbeat. A doctor came in and said they couldn't do surgery unless her heart had a regular rhythm. We prayed together, and, finally, her heart transitioned into regular beats and the surgical preparation could continue. Her orthopedic surgeon came into the pre-op room to speak to us about the procedure and what to expect. He seemed very calm and confident. He then said and did something quite unexpected:

"Now, Linda, you know I am going to do my very best for you. For your cervix to completely heal, you will need to do your part. You will have to quit smoking. If you don't, your cervix will not heal, and you will ruin my work." He walked to the other side of her bed, leaned over, and kissed her gently on the cheek. He said, "I want you to remember this kiss, the next time you want a cigarette." Darlene had a big smile on her face and chuckled when he said that.

It wasn't long before they wheeled her on down to the operating room. I sauntered over to the waiting room and waited and prayed with Shane.

After two hours of waiting, I was starting to get concerned and wondered if Darlene was okay and if the surgery was going well. Almost three hours later, her surgeon appeared from a back door. He hurried to me and pronounced with joy for all to hear, "We did it. We did it."

I said, "Did what?"

He replied, "The surgery was a success."

"Praise God," I said. Then the doctor and I held hands, laughed aloud, and said a short prayer of praise and thanks to God. I asked him with a certain amount of hope and expectation if she would no longer be paralyzed. He told me he couldn't promise it. He said even though the spinal cord was no longer compressed, there was no guarantee she would be able to walk and use her hands again. She would have to go through intensive physical therapy to have any chance of her body coming back to life. The good news was she would no longer be in severe nerve pain, now that the spine was decompressed.

Later, I was able to visit with Darlene in post-op, and then, we settled into her room. I noticed they didn't have a bed for me, only a recliner, but made the most of it. Not having a real bed didn't matter. I was just happy she was out of surgery and doing better. During the night, I would lay on my back and reach over to Darlene and touch her hand to make sure she knew I was there. When she would call out for a nurse, I would respond quickly, and she would be more at ease. I tried to help in any way I could. I slept there for four nights, standing guard next to my beloved wife.

On January 19, the fifth day, she was discharged from the hospital, and I took her home. She was still paralyzed, but she had no more spinal cord pain. She tried to move her toes, but she had little success. Nevertheless, we rejoiced together over that small victory. The following Monday, we had a follow-up visit with her orthopedic surgeon, and the x-ray showed excellent results. He required her to wear the neck collar and reminded us he couldn't promise she would ever be able to walk or use her hands again. We thanked him for all he was able to do, and then we left for home.

We had a few days and nights together at home, trying to adapt to post-surgery life. Even though the spinal pain was gone, my wife still was unable to use her hands or legs. The home nurse told us she would have to go through extensive physical therapy to walk and use her arms and hands again. I was on board with physical therapy and other activities to help my wife recover. She wasn't as invested in this next phase, however, because it was physically challenging to exercise with all of her medical challenges. Nevertheless, during her physical therapy appointments, I started to notice her chuckling and a little smile on her face from time to time. She wasn't about to argue with her home nurse or me when it came to her scheduled activities. She had no more neck pain, but she still struggled with several other challenges, including COPD, as her oxygen levels continued to be dangerously low.

One night, after I tucked Darlene in bed on the sofa in the living room, Shane relieved me, and I went to bed. I didn't sleep well that night because I kept hearing Darlene call out during the night. Near the morning, I heard her say to Shane, "I don't want you. I want my husband. Where is my husband?"

I immediately jumped up out of bed and came to Shane's rescue. I said, "Here I am, Dar. It's okay. I'll stay with you."

Shane thought it was funny that she wanted only her husband and not him. I laughed to myself and felt very privileged

On the morning of January 24, I came out of my bedroom and went to Darlene on the sofa. Shane had been up all night caring for her needs. She asked me to prop her up on the sofa, which I did. I checked her oxygen level and saw she was below 70%. Shane told me her oxygen levels had been low all night. I got worried, as her home care nurse had said that readings below 70% were extremely dangerous, causing oxygen deprivation to the brain. I decided to call 9-1-1.

The ambulance took her back to Mary Washington Hospital, and I followed and arrived at the same time. While they checked her into the Emergency Room, I was suddenly very sick to my stomach. Around noon, I called Shane and Alita and asked them to relieve me because I knew I was too ill to stay with her. I thought I had contracted a stomach virus. Within the hour, both Alita and Shane arrived on the scene. Darlene was calm if a family member was there. I told Darlene I was sick to my stomach, and I needed to go home and rest. Alita and Shane promised me they wouldn't leave her alone, and they would keep me posted. I kissed her cheek, went back home, and went to bed, hoping to sleep off the virus. After I left, the ER doctor decided to admit her into the hospital because of the severity of her low oxygen levels and their effect on her heart, lungs, and other vital organs.

Shane and Alita were unable to stay through the night with their mom. Alita had planned for her daughter, Alisha, to stay through the night to keep her grandmother company, and Alisha also brought her one-year-old son, Cameron. Being with Alisha and Cameron during the night seemed to bring great joy to Darlene, and I was so happy they could provide grandma with respite through the night.

Early the next morning, on January 25, Shane and Alita returned to the hospital to be with their mom. Alisha and Cameron remained, as well. I was still at home feeling a little better. During the previous night, the hospital had run several heart and lung tests to determine the cause of her low oxygen levels. The cardiologist arrived and stated he was considering doing an angiogram to determine if any of her blood vessels were blocked. He then seemed to change his mind and state that, perhaps, all she needed to do was to take heart medication at home to help raise her oxygen levels. After careful consideration, he ended up recommending she stay another day to monitor her levels. Once my wife heard the two alternatives, she spoke up and said she wanted to go home. The cardiologist was not supportive of that request, but, regardless, Darlene signed herself out of the hospital that day and returned home with Shane.

22
HOMEWARD BOUND

Psalms 27:4 (NASB) "One thing I have asked from the LORD, that I shall seek: That I may dwell in the house of the LORD all the days of my life, to behold the beauty of the LORD and to meditate in His temple."

Steve's Dream - January 16, 1987

I had a beautiful dream last night. I dreamed that Darlene and I were very much in love with each other. We had very quiet spirits and didn't have to talk much to communicate our love for each other. One evening we invited a group of our married friends to our house to watch the movie "Sound of Music" on our TV. I remember standing behind the living room watching the show, and then a commercial came on. I asked Darlene why she didn't show it using our VCR tape since we had taped it. She and I both laughed together because we realized it didn't really matter. Commercials didn't bother anyone. It was as if this movie was about our life together and marriage to each other. I couldn't keep my eyes or heart off of my Love, Darlene. And she couldn't either. We were so deeply in love. We were like two kids, very giddy and playful.

* * *

"Honey," she said. "I want to go home."

"Sweetheart," I replied. "I want you to get well. We can do this together."

"No, Honey. It's time. Please, I want to go home to Jesus."

It was Friday afternoon, January 25, 2019. My wife was at peace and seemed ready and willing to die. She had lost the will to live in the flesh, and had no fear of death because she was assured of salvation. In a blink of an eye, she knew she would be in the loving arms of Jesus. Darlene was waiting on me to come in agreement and honor her request. I believed God showed her that, soon, she would be coming home. However, this made no sense to me. I wanted her to live and to get well and walk again. I didn't want to lose her. She had been my helpmate for almost 49 years, and I selfishly wanted her to remain by my side.

Earlier that day, I had called a hospice office in Charlottesville and asked them for guidance. I explained my wife's medical condition, including complete paralysis, COPD, kidney disease, and type I diabetes. Hospice immediately dispatched a male nurse to our house to meet with us and discuss our options.

Ironically, the fact that my wife had COPD was the key to getting hospice approval for treatment. When the nurse arrived, he explained the mission of hospice is to help the patient who is ill and dying and help their family have a smoother transition with their impending death. Hospice care is a form of palliative care. In other words, hospice deals with the pain and not the cause or condition and is meant for people who have six months or less to live. Rather than trying to cure an illness, hospice aims to make the patient comfortable, ease their pain and other symptoms, and support the family through a sad and challenging time. All in all, I was struggling to accept this diagnosis for my beloved because I wasn't ready for her to leave me. The nurse reiterated all the benefits of the program, including medication and 24/7 support as required. He mentioned the medication would make my wife feel "more comfortable." I didn't understand what he meant by the words "more comfortable." In my mind, she was already more comfortable because her recent neck surgery had relieved all the physical pain caused by her spinal compression, but I didn't want to argue with him, because I was so emotionally drained and troubled by this new information. I just had to get away for a moment and pray.

When my son, Shane, arrived in the bedroom, I asked him to stay with his mom and the nurse for a few minutes. I excused myself, went to my bedroom and laid down on the bed. I started pleading with God to make her well. Suddenly, I felt His presence. He gently whispered that I had had her for 49 years, and now it was time for her to come home. Despite my continual request that she remain with me in this life, He wouldn't relent. I was lying on my side with my back to the door. All at once, I felt a gentle hand touch me on my lower back. I turned quickly, thinking my son Shane had touched me, but no one was there. I then realized it must have been an angel. With this manifestation, I took it as a sign. I must obey God and allow my beloved bride to go home. So, I surrendered her to God, got up, and went back into my wife's bedroom, where she was waiting on me to return.

"Honey, I prayed, and God gave me a sign. It is time for you to go home. I give you permission, Dar. I release you, my love, even though I don't want to. I want you to get well. God wants you to come home."

"Thank you, sweetheart," she said. She looked at the hospice nurse and said, "Yes, I am ready for hospice care."

The nurse took a blank form out of a 3-ring binder and gave it to me to review. It detailed the hospice program and the support to be provided. After reading it, I signed the form and handed it back. The nurse also signed it and placed a copy in the inside pocket of the binder. He then wrote out three prescriptions of medications for me to pick up from a local pharmacy. The meds were morphine, lorazepam, and glycopy. The nurse handed me the binder and suggested that I should read all the material to ensure I fully understand the hospice program when I had time. He also said, if I had any questions or needed any support whatsoever, to call the office immediately, and they would send a nurse out if necessary. I thanked him for coming out and meeting with us and for all his help. He then left.

When the nurse left, I felt like I was on my own. I was hardly qualified to care for my wife. Although I had been by her side caring for her throughout her illness, I wasn't trained for this. I was in over my head, and I knew only by God's grace and wisdom was I going to be able to handle this. The biggest question I still had, which wasn't answered, was how long my wife would live before God would take her home. My older brother, Michael, was on hospice for several weeks before he passed away in July 2018 from Alzheimer's disease. I had several other questions and concerns, such as, was Darlene going to be on hospice care for several weeks or months? Do I still administer her other medication that she took before hospice care started? Of course, if she's unconscious, I wouldn't be able to give her the pills. I could still check her blood sugar and give insulin injections as needed. I didn't understand why a hospice nurse wouldn't just live in our house and administer all the medication and care.

My mind was spinning, and I decided to call my older sister, Carolyn. She had been a hospice nurse for more than 30 years, and she helped to calm my emotions and enabled me to understand better what we were facing. She said the hospice program was excellent, and the nurses were very caring and supportive to the patient and the family in all matters. Carolyn really blessed me by giving me more assurance in the program, and she was there to help me in any way possible as well. All I knew for sure was Darlene was going to go home to be with Jesus. I just didn't know when, yet I was thankful the meds would make the transition process less painful and more comfortable for my beloved.

I decided to leave Darlene on the couch in the master bedroom. She was already settled in, and I didn't want to move her to the bed. That evening, I propped her up and we sat together on the couch, holding hands, and shared pleasant memories of our life through the years. Later, we watched our last movie together on TV, "Jaws." It wasn't a great movie, but it helped to take our minds off the situation, and, as we laughed at certain parts of the movie, it reminded me that a few weeks before, she had picked up a little chuckle and smile whenever someone would make a comment or say something about God or heaven or getting well. Looking back, I think even then she knew God's plan. She was going to go home soon to be with Him, and she was waiting on me to catch up to the reality of her imminent death.

23
WONDERMENT

Proverbs 31:28-29 (NASB) "Her children rise up
and bless her; Her husband also, and he praises her, saying:
'Many daughters have done nobly, But, you excel them all.'"

On Tuesday, January 29, 2019, my beloved wife lay motionless on the couch in her bedroom. She hadn't really stirred or been awake since her 67th birthday, January 26, 2019, when she had first started taking the meds Shane and I administered. Shane would care for her all through the night, and I would relieve him in the morning and stay with Dar all through the day until evening. Shane and I repeated this labor of love for three days and three nights. On the morning of the fourth day (Tuesday, January 29), I relieved Shane and knelt in front of my blessed wife. Before Shane left the room, he mentioned he had thoroughly cleaned his mom during the night. I thanked him for his love and faithfulness in caring for his mom. I could hardly talk because I was crying so much and so was Shane. We both knew it would be only a matter of time before she would be in eternity forever. I continually prayed aloud and sometimes quietly and spoke to her gently and lovingly all the while holding her hands and stroking her hair. I asked God to take her home sooner rather than later. I believed the Father heard my prayers. I also believed Darlene could hear me, as well.

I put my head close to her face and listened to her breathing, which was more labored now. Her breaths were shallow and irregular, and it was a struggle for her to stay alive. I wept and prayed and sang aloud to the Father of Lights to comfort and embrace her and bring her home. I checked the whiteboard in the small coffee bar adjacent to her bedroom where I had listed the three meds she was required to take and the times I needed to administer each. At the appropriate time, I would put a couple of drops of the morphine under her tongue, which helped to ease her pain.

That morning my granddaughter, Alisha, and her two boys, Cameron and Jayden, were in the living room. Sometimes Alisha would come in and pray and get very emotional. I didn't mind her stopping in and praying for grandma, especially since she kept her distance. I was, however, very concerned about her little children. I didn't want them to see great grandma in that condition. Alisha was very respectful and honored my request. I knew that Alisha and my four children were going to be broken when their mom passed away. She was the light in our home and demonstrated God's love unconditionally to all the kids. She opened her heart to them night and day, and always listened and offered love and kind words and prayers for God to touch them personally.

My friend Mike Zello was at my house that morning, as well. He had called me the night before and asked if he could stop by and pray with me. He was the director of Teen Challenge, a Christian ministry based in Fredericksburg, and had only been to my house once before. Looking back, I know that God wanted my granddaughter, great-grandsons, and my friend with me in those final hours and minutes of Darlene's life on earth.

Around noon, a couple of hospice ladies stopped by to discuss religious and social matters. They had called me a few days before, and I agreed to meet with them. One was a chaplain and the other was a social worker. I talked to them for maybe 15 minutes in the dining room. The discussion was about the services offered by the hospice in the areas of social well-being and spiritual matters. I must admit, I hardly listened to them because all I could think about was my beloved bride struggling to breathe in the master bedroom. After 15 minutes, I excused myself and told them I needed to get back to my wife. I wasn't sure what they were going to do, and I really didn't care. The hospice workers slowly entered the bedroom after I had taken my position on my knees in front of my beloved. She was lying on her back with her face towards me. Her eyes remained closed, and her breathing was staggered and shallow. I sensed she needed medication, so I got up and checked the whiteboard to verify. I saw that morphine was required, so I applied a couple of drops under her tongue. A couple of minutes went by, and she seemed to settle down; her breathing was more consistent but still very shallow. I wanted to make sure I took advantage of every moment with my beloved because she was so precious to me.

I continued to kneel in front of my wife, stroking her blond hair gently and talking about Jesus and heaven and how much I loved her and would miss her. Tears came easily, too easily. A couple of minutes went by, and then she suddenly opened her eyes, flailed her arms, and made guttural sounds. I thought she was in pain and jumped up to administer another drop or two of morphine. However, the hospice social worker spoke up and said she felt my wife was trying to communicate with me. I paused and went back over to the couch and got close to Darlene's face. Her eyes were opened wide but had a vacant and distant look. I gently told her that it was okay, and she could go home to be with Jesus. I repeated myself a couple of times. Within a few moments, she calmed down and closed her eyes again. I held her hands and kissed her face ever so softly. A few minutes passed, and I noticed she was no longer breathing. It was 12:31 pm when she took her final breath and passed into the arms of God.

"Wonderment!" That was the word the Lord gave me when I gazed upon her face as she transitioned into the loving arms of Jesus. She had the look of wonderment on her face. The look of peace that passes all understanding. No more pain or suffering. She had the look of someone who was and is in the arms of the Great I AM. I had never used the word "Wonderment" before that I could remember, and that is why I firmly believe God gave me that word to assure me that she had gone to HEAVEN with the Father, Son, and Holy Spirit.

When she passed, I must have called out for Alexa, the Amazon electronic robotic music wizard, to play the song, "Adoration" by Mike Adkins. The music started immediately. Mike Zello and I raised our voices and lifted our hands in praise as we sang and wept for my beloved Darlene's departure. I was in a fog, lost in sorrow because my blessed bride had gone home. The hospice ladies said a few words and departed.

Sometime later, I called the Found and Sons funeral home. Two men in a hearse arrived a few hours later that day and removed my beloved's body. My son, Shane, and I wept as we stood on the porch together, looking out at an unbelievable sunset as the hearse drove away. The woods appeared to be on fire. I had never seen anything like that before and knew it must have been another sign from Papa. My sweetheart was home with Jesus, and all heavenly hosts were rejoicing.

My life on this earth will never be the same without Darlene. Even as I complete this book, I can hardly get through each day without something reminding me of our life together. I saw monarch butterflies everywhere for several months after her passing and remembered how she used to love watching these special butterflies. So, when I saw them, I was amazed but not surprised. I see evidence of her in my four children, six granddaughters, and three great-grandsons. Plus, there are so many others who she had touched throughout our life, many of whom we will not see until we all rejoice together in the kingdom of God. I miss her so very much, and my heart is broken. I was married to my Blessed Bride for almost 48 years. My hope and prayer is that I will be with her in eternity forever, worshipping our Lord and Savior Jesus Christ.

Dar and I lived together for 49 years. I asked Darlene all the time to please quit smoking. My beloved bride told me she had smoked since she was a small child, and she wasn't going to stop unless God took away the desire to smoke. Ironically, two weeks before my Blessed Bride passed into the arms of Jesus, Papa delivered her from cigarettes. He replaced the habit with His peace and tranquility, and I was truly amazed. I was reminded of how God honored His Word. He answered my prayer in His time and His way. God is so good.

Darlene's ashes were laid to rest at Quantico National Cemetery, Section 23A, Dumfries, VA. The headstone was engraved with her full name. It also included Proverbs 31: 28 – 29 and our two code words: ITALY and HOLLAND.

I Truly Always Love You

Hope Our Love Lasts and Never Dies

My beloved and I were the only ones who knew the true meaning of those two words that expressed our love beyond the grave.

Last Picture of Sunset
This picture was taken from my front porch looking west as the hearse took Darlene's body away from me. I have never ever seen a sunset like this ever from where I live. It was an indication to me that God's angels were rejoicing and having a party with Darlene as she entered with the Father.

AFTERWORD

"And God shall wipe away every tear from their eyes;
there shall be no more death, nor sorrow, nor crying.
There shall be no more pain, for the former things have
passed away." Revelation 21:4 (NKJV)

A poem by Darlene

My love is pure; My love is true,
Not sad nor blue it's just for you.
Love me now while I am living.
Don't wait I pray until I am sleeping.
Then have it chiseled in marble those sweet words on ice
- my tombstone.
Here lies my wife whom I do love.

To Those I love and Leave Behind

When I am gone, release me. Let me go.
I have so many things to see and do.
You must not tie yourself to me with tears.
Be happy that we had so many years.
I gave you my love. You can only guess
how much you gave me in happiness.
Now it is time I traveled on alone.
So, grieve a while for me, if grieve you must.
Then let your grief be comforted by trust.
It's only for a while that we must part.
So, bless the memories within your heart.
I won't be far away, and life goes on.
So, if you need me, call and I will come.
Though you can't see or touch me, I'll be near.
And if you listen with your heart, you will hear
All my love around you soft and clear.
And then when you must come this way alone,
I'll greet you with a smile and say, "Welcome Home."

Several months later, in the Summer of 2019, I had a dream one night. It was so real. I dreamed I was near a deep pool of liquid that was crystal clear. It looked like water, but it was more gel-like in movement. I voluntarily plunged into the pool only to find it quite refreshing and cool. I was amazed I was still able to breathe and to take in all its beauty as I floated through it. The substance seemed to envelope all my senses. I could drink of it and not be filled or lacking in any manner. In a flash, I penetrated the wall and was floating out into a wide-open space of lightness. It appeared food-like substances were floating all around me. Some would come near, and I would taste, and it was so delectable. Other food would touch me and penetrate my skin, bringing such delight to my complete being.

I awoke from the dream and realized it was only a dream. It was around midnight. I prayed and called out to God to tell me if this dream was from Him. I sensed it was an answer to prayer. He wanted me to know Darlene was in heaven with Him, and she wanted me to have a little taste of heaven through my dream. I was so happy, and I started singing and praising Father God for revealing these truths to me. As I said the name "Jesus" repeatedly, I physically felt a vibrating force up and down my spine. The more I praised and said the name of Jesus, the more it continued. I knew there was an angel in my bedroom. I was so at peace with this revelation from God.

Thank you, Jesus, for my Blessed Bride.

Quantico National Cemetery

ABOUT THE AUTHOR

Steven Joseph Fortner — the author of *My Blessed Bride*---was born June 6, 1950, in Covington, Kentucky, the 3rd oldest of nine children of Paul and Eileen Fortner. Steve's parents were devout Catholics, with his father having converted to Catholicism early on in their marriage. Steve attended Catholic schools through the first 12 years of education. Upon graduation from Covington Catholic High School in 1968, Steve decided to enlist in the Naval Submarine Service for six years. After a year of formal Fire Control electronics training at the Guided Missile School in Dam Neck, in Virginia Beach, Virginia, he received orders to serve on the *USS Simon Bolivar* (SSBN-641) Blue Crew, which was stationed in Charleston, South Carolina.

After returning from his first submarine patrol, having hitched a ride with a shipmate to the Naval Base, who stopped in his non-discrete mobile home first to change clothes and greet his wife, Steve had a life changing yet brief encounter with the most beautiful woman he had ever seen, Darlene. They fell in love and a year later were married in a small Catholic Chapel in Newport News, Virginia. He received an honorable discharge on August 11, 1978, having served for almost 10 years. Steve worked as a Defense Contractor following his Navy career and moved to Blackwood, New Jersey.

On 11 November 1983, Darlene's life radically changed when their next-door neighbor prayed with Darlene to receive Jesus as her savior. Eight days later the neighbor prayed with Steve and their kids to also receive Jesus Christ in their hearts. "Radiant" was the word God gave Steve as a description of Darlene's inner beauty and permanent heart change. "Promotion to promotion to promotion" were words spoken over Steve by an evangelist the next evening in Church.

God became the center of their marriage, family and business life. From that point on, Darlene was on fire to share Jesus with everyone anytime. From the beginning she was anointed as a prophet and teacher by God. In July 1988 Pastor John David Bateman, of Open Doors Community Fellowship, licensed her to preach and teach the Gospel. She held Bible classes for neighborhood kids in their house every Friday. She also prayed and led more than 50 children and adults to the Lord over the years.

In September 1990, God opened an opportunity for Steve and a Christian friend, Herb, to start a new business, Quality Performance, Inc. (QPI). The business grew rapidly in the military market. In March 2002, the Navy awarded QPI a multi-million-dollar, five-year contract for the design and development of the Moriah Wind System. After 27 years of successful business, in August 2017, Herb and Steve sold QPI to Valkyrie Enterprises for millions of dollars.

While Steve's business life was a success, his wife's health continued to decline. Darlene struggled all her life with various serious illnesses, including type I diabetes, congested heart disease, kidney disease and chronic obstructive pulmonary disease (COPD). In November 2018, Darlene fell in the shower and fractured her cervix, which resulted in a compressed spinal cord and paralysis from the shoulders down. After back surgery, Darlene's health took a turn for the worse, and she was placed in hospice. On 29 January 2019, in their house at Lake Anna, Virginia, Darlene transitioned into the arms of Jesus. As Steve kissed her face one last time and held her closely, God gave him the word "Wonderment." She had the look of Wonderment as she entered the kingdom of heaven. Steve was married to his Blessed Bride for almost 48 years. They were blessed with four children (Joe, Alita, Shane, Charity), six granddaughters, and three great grandsons.

Since 2008, under the direction of Chaplain Ray Perez of Good News Jail and Prison Ministry, Steve volunteers to teach the Gospel to men who are incarcerated at Prince William County Detention Center. In 2018, Steve helped to start a 501(c)(3) public charity in the community and serves on the board of directors. The Belmont Foundation supports the local public schools with food for needy kids, educational projects, and other tasks assigned. He also serves the local rural community in Central Virginia as a member the Belmont Ruritan Club.

CONTACT INFORMATION: Steve Fortner,
Email: SaintLurch@gmail.com

ACKNOWLEDGEMENTS

I want to personally thank God for giving me, Darlene, the love of my life, for almost half a century on earth. I also want to specially thank my children (Joseph, Alita, Shane, and Charity) for putting up with me and my irritable ways as I read and studied all of their mom's notes, prayers, prophecies, words from God, poems, songs, and teachings, from her enormous collection she saved through her life's journey with me.

Thank you, Gayle, for being a great and loyal sister to Darlene throughout her entire life. Your love and many cards, letters, pictures, and video phone calls brought such joy to her soul.

I want to also thank Pastor Carol Bretz for praying with Darlene that November afternoon in 1983 and helping Darlene understand that Father God loved her for just who she was. Also thank you so much for leading me and our kids to Christ Jesus, eight days later in our living room.

Dear Pastor John David Bateman, you knew right away that Darlene was a unique child of God and called as a prophet and teacher of the Word. Thank you so much for empowering and licensing Darlene to preach the Gospel under your ministry, Open Door Community Fellowship.

Finally, I couldn't have written this book without the tremendous support and professional expertise from my good friend and editor, Michelle Wilson. Besides being a Godly woman with a servant's heart, she cheered me on to complete the work that God had called me to write.

Thank you all so very much.

ITALY ~ HOLLAND

My Blessed Bride is more than a love story between two people. It is the life-long journey to know and to experience God's love in a real and practical way in this life on earth, through the leading of the Holy Spirit within. Father God truly BLESSED my beloved Darlene and me with 48 years of marriage, four children, six granddaughters, and three great-grandsons.

In Kenneth Wuest's Word Studies in the Greek New Testament, Volume III, the NT Greek word for BLESSED is Makarios, which, "was chosen by the Bible writers to describe the state of the man (woman) who is the recipient of the divine favor and blessing." Furthermore, "It denotes a state of true well-being." ...."but is enjoyed only when there is a corresponding behavior towards God; so that it forms the hoped for good of those who in this life are subject to oppression."

My Blessed Bride illustrates God's master plan for Steve and Darlene individually, and together in one flesh through marriage. Darlene was called as a prophet and teacher by God and led scores of souls to Christ through her prayers, ministry, and bible classes. Weak in the flesh, yet powerful in His Word, she persevered until finally being called to her heavenly home with Jesus. Her love lasts forever beyond the grave.

My Blessed Bride Highlights
• A Divine meeting
• Miracles
  ◦ Personal
  ◦ Business
• Spiritual warfare
• Power of hearing and obeying the Holy Spirit

STEVE FORTNER

Steve served in the U.S. Navy submarine service for nearly ten years and was honorably discharged as a Petty Officer 1st Class, Fire Control Technician (FTB1). He met Darlene after his first patrol, fell in love and married a year later. On January 29, 2019, (3 days after her 67th birthday), Darlene went to her eternal resting place in Heaven. Steve is a retired businessman, where he co-founded a military consulting business, Quality Performance, Inc. in 1990. Over the years, QPI grew into a multi-million-dollar manufacturer and distributor of military parts and electronic equipment. After 27 years of successfully selling military parts and modern meteorological systems to the Navy, he and his partner sold the company. Today, Steve resides in Central Virginia with two of his four children, Shane and Alita (and her husband, William). Charity lives in Greensboro, NC, with her husband, Wallace, and their four daughters. Joseph and his wife, Carmen, reside in Montgomery, AL. Steve has six granddaughters and three great-grandsons. Steve is an avid golfer who loves reading and ministering to men incarcerated at the Prince William County Adult Detention Center. He also serves the local Lake Anna community through the Belmont Ruritan Club and the Belmont Foundation, a local 501(c)(3) charity that supports children in need.

$22.50
ISBN 978-1-7350611-4-6
52250>

9 781735 061146